WITHDRAWN   2 4 JUN 2022

D1349584

VOLUNTEERING AS LEISURE/LEISURE AS VOLUNTEERING

AS VOLUNTEERING

An International Assessment

Volunteering as Leisure/ Leisure as Volunteering

An International Assessment

Edited by

Robert A. Stebbins
University of Calgary

and

Margaret Graham
Caledonian University

CABI Publishing

CABI Publishing is a division of CAB International

CABI Publishing
CAB International
Wallingford
Oxfordshire OX10 8DE
UK

Tel: +44 (0)1491 832111
Fax: +44 (0)1491 833508
E-mail: cabi@cabi.org
Website: www.cabi-publishing.org

CABI Publishing
875 Massachusetts Avenue
7th Floor
Cambridge, MA 02139
USA

Tel: +1 617 395 4056
Fax: +1 617 354 6875
E-mail: cabi-nao@cabi.org

A catalogue record for this book is available from the British Library, London, UK.

Library of Congress Cataloging-in-Publication Data

Volunteering as leisure/leisure as volunteering : an international
assessment / edited by Robert A. Stebbins and Margaret Graham.
      p. cm.
Includes bibliographical references and index.
   ISBN 0-85199-750-3 (alk. paper)
   1. Voluntarism. 2. Leisure. I. Stebbins, Robert A., 1938–
II. Graham, Margaret, 1952–   III. Title.
   HN49.V64V64   2003
   302′.14—dc22   ·   2003016240

ISBN 0 85199 750 3

Typeset by Servis Filmsetting Ltd, Manchester
Printed and bound in the UK by Cromwell Press, Trowbridge

Contents

Contributors

Susan Arai, PhD, is an Assistant Professor in the Department of Community Health Sciences at Brock University in St Catharines, Ontario. With an MA in Leisure Studies (Waterloo) and an interdisciplinary PhD (University of Guelph), Susan's work on volunteering as leisure incorporates perspectives from psychology, planning, public administration, macro social work, sociology and political science. Working within a community development and critical pedagogy framework, Susan practises and conducts research on the involvement of citizens in community initiatives and non-profit or voluntary associations. She possesses previous experience with healthy communities initiatives, community health centres, social planning councils, municipal recreation departments, hospitals and other human services. Previous studies and publications focus on the role that volunteering plays in the development of community, citizenship, civil society, empowerment, social capital and social change.

John Benoit has spent the last 30 years as a sociologist, studying complex organizations. For the last 20 years at Dalhousie University in Halifax, NS, Canada, he has developed and directed management education for Canadian fire officers. During this time he has spent many enjoyable moments observing volunteer fire departments conduct actual firefighting, train for firefighting, or administer their organizational activities. This research has led to enjoyable and fruitful collaboration with Kenneth B. Perkins, resulting in two books on the volunteer and composite fire service as well as several articles and book chapters. John's doctorate is from the Johns Hopkins University.

Graham Berridge is Senior Lecturer, Teaching Fellow at Thames Valley University, London, UK, since 1990. Course Leader for BA (Hons) Event Management, having previously developed areas of study in leisure management and health and fitness management. Member of the Leisure Studies Association (UK), serving on Executive Committee between 1996 and 2000 and acting as newsletter editor 1998–2000. Accredited member of the Institute of Learning and Teaching. Previously served as Race Director for the British Mountain Bike Federation and (MTB) Representative to the British Olympic Association. Member of online cycling forum (Londoncyclesport) and London Phoenix online cycling club. Active cycle event coordinator for mountain biking, road racing and cyclo-cross. Academic and research interests centre around event experiences and event planning, planning active lifestyles for young people and the classification systems used for computer games.

Laurence Chalip is a professor in the Department of Kinesiology and Health Education at the University of Texas at Austin, where he also serves as coordinator of the graduate and undergraduate sport management programmes. His research focuses on sport marketing and policy. He has published three books, three research monographs, and over 50 articles and book chapters. He is a Research Fellow of the North American Society for Sport Management, and has won two service awards from the Sport Management Association of Australia and New Zealand. He was the founding Editor of *Sport Management Review*, and is currently Editor of *Journal of Sport Management*. In addition, he serves on the editorial board of five other journals in the field. In 2000, Dr Chalip was elected to the International Chair of Olympism by the International Olympic Committee and the Centre for Olympic Studies.

Antonio Carlos Bramante is a professor in the Department of Leisure Studies at the State University of Campinas, São Paulo State, Brazil. He has been in the field of recreation and leisure for the past 30 years, intercalating his academic work with several positions held in the public and private sectors such as Secretary of Childhood and Youth, Education and Culture, Sports and Leisure at the municipal level as well as Director Technical Support of the National Sport Development Institute at the federal level. He was consultant to the National Leisure Policy of the Social Service of Industry, an NGO with over 500 leisure centres in the country and, presently, he is conducting a research and professional preparation programme for managers of the Banco do Brasil Athletic Association, another NGO with over 1200 social clubs spread throughout the country. His major areas of study centre on the development of public and private leisure policy and on comparative leisure, with a focus on Latin American countries.

Deborah Edwards coordinates the Bachelor of Business Tourism Management degree at the University of Western Sydney (UWS), New South

Wales, Australia. Her Graduate Diploma is in Tourism Management and she is currently undertaking her doctorate on the organization of volunteers at visitor attractions. She has worked overseas and has publications in both journals and conference proceedings. She assisted in a study of volunteers at the Sydney 2000 Olympic Games under Christine Green and Laurence Chalip. She has recently been co-author of sustainable tourism modules in tourism operations management and tourism planning. She is a member of the module development committee for Best Enterprises for Sustainable Travel (BEST) and has recently been involved in the curriculum development for Sustainable Tourism Modules arising out of the Best Think Tank III. Her research interests are in volunteerism, tourism planning, sustainable tourism and regional development.

Margaret M. Graham (PhD, museum volunteerism) is Research Fellow at the Moffat Centre for Travel and Tourism Business Development. Margaret is responsible for providing leadership of the Centre's research arm, which complements that of the business development team. Her role involves working closely and collaboratively with industry partners (from large national tourist boards to small not-for-profit organizations) as well as with other academics. She was recently involved in the inception of the Caledonian Heritage Futures Network, which is a multi-disciplinary network of academics from Caledonian University who have an interest in cultural heritage-related research. Margaret's research interest in cultural heritage volunteerism has been influenced by her former curatorial role within the independent museum sector. Enhancing her commitment to build and promote the University's research strengths in research and knowledge transfer she wholeheartedly supports the work of the WLRA's Commission on Volunteerism.

B. Christine Green is an Assistant Professor in the Department of Kinesiology and Health Education at the University of Texas at Austin, where she coordinates the activities of the Sport Development Lab. Her research focuses on sport development and the marketing of sport events. Her research has appeared in such journals as the *Journal of Sport Management, Sport Management Review, Annals of Tourism Research, Journal of Leisure Research, and Leisure Sciences.* She is a member of the editorial board of four journals in the field, and serves as Associate Editor of the *Sport Management Review.* She designed and managed the volunteer systems for the British Olympic Holding Camp for the Sydney Olympic Games, and directed an eight-member team evaluating the volunteer programme at the Sydney Olympics.

Linda Bridges Karr was inspired to begin her study of processes within volunteer organizations through her experiences as both a volunteer and executive staff member in a large volunteer youth-serving organization. She holds both a Master of Public Administration and a PhD in sociology from the University of South Carolina. Her dissertation considered the dynamics of different configurations of paid staff and volunteers in management positions. Her most recent work includes a large-scale study, conducted at the University of Groningen (The Netherlands), of motivation and commitment among Scout leaders in The Netherlands and the United States. She has worked extensively with Lucas C.P.M. Meijs to develop integrated models of motivation and management in volunteer organizations.

Lucas C.P.M. Meijs (1963) graduated in 1991 at the Faculty of Business Administration/Rotterdam School of Management, Erasmus University, Rotterdam, The Netherlands. He joined the doctorate programme in general management at the same institute. In 1997 he defended his PhD dissertation 'Management of volunteer organizations'. He is Assistant Professor in the Department of Business-Society Management at the Faculty of Business Administration, Erasmus University, Rotterdam. He teaches non-profit management and business–non-profit partnerships. He has published articles on issues relating to volunteer management, non-profit management, how to support/promote volunteering and volunteer organizations and the relationship between business and non-profit. He is a member of the National Policy Committee on volunteer policy, aimed at getting local municipalities to create policies to support volunteerism. He is member of several advisory boards, such as Scouting Netherlands and X-zorg (a national volunteer care organization).

Geoff Nichols (BA (Hons) MSc, MSc) is a lecturer at Sheffield University, where he has taught courses in sport and recreation management since 1990. Present research interests include evaluating leisure programmes' impact on crime reduction, and volunteers in sport. He was part of a team which surveyed volunteers in UK sport in 1996, and completed an update of this work in 2002, conducted for Sport England. He has also conducted a major survey of volunteers in Guiding in the UK, and recently wrote an overview of volunteering in sport for the Central Council of Physical Recreation. Between work and looking after a young family, he takes part in fell running, rock climbing and mountaineering.

Kenneth B. Perkins is a sociologist at Longwood University in Farmville, Virginia. After moving to the Farmville area in 1984 from Virginia Tech, he joined the Prospect Volunteer Fire Department. and has remained a member. He has conducted applied research on a federal grant to study wildland fire safety in the USA and has done resource assessments and conflict resolution involving public safety personnel for local governments. Prior to the current work, his most recent publication was 'Understanding volunteer EMS: beyond gloom, doom and benign neglect', with longtime collaborator John Benoit, in *The Gold Cross* (Magazine of the New Jersey State First Aid Council), Summer 2002.

Kenneth E. Silverberg, PhD, is an Assistant Professor in the Department of Parks, Recreation and Tourism, at the University of Utah. He specializes in topics and issues related to municipal and community parks and recreation. He has also done extensive research and published a number of articles specific to the complexities of volunteerism, including the motivations and job satisfaction of volunteers in municipal parks and recreation settings. He also has a number of years of experience working in municipal recreation in Phoenix, Arizona, and has worked as the Recreation Director for a number of rural communities in Colorado and Wyoming. In addition, Dr Silverberg is a 5th year Regent with the NRPA Pacific Marketing and Revenue Sources Management School, and was just elected to the board of directors of the Society of Parks and Recreation Educators (SPRE).

Robert A. Stebbins, FRSC, is Faculty Professor in the Department of Sociology at the University of Calgary. He received his PhD in 1964 from the University of Minnesota. Author of 28 books and monographs as well as numerous articles and chapters in several areas of social science, his most recent works include: *New Directions in the Theory and Research of Serious Leisure* (2001), *Exploratory Research in the Social* Sciences (2001), and *The Organizational Basis of Leisure Participation: a Motivational Exploration* (2002). His book *Between Work and Leisure* will appear in spring 2004. He is presently writing up a study of hobbyists in kayaking, snowboarding, and mountain climbing as well as gathering data on the role of grassroots associations in the lives of amateur, hobbyist, and volunteer members and participants. Stebbins was elected Fellow of the Academy of Leisure Sciences in 1996 and, in 1999, elected Fellow of the Royal Society of Canada.

Stephen Wearing, PhD, is an Associate Professor at the University of Technology, Sydney (UTS). He has been responsible for a variety of projects in the area of leisure and tourism studies at an international and local level. Dr Wearing has directed a number of leisure and tourism community-based projects in Costa Rica, Solomon Islands, Guyana and Australia, receiving a special citation from the Costa Rican government for services towards community, conservation and youth and an outstanding contribution award from Youth Challenge International in Canada. He is the author (co-author) of seven books and over 80 articles dealing with issues surrounding leisure and tourism. He has been project director for a range of social sciences in natural resource management projects and research, and a team leader for a variety of ecotourism, volunteer tourism and outdoor education activities.

Brian E. Wilson graduated from The University of Nottingham in 1953 and became a management consultant. Most of his work involved devising and interpreting mathematical models of logistic and information systems in a variety of commercial and governmental organizations. These required the simultaneous use of both quantitative and qualitative concepts. All his life he has been active in voluntary organizations involved in social work, environment, hunting and sport. He rowed for London Rowing Club and was, until recently, a coach of 400 m in track and field athletics, up to Olympic level. After he retired, he lectured in Sports Science at the University of Surrey, where he also took his PhD in the Department of Education. The subject of his thesis forms the basis of his contribution.

Preface

Inspiration for this collection sprang from the conviction held by the editors that the idea of volunteering being, in its purest sense, leisure activity calls for further empirical and theoretical exploration. Such exploration is required to foster a different and badly needed conception of volunteering, because the reigning conception – volunteering as unpaid labour – is woefully inadequate both as an explanation of such activity and as a framework for describing it. In fact the Commission on Volunteering of World Leisure (formerly the World Leisure and Recreation Association) was founded on precisely this premise. Subsequently the Commission came to serve as the organizational sponsor of this collection, in that many of the contributors to the latter are members of the former and are actively studying volunteering from the leisure perspective. This collection, then, presents some of the results of their efforts in this field, demonstrating not only that volunteering can be fruitfully conceived of through the prism of leisure but also that this conception has substantial cross-cultural validity and applicability.

Acknowledgements

In the course of preparing this book, we have had the privilege and good fortune of working with an excellent team of editors, taking us through from the book's initial conception to its final stylistic polishing. In this regard we want to thank Rebecca Stubbs, Sarah Williams and Rachel Robinson. Additionally, we thank Elaine Coverdale for her fine work on the promotional features of this volume. We are also grateful to Claire Gwilt for overseeing the design of the cover. Finally we thank our contributors for their chapters and their prompt attention to editorial details and deadlines. They have been a most rewarding group with which to work.

Introduction

Robert A. Stebbins

University of Calgary

According to Jeremy Rifkin (1995), Aronowitz and DiFazio (1994) and others, the industrialized world has now entered the early years of the Information Age. Here it is gripped by dramatic declines in employment and public-sector service paralleled by a concomitant rise in the third sector as well as personal and collective dependency on the volunteers comprising it. Moreover, the twin ideas that work is inherently good and that, when it can be found, people should do it (instead of leisure) are being increasingly challenged. Applebaum (1992, p. 587) writes that 'with increases in the standard of living, consumerism, and leisure activities, the work ethic must compete with the ethic of the quality of life based on the release from work'.

Beck glimpses the near future as a time when there will still be work to be done, but a significant portion of which will be done without remuneration:

> The counter-model to the work society is based not upon leisure but upon political freedom; it is a multi-activity society in which housework, family work, club work and voluntary work are prized alongside paid work and returned to the centre of public and academic attention. For in the end, these other forms remained trapped inside a value imperialism of work, which must be shaken off.
>
> (Beck, 2000, p. 125)

Beck calls this work without pay 'civil labour'. Some of it, however, especially club work and voluntary work, is also leisure. Indeed some of it is serious leisure, since such work often goes with being an amateur, hobbyist, or skilled and knowledgeable volunteer (Rojek, 2002).

These reasons alone justify broad and deep exploration of the motivational and socioeconomic conditions that encourage vastly different demographic categories of people to take up volunteering. In this regard, it is now clear that each category is rather differently motivated and that the twin motives of altruism and self-interest are common to all categories. It is also clear that both motives serve as mainsprings for leisure behaviour. Examples of self-interested volunteering include working for a strongly felt cause and, as noted later, working to experience, as serious leisure enthusiasts do everywhere, the variety of social and personal rewards available in volunteering and the leisure (non-work) career in which they are framed.

Finally, it is known that substantial measures of coercion or obligation in volunteering sometimes obliterate for some people the rewards that other people derive from the leisure activity that satisfies these two motives. So, given the importance of altruism and self-interest and their intricate interplay in volunteering, a field whose star is becoming brighter in every country as the Information Age evolves, the time has come to explore systematically, both theoretically and empirically, the complicated link between it and leisure.

Yet, it is relatively rare in both the study of leisure and the study of voluntarism and citizen participation to find these two concepts considered together. In the first field, possibly because volunteering is seen 'as somewhat more lofty than . . . the fun and frivolity often associated with leisure' (Henderson, 1984, p. 58), volunteers, until very recently, have for the most part been ignored as subjects of research. Some exceptions to this indictment are discussed later in this Introduction. Researchers in the second field typically look on volunteers as helpers, as people filling a distinct, contributory role in modern society and, more particularly, in certain kinds of organizations. That this role is work or leisure or something else seldom stirs much interest. Thus, whether it is leisure studies specialists looking at volunteering or voluntary action specialists looking at leisure, the outcome has been much the same over the years: neither field has been inclined to view its own subject matter through the eyes of the other.

The Volunteerism Commission

It was in light of this situation that World Leisure (formerly World Leisure and Recreation Association) founded in 1997 and formally approved in 2000 its Volunteerism Commission animated by two main objectives. They are to organize and encourage research in all countries on all aspects of volunteering that relate to leisure and, to the extent they are deemed useful there, to disseminate to the applied sector the world over relevant research findings in this area. The applied sector consists of individual volunteers, their 'employers' (those who engage them), and various non-profit agencies and organizations. An important assumption here, which springs from the leisure perspective, is that volunteering is, among other things, a primarily creative, society-building activity, which nevertheless loses this quality when, as a money-saving strategy, it is foisted on altruistic citizens by agents of the public or private sector.

Concerning the first objective, a handful of theorists and researchers in leisure studies and the study of voluntarism and citizen participation have argued in recent decades that, depending on the writer, volunteering is frequently, if not invariably, a form of leisure. When collected together, however, these observations and studies still leave some critical issues unresolved, including how to reassure employers of volunteers that in seeking leisure the latter will have the commitment and perseverance needed to enact their roles effectively. There is also the issue of the reaction of the financial backers of non-profit organizations and even the general public to filling important volunteer roles with people they define as primarily motivated by a search for enjoyment. A third issue is whether 'leisurely' volunteers are dependable. And a fourth centres on the question of how to ensure the leisure sense of volunteering as expressed in its inherent creative and society-building components in the face of employers who want docile, no-nonsense, unpaid equivalents of the remunerated employees they have just declared redundant.

The Volunteerism Commission encourages researchers to adopt any theoretical or methodological approach to questions of this sort that promises to bear fruit. One that has already proved its utility in this regard is the serious–casual leisure perspective (Stebbins, 1997, 2001a,c). It sets out ways to resolve issues in the applied sector, like those just raised, to the advantage of all concerned. In particular, it shows that many volunteer roles, because they offer their incumbents special careers and distinctive sets of rewards, can be understood as serious leisure. This perspective applied to volunteering refutes the idea that conceiving of volunteering as leisure trivializes the former, implying in the extreme case that volunteers are, at bottom, selfish, unreliable and prone to giving least effort. Moreover, volunteers can simultaneously pursue their activities as serious or casual leisure, therein making substantial contributions both individually and collectively to the functioning of the wider community.

The Volunteerism Commission is a unique entity, both within and outside World Leisure. True, many independent centres and institutes as well as university-based departments and divisions operate with mandates to study one or more aspects of volunteering or to advance theoretical knowledge or practical knowledge, if not both. Yet it is equally true that researchers in these units seldom address themselves to the leisure facet. The goal of the Volunteerism Commission is to fill this critical gap.

The proposition that volunteering is a form of leisure is beset by a thorny definitional problem that is neatly side-stepped in the economic conception of volunteering as unpaid work. The economic conception, which dominates in volunteer studies, avoids this problem primarily by being amenable to objective measurement, as expressed in absence of payment as livelihood, whether in money or in kind. Thus it largely avoids the messy question of motivation so crucial to the leisure conception. The latter, on the other hand, revolves in significant part around a central subjective question; it must be determined whether volunteers feel they are engaging in enjoyable or satisfying activity that they have had the option to accept or reject on their own terms. A key part of the leisure conception of volunteering is felt to be the absence of moral coercion to do the volunteer activity, an element that, as argued later, may be experienced in degrees, as more or less coercive. It has therefore become necessary to speak of 'marginal volunteering' (Stebbins, 2001b), a new classification encompassing several types of volunteering, each driven by its own combination of three elements – choice, coercion and obligation. These elements are not always as contradictory as they might first appear.

Volunteering as Leisure

Notwithstanding the relative lack of scholarly attention given to volunteering by leisure studies specialists, making a case for it as leisure poses little logical difficulty. If the word 'volunteering' is to remain consistent with its French and Latin roots, it can only be seen, as all leisure is, as non-coerced activity. It follows that, as with all leisure, leisure volunteering is basically a satisfying or enjoyable experience (or a combination of both). For otherwise we are forced to posit that so-called volunteers of this kind are somehow pushed into performing their roles by circumstances they would prefer to avoid, a flat contradiction of terms. And, while it is true that, in rare instances, volunteers are paid, even beyond expenses (for instance, 3% of the sample were paid in a study conducted by Blacksell and Phillips, 1994, p. 13), these emoluments are much too small to constitute a livelihood or significantly obligate someone.

Finally, it is also true that volunteering normally includes the clear requirement of being in a particular place, at a specified time, to carry out an assigned function. But as Kaplan (1960, pp. 22–25) once observed, true leisure can be obligated to some extent, although certainly not to the extent typical of work. Such obligation is none the less real for volunteers, even if the powerful rewards of the activity substantially outweigh it and the participant has an option to quit the activity at a convenient point in the near future. Given this condition it is more accurate to describe obligation in volunteering as *flexible*; unlike work and personal obligations (e.g. shopping for groceries, enduring dental work) there is relative freedom to honour commitments (Stebbins, 2000).

Defining Volunteering

Cnaan *et al.* (1996) set out four dimensions they found running throughout the several definitions of volunteering they examined. These dimensions are free choice, remuneration, structure and intended beneficiaries. Our definition is built from these four: *volunteering is uncoerced help offered either formally or informally with no or, at most, token pay done for the benefit of both other people and the volunteer.*

Concerning the free choice dimension, we prefer the language of (lack of) 'coercion', since that of 'free choice' is hedged about with numerous problems (see Stebbins, 2002). The logical difficulties of including obligation in definitions of volunteering, treated earlier, militate against including this condition in our definition. As for remuneration, volunteers retain their voluntary spirit providing they avoid becoming dependent on any money received from their volunteering. Structurally, volunteers may serve formally in collaboration with legally chartered organizations or informally in situations involving small numbers of relatives, friends, neighbours and the like that have no such legal basis. Finally, it follows from what we said previously about altruism and self-interest in volunteering that both the volunteers and those who they help find benefits in such activity.

Three Forms of Leisure Volunteering

Viewed as leisure, volunteering comes in three main forms: *serious, casual* and *project-based leisure.* All three can be marginal, although not always in the same ways. Serious leisure is the systematic pursuit of an amateur, a hobbyist or a volunteer activity sufficiently substantial and interesting in nature for the participant to find a (non-work) career therein acquiring and expressing a combination of its special skills, knowledge and experience (Stebbins, 1992). Serious leisure, or career, volunteering is exemplified in such non-remunerated activities as working with autistic children, serving as president of a grassroots organization and coaching youth sport. Serious leisure is often compared with casual leisure, or immediately, intrinsically rewarding, relatively short-lived pleasurable activity requiring little or no special training to enjoy it (Stebbins, 1997, 2001c). Casual leisure activities like sunbathing, strolling in a park and sleeping until late on Sunday morning find their parallel in *casual volunteering*, for example, cooking hot dogs at a church picnic or taking tickets for a performance by the local community theatre. Finally, the serious and casual forms differ from another kind of voluntary action: magnanimous donations of blood, money, clothing and the like.

Serious leisure is further defined by six qualities which distinguish it from casual leisure, qualities uniformly found among its amateurs, hobbyists and volunteers. One is the occasional need to persevere. Participants who want to continue experiencing the same level of satisfaction in the activity have to meet certain challenges from time to time. It happens in all three types of serious leisure that deepest satisfaction sometimes comes at the end of the activity rather than during it, from conquering adversity along the way.

Another quality distinguishing serious leisure is the opportunity to follow a leisure career in the endeavour, as shaped by its own special contingencies, turning points, and stages of achievement and involvement. Nevertheless, in some fields, notably certain arts and sports, this career can include decline. Moreover, most, if not all, careers here owe their existence to a third quality: serious leisure participants make significant personal effort based on specially acquired knowledge, training or skill and, indeed, at times all three.

Serious leisure is further distinguished by several durable benefits, or tangible, salutary outcomes of such activity for participants. They are self-actualization, self-enrichment, self-expression, regeneration or renewal of self, feelings of accomplishment, enhancement of self-image, social interaction and sense of belonging, and lasting physical products of the activity (e.g. a painting, scientific paper, piece of furniture). A further benefit – self-gratification, or pure fun, which is by far the most evanescent benefit in this list – is also enjoyed by casual leisure participants. The possibility of realizing such benefits constitutes a powerful goal in serious leisure.

Fifth, serious leisure is distinguished by a unique ethos that emerges in each expression of it. At the core of this ethos is the special social world that evolves when enthusiasts in a particular field pursue over many years substantial shared interests. According to Unruh (1979, 1980), every social world has its characteristic groups, events, routines, practices and organizations. It is held together, to an important degree, by semi-formal, or mediated, communication. In other words, in the typical case, social worlds are neither heavily bureaucratized nor substantially organized through intense face-to-face interaction. Rather, communication is commonly mediated by newsletters, posted notices, telephone messages, mass mailings, radio and television announcements, and similar means.

The sixth quality – participants in serious leisure tend to identify strongly with their chosen pursuits – springs from the preceding five. In contrast, most casual leisure, though not usually humiliating or despicable, is for most people, none the less, too fleeting, mundane and commonplace to generate distinctive identities.

The second form is experienced as casual leisure. It comprises several types, one being casual volunteering and the others being play (including dabbling), relaxation (e.g. sitting, napping, strolling), passive entertainment (e.g. television, books, recorded music), active entertainment (e.g. games of chance, party games), sociable conversation and sensory stimulation (e.g. sex, eating, drinking). All types have in common the fact that they are considerably less substantial than serious leisure and offer no career of the sort found there. Furthermore, it is likely that people pursue the different types of casual leisure in combinations of two and three at least as often as they pursue them separately. For instance, every type can be relaxing, producing in this fashion play–relaxation, passive entertainment–relaxation, and so on. Various combinations of play and sensory stimulation are also possible, as in experimenting with drug use, sexual activity and thrill seeking in movement. Additionally, sociable conversation accompanies some sessions of sensory stimulation (e.g. drug use, curiosity seeking, displays of beauty) as well as some sessions of relaxation and active and passive entertainment, although such conversation normally tends to be rather truncated in the latter two.

The third form is expressed through project-based leisure: a short-term, reasonably complicated, one-off or occasional, though infrequent, creative undertaking carried out in free time (Stebbins, 2004). It requires considerable planning, effort and sometimes skill or knowledge, but is for all that neither serious leisure nor intended to develop into such. Examples include surprise birthday parties, elaborate preparations for a major holiday and volunteering for sports events. Though only a rudimentary social world springs up around the project, it does in its own particular way bring together friends, neighbours or relatives (e.g. through a genealogical project or Christmas celebrations), or draw the individual participant into an organizational milieu (e.g. through volunteering for a sports event or major convention). This further suggests that project-based leisure often has, in at least two ways, potential for building community. One, it can bring into contact people who otherwise have no reason to meet, or at least meet frequently. Two, by way of event volunteering and other collective altruistic activity, it can contribute to carrying off community events and projects. Project-based leisure is not, however, civil labour, which must be classified, as was done earlier, as exclusively serious leisure.

Inextricably entangled with any discussion of volunteering as marginal is the question of obligation and the observation that obligation is not necessarily morally coercive. That is, people can feel obligated to carry out volunteer activity from which they nevertheless derive significant satisfaction or pleasure. People are obligated when, even though not actually coerced by an external force, they do or refrain from doing something because they feel bound in this regard by promise, convention or circumstances. But, as just indicated, obligation is not necessarily unpleasant. For example, Mary, being treasurer of her tennis club, is obligated to attend meetings of its executive committee, but does so with enthusiasm because she finds considerable satisfaction in helping to direct the club's affairs and working to keep it financially viable. Thus, it is important to separate *disagreeable obligation* from what has just been described: *agreeable obligation*, which is both an attitude and a form of behaviour that, together, can constitute a central part of the leisure experience. When felt, agreeable obligation is part of leisure because it accompanies positive attachment to an activity, is associated with pleasant memories and expectations (Stebbins, 2000), and, as mentioned, is flexible.

The studies reported in this book apply the foregoing leisure perspective to volunteering, each showing in its own way that issues such as those raised earlier can be resolved to the advantage of both individual volunteers and non-profit organizations. In particular, many of the studies show that volunteer roles, because they offer their incumbents special careers and distinctive sets of rewards, can be understood as serious leisure or, without the career element, as project-based leisure. This perspective applied to volunteering works to negate the proposition that conceiving of volunteering as leisure trivializes volunteering. Still, the leisure perspective stresses that the primary reason for volunteering is self-interest and that volunteers remain largely unaware of how their actions ramify socially.

Past Conceptions of Volunteering as Leisure Activity

Whether it is leisure studies specialists looking at volunteering or voluntary action specialists looking at leisure, the result has been much the same: neither field has been inclined to view its own subject matter through the eyes of the other. Still, significant exceptions exist, some of which will be reviewed here to show how the theoretical link between leisure and volunteering has evolved in recent decades.

Some of the earliest theoretical stirrings in this area came from Bosserman and Gagan (1972, p. 115) and David Horton Smith (1975, p. 148), who argued that, at the level of the individual, all leisure activity is voluntary action. More precise statements were made then and somewhat later by Kaplan (1975, p. 394) and Neulinger (1981, p. 19), two leisure studies specialists, who observed in passing how leisure can serve either oneself or other people or both. It is presumed that they had volunteerism in mind. From the side of voluntary action research, Kenneth Boulding (1973, p. 31) theorized that voluntary service borders on leisure, frequently even overlapping it. Alex Dickson (1974, p. xiii) observed that leisure is seen in commonsense as part of voluntary action, and does in fact 'carry this spare-time connotation'.

Karla Henderson (1981, 1984) examined the leisure component of volunteering both empirically and theoretically. She noted that social scientists ordinarily regard volunteering in the same way as they regard paid work, as having an external, or extrinsic, orientation – the volunteer has a job to complete for the benefit of the community. This contrasts with the view they hold of leisure as oriented by internal, or intrinsic, interests – the participant enjoys the activity for itself and for the self-expression and self-actualization it may engender. Henderson found that her sample of volunteer farm workers in the USA defined their volunteering as leisure; for them volunteering was part of their leisure world.

A few years later Stanley Parker (1987) reported findings from research on a group of peace workers. He discovered that, whereas they worked as volunteers for the cause of peace, they considered this work to be part of their leisure. Parker also completed a second study around this time centred on the serious leisure activities of two samples of volunteers, one drawn in Britain, the other drawn in Australia (reported in Parker, 1992). Here he learned that one person in five engaged in some form of activity classifiable as volunteering. Almost invariably, the people sampled described their volunteering as leisure, primarily as a rewarding activity and secondarily as a helping activity. Their leisure was none the less most substantial; in reality it was serious leisure.

While Parker was studying peace workers, Chambré (1987) was examining elderly volunteers. She reached similar conclusions: her respondents also defined their volunteering as leisure activity. Like Henderson, she wrestled with the extrinsic–intrinsic and the altruistic–self-interested dimensions, both of which pervade leisure volunteering. Volunteering is a work-like activity wherein a person accomplishes a task without remuneration. At the same time, the activity, which is non-coercive, provides many a satisfying experience. Chambré (1987, p. 118) found, however, that the motives given by the elderly for taking up a volunteer role differ from those given for continuing in it. Although their sense of altruism often led them to volunteer in the first place, they were highly motivated by the intrinsic satisfaction they found there to continue in this role.

Working from Chambré's conclusion that volunteering is leisure, Fischer and Schaffer (1993, pp. 51, 106–108) set out to explore the patterns of costs and rewards the elderly experience when they participate in this kind of activity. Following a comprehensive review of the current research and case study literature, these authors concluded that certain costs (e.g. time, hazards, inconvenience) are typically offset by numerous special rewards. The rewards include the following: feeling competent to do the volunteer work, sensing ideological congruence with the organization and being satisfied with the job done (i.e. work is interesting, professional growth is possible, personal skills are used). Self-actualization, self-enrichment and opportunities for social interaction were also found to be highly appealing (Fischer and Schaffer, 1993, Chap. 10). Moreover, it appears, the elderly are not alone in their assessment that volunteering is highly rewarding leisure. Thompson and Bono (1993) found a similar outlook in their sample of volunteer firefighters, whose activities fostered self-actualization, a sense of group accomplishment and a special self-image.

Case studies like that of volunteer firefighters reveal that volunteering in a variety of leisure contexts can show common ground results as well as considerable diversification. For example, Graham's (2001) historical development approach to a comprehensive study of museum volunteers in one of the largest urban public-sector museum services in Europe drew parallels between volunteering and museums as a charitable cause. She argued that museums and volunteers both continue to reproduce a philanthropic legacy originating from the 19th century when both had a role to play in relieving social problems related to rapid industrial progress. It was from these origins that gendered stereotypes and altruistic associations with volunteering have emerged. The distinctiveness of museum volunteering from other forms of volunteering is best exemplified by the degree of flexibility in interpreting volunteer profiles and definitions. Often volunteer leisure experiences tend to cross the boundaries between work and leisure. For example, a volunteer may use his/her host museum to progress a lifelong hobby and have knowledge and skills that exceed those of the museum's paid staff, even those with a postgraduate qualification in the same field of interest. For others, such as those recovering from long-term illness, volunteering is a leisure pursuit undertaken in a non-threatening environment that may prepare them for the demands of returning to paid work.

The chapters contained in this book provide a rich diversity of contextual analyses of volunteer experiences and cutting-edge issues from the perspective of volunteering as leisure, be it of the serious, casual or project variety. Further, these chapters consider issues of volunteering that collectively make a significant contribution towards understanding a raft of issues concerning volunteers and the organizations that host them. However, this progress must not cause us to lose sight of the history of volunteering and the significant contributions it has made in the past. The next chapter first examines this history and then takes a practical line by applying theories of volunteering to real-life examples.

An International Set of Studies

This book centres on the international volunteer scene. To obtain a broad set of examples of theory and research on volunteering as leisure and leisure as volunteering, in 2001 we distributed a call for chapters to be included in the present volume to members of the Volunteerism Commission. Eleven researchers or teams of researchers working in six countries – Britain, Brazil, Canada, Australia, The Netherlands and the USA – responded with proposals. The chapters they subsequently wrote are organized according to four themes: (i) establishing long-term commitment: event volunteering; (ii) changing volunteer lifestyles: motivation and satisfaction; (iii) politics of volunteering and active citizenship: policy issues; and (iv) encouraging the next generation: sustainability and youth volunteering.

These chapters give evidence of the enormous variety of work going on in the name of leisure and volunteering, ranging from research on volunteer firefighting to that on sport volunteering. They also show that, whereas it is possible to find support for the serious–casual–project-based leisure approach in each, authors of several chapters have chosen to frame their findings in other theoretical perspectives. This is as it should be, for the original mandate of the Volunteerism Commission called for 'researchers to adopt any theoretical or methodological approach to questions of this sort that promises to bear fruit'. This does not, however, create untoward theoretical contradiction. Rather, the serious–casual–project leisure conceptual framework establishes *a priori* the phenomenon to be investigated – volunteering as leisure, leisure as volunteering. This focuses inquiry, while leaving open the question of choice of framework to be subsequently used for interpreting the data generated. At this point some authors opted to frame their data in the serious–casual–project-based leisure perspective, whereas others preferred to use, for instance, management theory, organizational theory or the social behaviour perspective. Our understanding of volunteering and leisure is all the richer for this variety.

Finally, in all these chapters, their authors touch in one way or another on the twin questions of effective scheduling of volunteer time and delivery of volunteer services. In a couple of them these two are considered under the rubric of 'best practices'. Margaret Graham, in the first chapter, sets the stage for the rest of this book by addressing herself to these questions as well as to that of the history of volunteering. Heritage volunteering in Scotland serves as an example.

References

Applebaum, H. (1992) *The Concept of Work: Ancient, Medieval, and Modern.* State University of New York Press, Albany, New York.

Aronowitz, S. and DiFazio, W. (1994) *The Jobless Future: Sci-tech and the Dogma of Work.* University of Minnesota Press, Minneapolis, Minnesota.

Beck, U. (2000) *The Brave New World of Work* (trans. by Patrick Camiller). Polity Press, New York.

Blacksell, S. and Phillips, D.R. (1994) *Paid to Volunteer: the Extent of Paying Volunteers in the 1990s.* Volunteer Centre UK, London.

Bosserman, P. and Gagan, R. (1972) Leisure and voluntary action. In: Smith, D.H. (ed.) *Voluntary Action Research: 1972.* D.C. Heath, Lexington, Massachusetts, pp. 109–126.

Boulding, K. (1973) *The Economy of Love and Fear.* Wadsworth, Belmont, California.

Chambré, S.M. (1987) *Good Deeds in Old Age: Volunteering by the New Leisure Class.* Lexington Books, Lexington, Massachusetts.

Cnaan, R.A., Handy, F. and Wadsworth, M. (1996) Defining who is a volunteer: conceptual and empirical considerations. *Nonprofit and Voluntary Sector Quarterly* 25, 364–383.

Dickson, A. (1974) Foreword. In: Smith, D.H. (ed.) *Voluntary Action Research: 1974.* D.C. Heath, Lexington, Massachusetts, pp. xiii–xx.

Fischer, L.R. and Schaffer, K.B. (1993) *Older Volunteers: a Guide to Research and Practice.* Sage, Newbury Park, California.

Graham, M. (2001) The impact of social change on the roles and management of volunteers in Glasgow museums. PhD thesis, British Library, London, UK.

Henderson, K.A. (1981) Motivations and perceptions of volunteerism as a leisure activity. *Journal of Leisure Research* 13, 208–218.

Henderson, K.A. (1984) Volunteerism as leisure. *Journal of Voluntary Action Research* 13, 55–63.

Kaplan, M. (1960) *Leisure in America: a Social Inquiry.* Wiley, New York.

Kaplan, M. (1975) *Leisure: Theory and Policy.* Wiley, New York.

Neulinger, J. (1981) *To Leisure: an Introduction.* Allyn and Bacon, Boston, Massachusetts.

Parker, S.R. (1987) Working for peace as serious leisure. *Leisure Information Quarterly* 13(4), 9–10.

Parker, S.R. (1992) Volunteering as serious leisure. *Journal of Applied Recreation Research* 17, 1–11.

Rifkin, J. (1995) *The End of Work: the Decline of the Global Labor Force and the Dawn of the Post-market Era*. G.P. Putnam's Sons, New York.

Rojek, C. (2002) Civil labour, leisure, and post work society. *Loisir et société/Society and Leisure* 25(2), 21–36.

Smith, D.H. (1975) Voluntary action and voluntary groups. In: Inkeles, A., Coleman, J. and Smelser, N. (eds) *Annual Review of Sociology*, Vol. 1. Annual Reviews Inc., Palo Alto, Calfornia, pp. 247–270.

Stebbins, R.A. (1992) *Amateurs, Professionals, and Serious Leisure*. McGill-Queens University Press, Montreal.

Stebbins, R.A. (1997) Casual leisure: a conceptual statement. *Leisure Studies* 16, 17–25.

Stebbins, R.A. (2000) Obligation as an aspect of leisure experience. *Journal of Leisure Research* 32, 152–155.

Stebbins, R.A. (2001a) Volunteering – mainstream and marginal: preserving the leisure experience. In: Graham, M. and Foley, M. (eds) *Volunteering in Leisure: Marginal or Inclusive?* Leisure Studies Association, Eastbourne, pp. 1–10.

Stebbins, R.A. (2001b) *New Directions in the Theory and Research of Serious Leisure*, Mellen Studies in Sociology, Vol. 28. Edwin Mellen Press, Lewiston, New York.

Stebbins, R.A. (2001c) The costs and benefits of hedonism: some consequences of taking casual leisure seriously. *Leisure Studies* 20, 305–309.

Stebbins, R.A. (2002) Choice in experiential definitions of leisure. *Leisure Studies Association Newsletter* 63(November),18–20.

Stebbins, R.A. (2004). Project-based leisure: theoretical neglect of a common use of free time. *Leisure Studies* (in press).

Thompson, A.M., III and Bono, B.A. (1993) Work without wages: the motivation of volunteer firefighters. *American Journal of Economics and Sociology* 52, 323–343.

Unruh, D.R. (1979) Characteristics and types of participation in social worlds. *Symbolic Interaction* 2, 115–130.

Unruh, D.R. (1980) The nature of social worlds. *Pacific Sociological Review* 23, 271–296.

Volunteering as Heritage/ Volunteering in Heritage

1

M. Graham

Caledonian University

Introduction

There is no doubt that a rise in demand for volunteering experiences world-wide is paralleled by an increase in demands being placed on non-profit-making organizations to schedule their volunteers more effectively while being more accountable to the communities they serve.

However, the haphazard and inconsistent delivery of volunteering has been a hallmark that has dogged the voluntary sector for more than a century. Volunteering as a leisure pursuit suggests motives to volunteer are informal and as such volunteers cannot be controlled in the same way as paid staff. Added to this, perceived stereotypical images of volunteers and ideo-logical assumptions have been reproduced and continue to colour percep-tions about volunteers, preventing them from being fully understood. Indeed, it could be argued that there is a moral panic within spheres of the voluntary sector that suggest that future volunteering will be compromised either through lack of interest among the younger generation or by policy interfer-ence that threatens the long-established 'spirit of volunteering' as a legacy of the past. However, as more people compete for volunteering experiences there is more potential for host organizations to be more selective to ensure that they recruit those with compatible skills and commitment. There is also the threat that the satisfaction and enjoyment derived from leisure volunteer-ing will be compromised through *excessive and unpleasantly inflexible obligation* (Stebbins, 2001).

This shift from informal voluntary action to formal voluntary action aims to raise the status of voluntary work by setting standards of best practice. All the chapters contained within this book consider issues of volunteering that collectively make a significant contribution towards understanding a whole raft of issues concerning volunteers and the organizations that host them. However, progress must not lose sight of the history of volunteering and the significant contributions it has made in the past.

This chapter takes a pragmatic approach by applying theories of volunteering to real-life examples. These examples are drawn from Scottish cultural heritage organizations that support national causes with an international reputation.

Objective

Change is always a challenge but depending on whether change is viewed positively or negatively, progress can be either meaningfully advanced or stiflingly hindered. Preserving volunteering as a leisure experience is crucial in its future development. At this point it is appropriate to consider Stebbins's (2001) marginal versus mainstream volunteering debate. Ideally, mainstream volunteering should be a motivation-driven 'freely chosen activity' that is a 'satisfying and enjoyable' leisure experience (Stebbins, 2001). On the other hand, marginal volunteering is distinguished by its marginalization of free choice and emphasis on 'disagreeable', inflexible obligation (Stebbins, 2001). Indeed, serious and casual leisure volunteering may contain aspects of marginal volunteering but in this case obligation is flexible with no 'moral coercion'.

Stebbins (2001) warns that the coercive emphasis of marginal volunteering must not threaten volunteer motivation as leisure and the agreeable personal rewards realized through mainstream volunteering experiences.

The objective of this chapter is to provide a foundation which subsequent chapters can relate to and build on to form a picture that will help to demonstrate the scope and diversity of volunteering as well as identify commonalities.

Research Field

This chapter will draw from several major national visitor attraction research projects undertaken in the UK during the past decade by academic research staff at the Moffat Centre for Travel and Tourism Business Development, based at Glasgow Caledonian University. The Moffat Centre has its own philanthropic origins. The Centre's benefactor, the late Jamie Moffat, founder of what was Scotland's largest travel agent, now known as ATM Travel, acknowledged that forging links with universities would provide the potential for the tourism industry to draw from academic expertise to improve the performance of tourism-related business operating within both the commercial and not-for-profit sectors. The Centre is committed to raising the status of tourism through developing the skills and effectiveness of those who work in the sector. It does this by employing highly skilled business development and research staff dedicated to encourage best practice through research, academic teaching and by providing student scholarships, placements and employment. Post-doctoral staff currently involved in heritage research at the Centre have significant experience themselves as volunteers which includes volunteering and paid work experiences in heritage organizations. Moffat Centre (MC) research publications and presentations are disseminated widely through a variety of academic and industry media, which is confirmed in the reference sources used to compile this chapter.

The research projects used in this chapter will focus on the visitor attraction sector in the UK, which is dominated by cultural heritage not-for-profit organizations that depend significantly on volunteers. The projects include national visitor attraction surveys that targeted approximately 6000 visitor attractions in England (English Tourism Council (ETC), 2001, 2002) and Scotland (Scottish Tourist Board (STB) and the MC, 1998, 1999, 2000; STB/VisitScotland and the MC, 2001; VisitScotland and the MC, 2002), a labour market skills forecasting survey targeting 700 visitor attractions in Scotland (Cultural and Heritage National Training Organisation, 1999), a volunteer survey targeting 2000 volunteers operating within National Trust for Scotland countryside and heritage properties (Graham, 2003), and a volunteer management programme delivered to paid staff at Scotland's Burns National Heritage Park.

It is appropriate that the theories and models contained within this chapter were originally devised from an empirical study targeting 2000 volunteers active in museums and galleries located in Glasgow (Graham, 1996, 2001). Firstly, this venue for volunteering activity is the largest public-sector urban museums service in Europe. Secondly, a significant number of volunteers are drawn from the independent charity, the Glasgow Art Gallery and Museums Association (GAGMA), which has been highlighted as a benchmark of good practice in active citizenship, by national museum and volunteer-related agencies. This argument is also supported by this Scottish city's philanthropic history. In order to explain this more fully readers will be invited to step back in time to compare the development of theories of volunteering with much earlier volunteering experiences. Finally, the effectiveness of volunteering as a leisure experience will be considered. This final approach to understanding volunteering is not so easily tied to the experiences of the past, when volunteering was more easily explained as that of unselfish service to the community. This chapter focuses on cultural heritage volunteering but the theories and models it presents are flexible enough to be applied to all the contexts contained within this book.

Volunteering as Heritage

This book celebrates volunteering as supporting *wholesome* causes that address the needs of host organizations as well as the needs of the volunteers themselves. Having a rational view of volunteering is the only way we can make sense of it, to try to understand its current role. However, so many pre-conceptions and stereotypes have become attached to volunteering that they make it difficult to conceptualize and define. Life experiences as volunteers clearly reveal the limitations that social change has had on the principles and long-established values that have become welded to volunteering and the types of causes volunteers support. Therefore, it is critical to view the current role of volunteering in the context of social change.

Kendall and Knapp (1996) identified a link between changing volunteer characteristics and social initiators. They argued that the altruistic label of *respectability* that remains attached to volunteering can be traced back to pre-industrial society. At this time volunteering activity emerged from the church connections of the British landed gentry and was delivered as acts of selfless duty to help relieve poverty. They added that it was during the rise of rapid industrialization and urbanization that the British voluntary sector became a distinct, value-laden tradition/The institutionalization of the volun-tary sector spawned rapidly during this period and became dominated by practical help charities. Volunteering became established as one of the few occupations suitable for middle-class women. It is from this period that vol-unteer gendered stereotypes have emerged. During the inter-war period increased pressure on the voluntary sector weakened its association with female volunteers as it tried to relieve the plight of the casualties of the Great War as well as those of the Great Depression that followed. However, gender stereotyping within some organizations persists, particularly in public-service organizations like health and education and those that continue to have links with the landed gentry, like heritage (McCrone *et al.*, 1995) and/or tasks associated with women's traditional domestic role.

Indeed, Britain's more serious volunteering tradition took off in the wake of rapid industrialization and urbanization during the 18th and 19th centu-ries/Various forms of volunteering provided a means to help address a whole raft of social problems linked to residential overcrowding, cultural deviance, deprivation and poverty (Graham, 1995, 2001)./Looking back, volunteering can be viewed from two perspectives – either as a duty undertaken by privi-leged people with superfluous leisure time 'to support worthy causes' or alternatively as a pursuit to further enhance privilege and social status. Volunteering action included providing gifts of time, skills, money and/or possessions.

Wholesome forms of volunteering are the most documented. Indeed, benevolent volunteering is one of the longest-surviving volunteering tradi-tions (Graham, 2001). In her thesis Graham uses the example of 19th-century Glasgow and the relative success of its Home Mission Service, which still exists today. Organizations like Glasgow City Mission (founded in 1826) continue to address similar problems although linked to current disadvan-taged lifestyles (Glasgow City Mission, 1926; Graham, 1995). Although the delivery of volunteering reform was inconsistent, 19th-century Glasgow was viewed as a role model by the British Charitable Organisations Society partially because of established strong links between local politicians, eminent churchmen, industrialists and voluntary-sector benefactors. Volunteering in Glasgow at this time involved a host of volunteering experiences, i.e. to develop and support church and medical missions, Magdalene societies, youth organizations, higher education, sport and more casual forms of recreational volunteering.

However, documentary evidence tends to rejoice in celebrating the *wholesome* aspects of volunteering development. Less visible forms of volunteering tended to be led by educated people but depended on the support of those who were poorly educated and was often 'driven underground'. These *less than wholesome* types of volunteering also included gifts of time, money and possessions to support causes like radical political organizations, blood sports and various forms of human capital trade. An example of the latter includes the parental sacrifice of a child to some form of legal or illegal labour process in the belief that such action would secure a child's future care and protection.

The parallel Graham (2001) makes with early developments in heritage and medical volunteering is revealing. She traces back the origins of student volunteering action in medical and museum research and the rise of professional occupations in both types of public-service organization. She draws parallels between the diagnosis of disease with the interpretation of museum artefacts, when both service professionals control such facts that up until recently have gone relatively unchallenged. This suggests that the work of early philanthropists makes it difficult to totally separate volunteering from paid work. Industrialists were also active philanthropists. Textile industrialist William Coates founded public-sector libraries throughout Scotland to encourage *educational opportunity for all* for altruistic as well as social capital benefits. For example, illiteracy abounded in 19th-century Glasgow at a time when rules and regulations began to touch on all aspects of daily life. Signs were as commonplace in the workplace as they were in recreational spaces, some of which still exist today, for example 'keep off the grass', 'do not touch', 'silence', 'no loitering'. The role of philanthropy in education was significant and recreational spaces like libraries, museums and parks were used as a means to educate the 'uncivilized' masses. Industrial philanthropists, including Coates, were responsible for establishing the public-sector museums in and around Glasgow that exist today. Although the policy of *free access for all* was established then, only those deserving of improvement were included and allowed to participate. Mode of dress, behaviour, language and cleanliness would form the division lines between *social inclusion* and *exclusion*.

It is little wonder that many commentators consider volunteering in the context of paid work. Geroy *et al.* (2000, p. 280) argue that employee volunteering '*spills over to the job by increasing employee morale and productivity*'.

The motivation to volunteer included the desire to interact with like-minded people, to further education and knowledge, to provide enjoyment and entertainment, to improve the environment, and to control society.

Although volunteering in 19th-century Glasgow undoubtedly raised social status and benefited the economy and society, it provided as many enjoyable and challenging experiences as the scope of volunteering contained within this book. A 19th-century mission agent's diary entry describing the dens and wynds of Glasgow as *scenes of blackest horror and unprecedented violence* shows how dangerous and challenging some volunteering experiences could be. Volunteer motivation is as diverse today as it was then, and, although it is a leisure pursuit, volunteering can improve lifestyles by achieving significant social and human capital benefits.

Current Attitudes Towards Volunteering

Voluntary action can be explained as acts of active citizenship that provide some form of benefit to the community without reciprocal financial reward being the primary motivator. Under the umbrella of this perspective all the volunteer contexts contained within this book fit comfortably. However, this chapter will present arguments that suggest that volunteering is driven as much by self-interest as it is by altruism. It is also important to mention that attitudes towards volunteering can be coloured by stereotypical labels that unjustly associate volunteering with the older middle-class community who support some form of public-service charity. From a management point of view volunteering tends to be viewed as an unstructured part of the labour market, which has no long-term dependability nor record of effective management control. This economic perspective values volunteering according to its low cost, the number of tasks completed, its role in developing human capital and its contribution towards the health of communities. This undervalues volunteering by failing to consider its worth in terms of social capital such as the quality of volunteering as a leisure experience and the lifestyle benefits to be gained as a consequential reward.

A Case Study of Heritage Volunteering in Scotland

Heritage as volunteer host

This chapter focuses on Scottish heritage organizations that make a distinct contribution towards the visitor attraction sector in the UK. The following definition of a visitor attraction was devised by all four National Tourist Boards in the UK, namely the English Tourism Council (ETC; now Visit-Britain), Northern Ireland Tourist Board (NITB), VisitScotland (VS) and Wales Tourist Board (WTB):

A permanently established excursion destination, a primary purpose of which is to allow public access for entertainment, interest or education, rather than being principally a retail outlet or a venue for sporting, theatrical or film performances. It must be open to the public for published periods each year, and should be capable of attracting tourist or day visitors as well as local residents.

The visitor attraction sector in the UK is extremely diverse in terms of the type, size and purpose of organization. Employment within this sector is varied due to the seasonal nature of many visitor attractions and cost-related factors. Most visitor attractions are not-for-profit organizations and have an inherited legacy of providing non-conventional types of employment linked to philanthropy, community duty and furthering education.

Heritage is beginning to target and capture the interest of a wider audience and volunteers have a significant role in heritage interpretation and other tasks related to presenting heritage education to the public at large (Graham, 1995; Borman, 2003). Consumers of heritage have raised expectations about how views of the past should be delivered and interpreted. This is fed by the rise of popular choice benchmarks in heritage interpretation. Advances in interactive technology, educational literature, media broadcasting such as broadcast history documentaries, and the film industry, mean that heritage audiences are more knowledgeable and discerning than ever before. Lennon and Graham (2001) explain the dilemma faced by the not-for-profit sector as their philanthropic role is becoming challenged by pressure to compete with commercially orientated visitor attractions. However, they stress that the commercial sector is also becoming pressed to draw from the principles of heritage organizations in the drive to interpret heritage in an authentic and creative way that will capture the interest of a much wider consumer market.

It was estimated that there were 114,000 paid employees, either full time or part time, working in the UK visitor attractions sector in 2001. However, it was also estimated that a further 102,500 volunteers were also active in the visitor attraction sector at this time (ETC, 2002, pp. 140–141). Some 2662 visitor attractions in the UK provided actual employment-related information confirming that they used the skills of 87,000 people, of which 44,000 were paid employees and around 43,000 were volunteers (ETC, 2002, p. 102). In Scotland, of the 475 visitor attractions that provided labour market-related information, 33% of an identified 8339 workforce were volunteers (ETC, 2002, pp. 106–107). Attraction operators also expressed concerns for the future as volunteers were 'becoming more difficult to find' (ETC, 2002, p. 108).

There is no doubt that in terms of volunteer role, commitment, skills profile and responsibility, volunteers within the UK attraction sector encompass considerable diversity. Their involvement with their host organization can involve levels of time commitment equivalent to full-time paid staff down to involvement in short-term projects of less than half a day.

Heritage as cause

At the heart of volunteering lies the worthy causes that volunteers support. In cultural heritage these worthy causes form the basis of a distinct code of ethics and values that guide organizational decision making. For over a decade, management theory has been instrumental in providing new solutions to organizational problem solving to reduce the dependence of not-for-profit organizations on various sources of public funding. Recent reviews and restructuring programmes within cultural heritage not-for-profit organizations have aimed to ensure their worthy causes are pursued and achieved at least cost. For example, the importance of volunteer support was evident when it was included in Glasgow Museums' recent Best Value Review. This review served to encourage this large public-sector museum service to manage itself more effectively. In turn it made the museum profession accountable to adopt a more formal approach to the way it encouraged and organized its volunteers. In the process of this perspective shift, not-for-profit organizations have needed to adopt a new set of values and priorities more in line with commercial business. Therefore, organizations hosting volunteers are increasingly under pressure to ensure self-interest among volunteers is channelled to promote organizational values that enhance performance. A closer consideration of these cause-related goals will demonstrate how the balance has been tipped to include more economic priorities. For example, achieving the competitive edge over other leisure pursuits is becoming just as important when attracting and retaining good volunteers as it is in increasing popularity and widening access.

Four types of causes have been identified, with many of them having the potential to achieve as many benefits for volunteers as the potential benefits to be gained by the organizations that act as their host. The four cause-related types, detailed below, are: (i) primary special interest; (ii) social responsibility; (iii) environmental concern; and (iv) economic duty.

Primary special interest

In cultural heritage organizations the special interest cause is related to the subject matter of the organization and is the focus of its primary function. The main themes encompassed in the research projects being scrutinized consider causes related to the care and protection of historic properties, gardens, a variety of different countryside landscapes, museum and art collections, and the life and works of the Scottish Bard, Robert Burns. A hierarchy of special interest causes can be drawn after scrutinizing them more forcibly. This model helps explain why special interest causes are likely to generate either a narrow or popular interest among potential volunteer recruits.

NARROW INTEREST FOCUS   This includes organizations that preserve and interpret heritage topics not associated with popular interest. One of Glasgow's small independent interpretation museums, Heatherbank Museum of Social Work, fits this category (Graham, 2001). Heatherbank presents changing exhibitions on the history of care in the community. The organization has a small pool of ten volunteers, and has a history of attracting people from the service professions including people with work experience in social work, teaching, the Church and health. Their contacts, knowledge and sympathy concerning issues close to the caring profession were strengths that helped in tasks related to artefact acquisition, research and interpretation. Most volunteers were used for *ad hoc* projects, with a minority being used regularly as museum attendants and guides.

COMMUNITY INTEREST   Cultural heritage organizations that interpret the history of a locality depend on attracting community volunteers. Graham (2001) argues that interest and volunteer experiences vary considerably between one community organization and another. For example, small organizations like Glasgow's Springburn Museum depend significantly on volunteers to manage and undertake day-to-day routine operations (Graham, 2001). Without regular volunteering to maintain sufficient funding to survive, many organizations like it struggle to exist. Indeed, with declining interest among a pool of 12 to 20 volunteers, Springburn Museum struggled in vain to maintain sufficient funding to maintain vital income streams needed to survive. Although the subject matter of this museum interpreted the international importance of Springburn and its role in innovative developments in the heavy industries, volunteers tended to be retired from transport-related occupations like mechanical engineering. This employment history among volunteers was particularly important in transport conservation as it involved volunteers with outdated and highly skilled abilities that are increasingly difficult to come by.

On the other hand, large community museums demonstrated the potential to attract wider interest particularly for innovative and creative volunteering projects. Glasgow's People's Palace and Open Museum generated three waves of volunteering support during its '2000 Glasgow Lives' oral history project. More than 100 volunteers representing a wide spectrum of Glasgow citizens were trained in interview and technical skills to gather and record an archive of the life experiences of 2000 Glasgow citizens. The main strength of this group of volunteers was their collective community connections, which led to a comprehensive oral history archive that was representative of the whole of the city.

MEMBERSHIP INTEREST   Subscription volunteering to support the cause of cultural heritage organizations takes many forms. Graham identified the significance of Friends membership in contributing towards funding projects and as the most important source of regular and long-term volunteering in Glasgow's public-sector museums (Graham, 2001). Membership normally suggests more than a passing interest in the cultural heritage organization as a cause. Volunteer guides drawn from both the Friends of Glasgow Museums and members of the National Trust for Scotland demonstrated a high level of interpretation-related knowledge as well as an enthusiasm to develop it further (Graham, 2001, 2003).

NATIONAL INTEREST   Conservation volunteers involved in the preservation of artefacts of national importance are particularly prevalent in the cultural heritage sector. Tasks range from land management tasks involving retaining and enhancing the Scottish landscape, such as repairing fencing, traditional dry stone walling, horticultural and forestry work, to caring and protecting artefacts that interpret Scotland's industrial and colonial heritage (Graham, 2001, 2003).

INTERNATIONAL INTEREST   The primary cause of some of the cultural heritage organizations can be viewed in the context of international interest in the national culture of Scotland. Examples of this include the National Trust for Scotland Property, Fingal's Cave on the Isle of Staffa, made famous by Mendelssohn and the poet Robert Burns, who is as much a part of the Scottish brand as whisky, bagpipes and tartan. However, international visibility has been challenging for some Scottish heritage organizations and has resulted in requests for the repatriation of colonial objects. This was one issue faced by Glasgow Museums when it was compelled to return The Ghost Dance Shirt to its owners the Lakota Sioux following a public debate (Morris, 2000).

Social responsibility
This cause serves to advance research in and access to culture and heritage by widening community and tourist involvement for employment, educational, leisure and health-related purposes.

Environmental concern
Opening up access to the countryside for recreation is currently being advanced. Sustainability and the care and protection of the natural environment is one of the primary concerns of land management projects such as those involved in repairing the Scottish landscape and protecting endangered animal and plant life.

Economic duty
Cultural heritage organizations have become responsible for their role in interpreting the uniqueness of Scotland as a destination for domestic and international tourists. Marketing to tourists has become a civic duty encouraging the development of the local tourism economy. Volunteer guides in the museums surveyed specified the importance of their role in interpreting Scottish heritage to international tourists. The National Trust for Scotland staff also identified international tourists as an important market niche to

target in their volunteer holiday campaigns. In 2001, 3% of volunteers applying for volunteer positions in the National Trust for Scotland Thistle Camps were from overseas countries including the Republic of Ireland, USA, Japan and Zimbabwe (National Trust for Scotland, 2001).

Volunteer location model

The volunteering location model looks at three levels of supply and demand for heritage-related volunteering experiences. Two levels, the urban and rural model, apply to volunteering undertaken inside or directly outside historic buildings and properties, such as historic houses, museums and galleries, and other civic buildings. The third model considers more challenging forms of volunteering, in this case volunteering undertaken in a variety of countryside landscapes.

Rural model
Dependence on volunteers tended to rise alongside a declining supply of potential new volunteer recruits according to the size and rural aspect of the heritage organization. Indeed, some of the most isolated independent heritage organizations would not survive without the support of volunteers, particularly those which employed no paid staff.

Urban model
Organizations located in or near urban centres had a much larger supply of volunteers from whom to select. Although there is more investment in paid staff, project volunteering is a major growth area that pulls in volunteers on an *ad hoc* basis for a one-off project that may be short or long term.

Wilderness model
Countryside and outdoor heritage volunteering ranged from outdoor gardening and archaeological projects through to some of the most challenging conservation projects undertaken on treacherous mountainous regions in the Scottish Highlands. The number of volunteering experiences is decided by the host organization, who sells a limited supply of volunteering conservation holidays of 1–2 weeks' duration.

Volunteer characteristics

Graham (2001, 2003) identified that:

- More than 50% of long-term volunteers were predominantly from professional households, were female and were aged over 54 years.
- Short-term community project volunteers straddled class, gender and age categories fairly evenly.

- A significant sprinkling of male volunteers retired from public-service professions such as teaching and medicine had more recently emerged within the over 54 years age-band, particularly in the Glasgow museum survey.
- Female volunteers dominated all age ranges with the exception of the 35–44 age-band, which was predominantly male.
- Both male and female volunteers were equally represented in roles related to education and interpretation.
- Clusters of male volunteers demonstrated particular interest in fine art, transport and land management.
- Clusters of female volunteers were identified undertaking tasks related to sewing and flower conservation.
- Younger volunteers were involved in tasks related to work experience, student study programmes, information technology, computer database compilation and outdoor volunteering projects.

Levels of satisfaction and commitment to the host organization tended to decline the younger the volunteer. Staff who supervised volunteers agreed that the youngest volunteers tended to require maximum coaching and supervision. The following profiles consider differences and commonalities between the volunteer location model.

Urban and rural model
Volunteers operating inside/or nearby historic buildings, museums and galleries tended to be referred to as more 'active volunteers' and as such mirrored the profiles of visitors to the organizations. They were generally elderly, from middle-class households and had interests, careers or hobbies related to the subject matter of their host heritage organization. Both Scottish volunteer surveys confirmed that on average 75% of volunteers who fitted the urban and rural model were aged over 54 years with over 70% of total volunteers being female.

Urban model
Student and community project volunteering was more evident in the urban museum model and accounted for most volunteering undertaken by volunteers under 45 years of age. This group included a fairly equal mix of university students, unemployed people and those working full or part time.

Wilderness model
Most wilderness volunteers (58%) were aged between 25 and 44 years; 35% were aged over 44 years, with 65% of this older group being aged over 54 years. Only a minority (6%) were aged between 16 and 24 years.

Motivation

Motivation can be explained in three ways, as passive, special interest or active.

Passive motivators

There were two different types of passive motivator identified in heritage. In the first example, initial introductions to volunteering were instigated through some form of media and/or social networking. Sources of information included multiple sources of media publicity generated from host organizations including membership and promotion literature, community and press advertisements, and word-of-mouth networking through existing volunteers.

The second type of passive motivator involved initial introductions to volunteering being generated through obligations to friends and relatives or other community institutions, particularly in the voluntary and public sector. Volunteering in this case fulfilled either a desire to be with other volunteers who were friends or relatives or obligations linked to paid employment. For some volunteers this posed an unwelcome challenge while for others volunteering generated unexpected benefits, the scope of which is listed below using appropriate quotes from volunteers:

- Provided new friendships: 'Met other local people who are now my friends'.
- Increased confidence: 'I am no longer tongue tied'.
- Stimulated an interest in the subject matter of the organization: 'Generated an interest in the building'.
- Improved language skills: 'Improved my English'.
- Achieved personal satisfaction: 'Makes me feel not entirely useless'.
- Increased enjoyment: 'I was surprised that it was so much fun'.
- Improved feelings of well-being: 'Health improvements'.

Active motivators

Active motivators can be divided into two camps, *active citizens* and *challenge seekers*. Active citizens are driven by the desire to 'make a difference' to the local community, to the host organization or to the skills, social connections or well-being of the volunteer themselves. Various forms of active citizens were identified and are explained as follows using some quotes from volunteers.

- Commitment to the community: 'I enjoy putting something back into the community'.
- Commitment to the host organization: 'Our work has become essential as conservation standards are in decline as there are fewer paid staff'.
- Instrumental purpose: 'My main challenge is in research as I am keen to learn more about the collection'.

A variety of challenge seekers were identified, the scope of which can be explained using the following quotes:

- 'The odd challenge helps break with routine and keeps me motivated.'
- 'Archaeological fieldwork can be quite hazardous but it gives me immense satisfaction.'

- 'Hard work and strenuous exercise undertaken with a variety of different people working towards a common goal gives me an enormous sense of well-being.'
- 'My knowledge about the countryside and conservation helps me accomplish many challenging feats and instils a sense of pride and purpose.'
- 'Great working weekends away even although the weather, the midges and the accommodation are dire.'
- 'Stressful, but rewarding.'

Special interest motivators
Special interest motivators centre around an interest in the host organization's subject matter or project cause and the opportunity to meet like-minded people. For this group volunteering increased their knowledge of the local area or special interests related to the subject matter of the organization, such as Scottish and period history, architecture, the arts, crafts or practical outdoor conservation skills.

Typology

By bringing together all the Scottish surveys, a volunteer typology in heritage has been further advanced (Graham, 2003). The typology considers volunteer types, the cause they support that benefits the host organization and primary volunteer motivators. Table 1.1 shows different volunteer types alongside the mutual benefits achieved by them as well as the organization that their volunteering activities support.

Volunteer expectations

The current competitive nature of heritage in providing meaningful visitor and volunteering experiences has led to volunteering recruitment being more selective. In the future, organizations providing the best volunteering experiences are likely to secure the best volunteers. On the one hand, over 75% of all volunteers in the Scottish surveys expected to be treated informally. There was a fear that the philanthropic ethos of volunteering would be marginalized if more control was exerted over the support volunteers provide. On the other hand, a significant number of these volunteers expected their work to be recognized in a more formal manner. However, almost 25% of volunteers expressed the desire for a more formal relationship with their host organization provided volunteers' needs were met alongside those of the organization they supported.

Table 1.1. Volunteer typology in heritage.

Volunteer type	Primary benefit to host organization	Primary volunteer motivation
Discoverers	Develop knowledge/people	Develop skills and knowledge
Conservers	Preserve culture/heritage	Share/further existing skills
Educators	Convey knowledge	Socialize and coach
Learners	Education	Internalize skills and knowledge
Befrienders	Widen access to recreation and learning	Socialize and network
Adventurers	Preserve remote heritage assets	Experience challenge
Investors	Generate income/ self-sufficiency	Donate/fund-raise
Leisure seekers	Provide leisure experiences	Further personal interest/hobby
Activists	Support heritage profession	Make a difference and engage with paid staff
Health seekers	Contribute to well-being of community	Improve health and lifestyle
Organizers	Organize and develop volunteering	Lead and instruct

Volunteer leadership and organization

Graham (2001, 2003) identified two types of volunteer leadership, which can be defined as either formal Management centred or informal Team centred. At one end of the spectrum, in Management-centred leadership, management is closely involved with organizing volunteers, while in Team-centred leadership volunteers are self-organizing. All heritage organizations involved in the Scottish surveys were under pressure to become more formalized, even those with a strong history of Team-centred leadership.

The main drivers for changing the way volunteers were supervised was the realization that the performance of volunteers can directly or indirectly affect the performance of the heritage organizations they support. It is critical at this point to separate heritage from commercial business. Providing effective volunteering experiences that achieve the diverse range of community objectives is as important an objective as achieving financial self-sufficiency.

Glasgow Museums applied both approaches, the Team-centred leadership to the day-to-day operation of routine volunteering tasks, in particular guiding, and the Management-centred model for short-term projects. Indeed, Glasgow Museums had developed an increasingly formal model of Team-centred leadership which was led by committee-appointed 'organizers' who were responsible for engaging and involving volunteers. Liaison with management was particularly robust, with policy being implemented by volunteer organizers and dedicated paid members of staff at the initial volunteer recruitment stage. Although volunteer organizers controlled the selection, direction and supervision of the museum's volunteer guide service, formalization was driven by management and various public-sector training agencies. For example, more emphasis was placed on the existing knowledge and skills of volunteers during the recruitment process, with volunteering being more formally appraised in re-development plans currently under way in this organization.

Management-centred leadership was more prevalent in the university sector. This involved paid staff formulating policy and delegating and directing individual volunteers or groups of volunteers usually on specific *ad hoc* projects. There tended to be a strong element of on-the-job training and coaching.

The independent, public sector and National Trust for Scotland operated a mix of Team- and Management-centred approaches. Policy for the independent sector was implemented by boards of trustees which were made up of a mix of paid and honorary board members. Management was enforced primarily for health and safety and to ensure proper work practices were adhered to.

The Management-centred approach provided several advantages for volunteers. Formal management policy meant that their distinct supportive role was formally recognized and integrated alongside that of paid staff. From management's point of view they held the authority to implement essential policy, such as essential employment law and organizational objectives for the protection and benefit of the organization, heritage collections and volunteers. Some volunteers felt that this formalization process made them feel more involved and appreciated. However, sceptics had the perception that their performance as a volunteer was being monitored as if they were paid staff (Graham, 2000).

Conclusion

Political pressures have challenged the not-for-profit sectors to reassess the way they operate. Governments worldwide are realizing the social and economic benefits to be gained through developing volunteering as a leisure pursuit. There is no doubt that more dependence is being placed on volunteering activity as a means of addressing current socioeconomic problems. However, from a practitioner's point of view lack of knowledge and skill means they are unable to provide volunteering experiences that will provide mutual benefits to their organization as well as to their volunteers. Many not-for-profit organizations who host volunteers are being encouraged to consider management techniques to help them improve the way they administer and recruit volunteers. However, organizations that host volunteers have no strong links with management expertise. Added to this there is a popular belief within the not-for-profit sector that management is in conflict with the ethos of volunteering.

In the UK, funding sources for the not-for-profit sectors are becoming highly competitive and formalized. Expectations among philanthropists and volunteers have also heightened. Increasingly they expect that their contribution will be used to maximum benefit.

- What is the impact of policy pressures on future developments on volunteering?
- Do the social benefits being gained by volunteers outweigh the benefits they provide?
- In terms of social capital, skill and ability, are volunteers assigned to the correct volunteering positions?
- What do volunteers expect to gain from their volunteer experiences?

Practitioners who depend on the support of volunteers are increasingly being pressed to schedule them more effectively. On the one hand, there are raised expectations concerning the level of skill and ability presented by volunteers while, on the other hand, people who give of their time expect their role as a volunteer will be instrumentally fulfilling.

This chapter has paved the way for future chapters and provides a practical approach that can be applied to all the contributions that follow.

References

Borman, T. (2003) Face to face with history. *Journal of the Association of Heritage Interpretation* 8(1), 7–8.

Cultural and Heritage National Training Organisation (1999) *Skills Forecasting Scotland*. CHNTO, Bradford.

English Tourism Council (ETC) (2001) *Sightseeing in the UK 2000*. English Tourism Council, London.

English Tourism Council (ETC) (2002) *Sightseeing in the UK 2001*. English Tourism Council, London.

Geroy, G.D., Wright, P.C. and Jacoby, L. (2000) Toward a conceptual framework of employee volunteerism: an aid for the human resource manager. *Management Decision* 38, 280–286.

Glasgow City Mission (1926) *Glasgow City Mission Centenary Report: 1926*. Glasgow City Mission, Glasgow.

Graham, M. (1995) Religious philanthropy. Unpublished dissertation, Glasgow Caledonian University, Glasgow, UK.

Graham, M. (1996) Volunteering in an urban museums service. In: Ravenscroft, N., Phillips, D. and Bennett, H. (eds) *Tourism and Visitor Attractions*. Leisure Studies Association Publications, Eastbourne, pp. 21–40.

Graham, M. (2000) Who wants to be a volunteer? *Museums Journal* 100(3), 28–29.

Graham, M. (2001) The impact of social change on the roles and management of volunteers in Glasgow museums. PhD thesis, British Library, London, UK.

Graham, M. (2003) An exploration of volunteering support within the National Trust for Scotland, industry report. National Trust for Scotland, Edinburgh.

Kendall, J. and Knapp, M. (1996) *The Voluntary Sector in the UK*. Manchester University Press, Manchester.

Lennon, J.J. and Graham, M. (2001) The prognostication of the Scottish culture and heritage sector's skills profile. *Museum Management and Curatorship* 19, 121–139.

McCrone, D., Morris, A. and Kiely, R. (1995) *Scotland – the Brand: the Making of Scottish Heritage*. Edinburgh University Press, Edinburgh.

Morris, J. (2000) Repatriation report published. *Museums Journal* 100(2), 7.

National Trust for Scotland (2001) *Thistle Camps 2002*. The National Trust for Scotland, Edinburgh.

Scottish Tourist Board (STB) and the Moffat Centre (MC) (1998) *The 1997 Visitor Attraction Monitor*. Scottish Tourist Board, Edinburgh.

Scottish Tourist Board (STB) and the Moffat Centre (MC) (1999) *The 1998 Visitor Attraction Monitor*. Scottish Tourist Board, Edinburgh.

Scottish Tourist Board (STB) and the Moffat Centre (MC) (2000) *The 1999 Visitor Attraction Monitor*. Scottish Tourist Board, Edinburgh.

Scottish Tourist Board (STB/VisitScotland) and the Moffat Centre (MC) (2001) *The 2000 Visitor Attraction Monitor*. Scottish Tourist Board, Edinburgh.

Stebbins, R.A. (2001) Volunteering – mainstream and marginal: preserving the leisure experience. In: Graham, M. and Foley, M. (eds) *Volunteering in Leisure: Marginal or Inclusive?* Leisure Studies Association, Eastbourne, pp. 1–10.

VisitScotland and the Moffat Centre (2002) *The 2001 Visitor Attraction Monitor*. VisitScotland, Edinburgh.

Establishing Long-term Commitment: Event Volunteering

This section consists of two chapters, both presenting findings from research carried out on the practice of event volunteering in Australia, the USA and the UK. Both illustrate nicely the pursuit of one-off project leisure through volunteering.

Graham Berridge's comparison, in Chapter 2, of volunteering in British and American mountain biking competitions centres on the extent to which voluntary, or not-for-profit, organizations adopt sustainable practices when organizing outdoor events. Berridge sent questionnaires to a sample of organizers of outdoor biking events held in both the UK and the USA, with the intent of learning how they implement sustainable ethical practices and tend to environmental concerns. Data collection and analysis were guided by Chernushenko's 12 principles of sustainable sport, which offer some direction for the adoption of green practices, as related to the economic and political influences on sport and the costs of sport to athletes, society and the environment. His study culminates in several suggestions for ways that sports organizers can embrace a green ethic as well as adopt sustainable practices. He calls these suggestions the '12 principles of sustainable sport'.

In Chapter 3, Christine Green and Laurence Chalip observe that, as events are becoming increasingly dependent on volunteers, community and national development are becoming increasingly reliant on those events as an important component of the strategic development mix. Consequently, event volunteers have become vital, and not only to the success of the events for which they volunteer but also to the economic and social development to which events are expected to contribute. As a result of the increasingly significant role that event volunteers are expected to play, a parallel interest has emerged in the means needed to build and maintain an event volunteer workforce. To this end, Green and Chalip examine, by way of a survey of volunteers, the several factors that influenced the volunteers' motivation and commitment to serve at the 17-day 2000 Summer Olympic Games in Sydney, Australia. They found that the factors that promote and maintain a volunteer's commitment to an event as leisure activity are by no means the same as those that promote and maintain commitment to an employer as part of a person's livelihood.

Adopting Sustainable Ethics: Voluntary Practice Amongst Event Organizers

2

Graham Berridge

School of Tourism, Hospitality and Leisure, Thames Valley University, St Mary's Road, London W5 5RF, UK

Introduction

This chapter discusses the use of sustainable practices by voluntary organizers of mountain bike events in the context of the UK whilst offering a comparison with practices in the USA. The wider social context of this study is largely confined to the UK. The data from the UK build upon earlier work analysing the perceived recreational conflict between mountain bikers and other outdoor users that identified particular concerns over mountain biking's sustainable practices (Berridge, 1996).

The US comparison is included because it is generally regarded as the birthplace of mountain biking and because it has in the past experienced perception conflict between mountain bikers, landowners and other countryside users, which has been mirrored in the UK. The USA was also in its post-Atlanta Olympics phase, where mountain biking was introduced as a fully fledged Olympic sport for the first time. The Atlanta Games were promoted as part of a growing and significant attempt to make concerted attempts to apply sustainable principles to the organization of a major sporting event by extending practices introduced at earlier high-profile events such as the Pan-American Games and the Winter Olympics. The hope was that this would catalyse other organizers to follow where Atlanta led. In retrospect, the success of this programme was mixed to say the least, suffering several major sustainable blunders.

The research was conducted between February and June 1999. The aim of the study was to examine the extent to which Chernushenko's (1994) concept of a green games ethic for sports events was a feature of event organization. In particular, the interest lay in the extent to which voluntary

© 2004 CAB International. *Volunteering as Leisure/Leisure as Volunteering: an International Assessment* (eds R.A. Stebbins and M. Graham)

or not-for-profit organizations adopted sustainable practices in their organization of outdoor events. This chapter summarizes Chernushenko's 12 principles for sustainable sport and sets these in the context of wider social
initiatives on sustainability, such as Agenda 21. It then applies these principles, by means of a questionnaire, to the specific context of mountain bike
events.

Chernushenko's 12 principles

The concept for a sustainable green games ethic for sports events was developed (Chernushenko, 1994). This ethic, for looking at sport and sporting
events, reiterated the ability of sport to involve mass participation, to inspire
and to motivate people but it also identified that sport:

> when pursued without the limitations of a guiding ethic, [it] can cause severe
> and even irreparable harm – to people's health and well being and to the
> health and well being of the planet.
>
> (Chernushenko, 1994, p. xii)

The main thrusts of Chernushenko's argument were that: (i) organizational
practice (of sports events) contributed to global and environmental concerns
through energy consumption, air pollution, waste disposal, habitat loss, soil
erosion and so forth and (ii) ecological degradation made it difficult (and may
make it impossible) for some sports to be pursued. To support his ideas
Chernushenko uncovered the wanton wastefulness associated with sports
events and called for a green games ethic whereby organizers would embody
a combination of environmental stewardship, economic efficiency and social
responsibility. He catalogued how a number of sports events were damaging
to the environment and that such practice was wide in range across sporting
disciplines. This viewpoint of sports event organization was explored in
further detail down through international, regional and local events to illustrate that sporting events were being organized in a manner that exacerbated
waste and which was potentially and explicitly harmful to the environment,
participants and spectators.

   Chernushenko attempted to offer some direction for the adoption of
green practices as he explored the economic and political influences on sport
and the costs of sport to athletes, society and the environment. The outcome
of his study was to produce a way forward for sports organizers to embrace
a green ethic and to adopt sustainable practices. These practices he called
the 12 principles of sustainable sport; they are summarized in Table 2.1.
Some are relatively straightforward to adopt, such as the use of recycled
paper, whilst others, the idea of green sponsorship, require a more fundamental shift in attitude. It is these principles that this research is concerned
with, investigating them by collecting data from mountain bike event organizers to assess how effective they are in currently adopting green practices.

Table 2.1. Summary of Chernushenko's 12 principles of sustainable sport.

Conservation	The need to preserve natural resources, e.g. forests, habitat. Sport tends to take this for granted but does not have a strong code to protect such environments
Stewardship	Individuals, organizations have a duty to be 'stewards', to manage and safe-keep the resources we use for posterity
Eco-efficiency	To minimize the amount of materials used and wasted, to avoid costs and pollution and the problems linked to them
Partnership	Organizers and sponsors, host communities working together to limit waste/impact from the earliest stages
Leadership	Organizations can act as leaders to show good practice/solutions for others to emulate
Quality	Moving from 'higher, faster and stronger' ethic, which induces unnatural, synthetic and dangerous developments including bigger, better facilities. A more quality-based approach to sport should be adopted
Responsibility	Adopting appropriate attitude to participation, retaining ethical and moral stance, denouncing cheating
Democratization	Consulting with stakeholders over decisions
Investing in the future	Leaving a positive legacy for the host community via finance, facilities, community spirit etc.
Equity and access	Seeking to include potential social groups rather than excluding them
Diversity	Ensuring different conditions exist through different facilities rather than monoculture conditions and facilities
Active living	Recognizing activity and participation rather than high performance and sophisticated equipment

Wider social context

Such observations of the use (and misuse) of resources were not, of course, a new issue or a new discovery, especially where the focus is not only on effective land use but also on effective organizational process. However, for sport this kind of critical analysis was a new development, although it must be observed that the introduction of a planning guide for sport in the UK (Sports Council, 1993) did attempt to instil some sense of environmental awareness into planning for facilities if not into the actual event organization. In not recognizing the need for greater organizational ethics it could be argued that we are consequently undermining a central element of many sporting activities, which is that they are inextricably linked to ideas of health, well-being, pursuit of purpose and morality. Indeed, many of these ideals form the basis of our definitions of sport and leisure generally (Roberts, 1970; Neulinger, 1974; Kaplan, 1975; Kelly, 1982; Torkildsen, 1999) and leisure activities are seen as an ingredient that makes our quality of life much improved (Argyle, 1996). The UK Government's Sport For All policy has been part of a drive where the benefits of sport and recreation are being used to deal with social exclusion and promote health. Furthermore, in developing a code of practice on conservation, access and recreation, the Department of the Environment, Transport and the Regions (DETR) states that the:

> main considerations should, therefore, be to: use sporting and recreational activities as a way of increasing awareness of, and appreciation for, the environment and to increase support for its protection; provide and design facilities and activities which follow the principles of sustainable development.
>
> (DETR, 1999, p. 5.1)

Therefore, in offering such provision it is logical that we should be careful to assist in, and not destroy, the betterment of the environment we are using to provide such activities. Sport has been recognized as a central activity in the formation of leisure and leisure experiences (Rossman, 1989) and if the organization of it begins to harm the environment it can, from a sustainable viewpoint, be seen as neither an improvement nor perhaps an essential.

It is because some of the underlying premises of sport are reflected through this image of health and well-being, that the practices of the organizers of sporting events are of interest, in particular the extent to which a guiding ethic on the use of resources is present. Interest in this also reflects wider society concerns of how we manage the environment in general. While concerns for environmental practice in sport are not obviously apparent, concerns for environmental practice in society are. To the public at large the focus of such concerns stems from the 1992 UN Conference, the commonly referred to, Earth Summit. Agenda 21 was the main document to come out of the conference, and although it is not legally binding, it provides a blueprint for securing a sustainable future and a compelling practical and moral force for not only governments but also local democracies (Lipman *et al.*, 1995). Written by representatives of governments responsible for its implementation:

> Agenda 21 places a strong emphasis on people and their communities and an organizational approach, which stresses the needs of the poorest.
> Furthermore the conference recommended that each country should incorporate Agenda 21 at local level and coined the phrase 'think globally, act locally'.
>
> (Harris, 1997, p. 5)

Barber (1996) explains that this summit also helped concretize the definition of sustainable development that is universally acceptable and which is 'development that meets the needs of the present without compromising the ability of future generations to meet their own need' (Barber, 1996, p. 1). Whilst applying his argument to the role of sustainable leisure in cities, Barber also rationalizes the place of leisure activities in society as a belief that 'opportunities for recreation are essential to sustaining all that is best in society as well as improving the environment in which we live' (1996, p. 3). In other words, leisure activities should contribute meaningfully to our way of life and should act to enrich our social environment.

This view of the place of leisure is emphasized by the DETR, which states:

> The key sustainable development objectives are to maintain the quality of the environment in which leisure takes place, and which is an essential part of the UK's attractiveness to tourists, for future generations to enjoy; thus contributing to the quality of life of those taking part in leisure activities, and maximising the economic contribution of tourism, while protecting natural resources.
>
> (DETR, 1997, p. 1)

Whilst the inclusion of sustainable indicators for sport and leisure is welcome, the adoption of Agenda 21 missions is more commonly associated with tourism-based developments (Cater and Lowman, 1994; Lipman *et al.*, 1995; Harris, 1997). There are therefore wider social interests in sustainability and, particularly, the impact of tourism (Travis, 1982; Brockleman and Dearden, 1990). Having a sustainable component as a significant feature of tourism is a concept that has developed with the emergence of the concept of eco-tourism (Boo, 1990; Western, 1993; Wight, 1993), which, with the impetus of Agenda 21, has led in turn to the emergence of voluntary codes of practice as a method for promoting environmentally sound development and management (Williams, 1993). Codes of practice in tourism have been led, for example, through the United Nations Environment Programme and have been transferred into practice via organizations such as the World Travel and Tourism Council and the World Tourism Council. Sport is, by comparison, some way behind in a practice that is even for tourism, admittedly, still in its infancy. Associations like the Canadian Olympic Committee, Pan-American Games and the Sydney 2000 Organizing Committee issued documents on how sustainable practice featured in their events and have attempted to act as regional and global messengers. However, in the case of Atlanta, and despite the 1996 Organizing Committee having a well-publicized green programme, the actual practice and delivery of the event did suffer some well-publicized problems, for example high-pollution travel conditions and polluted competition environments. What therefore remains unclear is the extent to which ethical codes of practice are intrinsically present in the organization of sports, not just at high-profile international events but at regional and local ones as well.

If sport event organization is going to adopt a consistent green ethic how will it emerge? In some cases certain sports appear to already have a guiding ethic, whether intrinsically or one that has been thrust upon them, but usually as a result of the sport's need to address environmental issues at various stages of its evolution. Activities such as mountaineering, rambling, fell running and canoeing might well fit into this bracket, but so too do newer sports where voluntary codes of conduct have been established. This is especially the case where the sport uses natural outdoor resources and is exposed to the potential of recreation conflict with other users and landowners. Writing about jet-skiing, Anderson and Johnson observe that:

> Management of potential impacts in the UK has focused on the establishment
> of relevant byelaws, together with voluntary codes of practice for specific
> sports and non-statutory management plans for defined geographical areas,
> within the coastal zone . . . jet skiers are perceived by many as a problem
>   (Anderson and Johnson, 1998, p. 76)

Mountain biking, in particular, falls into this bracket as it has experienced a number of conflict issues since its introduction into the UK in the late 1980s and its significant development throughout the 1990s. Many of these conflict issues reflect similar ones experienced in the USA, where mountain biking was founded in the early 1980s and grew enormously as a proportion of the cycle market in the following decade (Berridge, 1996). As the above authors comment, the growth of mountain biking and snowboarding is similar in occurrence to jet skiing, which is part of the 'growth and challenge of a new "lycra" activity along side more well established activities' (Anderson and Johnson, 1998, p. 80).

Mountain bike context

Mountain bike events were selected to test Chernushenko's principles for a number of reasons, some of which are cited above. In the management of mountain bike events there exists a spread of organization types with a high proportion reflecting Parker's (1999) notion of volunteering, others having moved from voluntary into commercialism (Tomlinson, 1979), with a few being purely commercial. Like most sports whose infrastructure is made up of hundreds of volunteers (Watt, 1998) so too is mountain bike event organization, with the majority linked to mountain bike or cycle clubs who promote the sport and events without any direct personal financial gain. Whilst only a very few organizers exhibit commercial traits, most of these being linked to cycle retailers, there are several organizers who are quasi-voluntary in the sense that there is some financial gain but extensive use is made of volunteers and money donated to charitable causes. This profile would allow for a spread of opinions on the underlying principles of running a mountain bike event.

In addition, the development of the sport of mountain biking has reflected and raised green issues in a number of ways: access to the countryside; environmental impact concerns; promotion of activity as having green credentials; location of events; nature of land use. Mountain bike events take place outdoors at countryside locations using natural terrain as the location for challenge. The creation of courses for organized competition requires some inevitable shaping of land for the layout of a course and this may involve some terrain damage as a result. The impact of 500 plus riders travelling over a course, some up to four or five times, also causes erosion of the land. Recreational riding and the use of trails also has an impact and has been the issue of recreational conflict in the countryside in areas of the UK such as the Malvern Hills, Forest of Dean, Cannock Chase, Exmoor and the Lake District. In the USA similar, and sometimes more heated, conflict has arisen at popular mountain bike areas around the Marin Trails in San Francisco.

These issues have been debated and reflected in practice through many of the countryside landowning, managing and access control agencies such as the Forestry Commission, Countryside Commission, National Parks Authority, Countryside Landowners Association, as well as the Ramblers and the Horse Society, in some cases leading to the banning of events and restrictions imposed on riding in specific areas (Berridge, 1996). As a sport there exists an established governing body, British Cycling, and an international authority, the Union Cycliste International (UCI), and as such there is a hierarchy responsible for racing sanction, management and development. The importance of a governing body is noted by Watt (1998), who states that 'they act as the representative voice of a specific sport at all levels, the demands on the organization are substantial' (Watt, 1998, p. 59). As a disseminator of initiatives, developments and government policy, the governing body has a crucial role to play in the direction a sport may take, and its involvement and influence is highly significant. The organization of mountain bike events, then, reflects a number of issues that have a direct relevance to wider concerns over how we use resources and the impact this has on the environment.

Methodology

The first stage of the research consisted of adapting Chernushenko's 12 principles so that they were specifically relevant to the nature of mountain bike events. This resulted in a 20-item questionnaire with the vast majority having option check/button boxes relating to specific green issues reflected in organizing mountain bike events. Organizers of local, regional and national mountain bike events were then contacted. Two methods were used to collect data. A traditional paper questionnaire form was available and there was also an online questionnaire made available, which was accessed via a 'mountain bike events survey' website. The website was specifically set up for the survey and posted via Freeserve, a popular UK internet service provider. This site was then meta-linked to the internet portal search engines Yahoo!, AltaVista and Lycos. A link was also established through an existing website, www.cyclelondon.com. Using this approach served a number of purposes. It allowed remote access to the survey from event organizers who did not form part of a direct mailshot. It also gave those organizers contacted via a land mailshot the option of completing either a paper survey or an online one. Furthermore, organizations that were listed with e-mail could be contacted directly as part of an internet mailshot.

The last method was aimed at US organizations. Organizers were selected from events diaries in specialist magazines, direct promotional material and website addresses, and all were promoting competitive events. Additional e-mail addresses were obtained from the public domain website CyberCyclery.com, which lists cycling organizations and clubs and a brief summary of their activities/events. UK organizers were then contacted and asked to complete either a hard copy or an online copy of the survey. US organizers were asked to complete an online copy only. The total number of responses used in the survey accounted for over 75 separate mountain bike events, with the majority of these classified as regional or local based.

Results and observations

The results were categorized according to which one of the 12 principles the answers related to. The principle from Table 2.1 of *quality* is addressed in the conclusion. In the following figures the UK is first with the USA in brackets.

The principle of organizational *responsibility* asked organizers if they actively promoted no cheating/no bad behaviour: 65% (55%) actively did so in their literature and public address announcements, with reminders of the rules of participation and race etiquette being rigorously employed, especially at the race sign-on area. This reflects what is known as the self-sufficiency rule in mountain bike events. This rule, which is the formal and moral core of mountain bike racing and has been a feature of mountain bike racing since its first inception, states that solely the rider must repair any mechanical failures during the duration of a race. This means that any rider getting a puncture, for example, has to carry with them the appropriate tools to fix the puncture (new inner tube, tyre levers, air pump). If they do not then their race is effectively over since any rider seeking outside assistance from spectators or team support is disqualified. On occasion, riders at national and international levels have tried to bend this rule and have been instantly disqualified. The retention of the self-sufficiency rule maintains the equal chance aspect of the sport and in doing so also retains an element of quality of purpose instead of quantity of finance and support.

A further issue of *responsibility* is that of ethical behaviour. Every single organizer in the survey (100%) stated that they made it clear about race and trail behaviour in the entry form. Mountain bike racing has an established race etiquette that is used in cases of overtaking and general trail behaviour and this forms part of officially sanctioned rules of racing. It espouses fairly good etiquette such as lapped riders should give way to leading riders and riders overtaking should inform the rider in front which side they will pass on. Equally, boisterous abuse of slower riders and physically aggressive rider contact is not permitted, neither is abuse of officials. Transgression of this principle, if discovered and reported to the organizer, can result in disqualification. One organizer, running a weekly set of races, made a practice of publicly humiliating any rider found to transgress such rules by calling their name out at the start line of the next race and in some cases banning them for one race. In another instance, an organizer of a national status event disqualified a rider of international renown and ranking for verbally abusing a course marshal. Enforcement such as this serves to remind riders of the need to practise race etiquette and supports the notion of a strong ethical element to organizational practice and a desire to ensure that intimidation of newer and slower riders is not acceptable. It should be noted, however, that such public actions of disqualification are very rare and in most instances there exists an internal ethical practice on the part of riders.

These actions are further supported through the principle of *active living*. Organizers were asked to grade the extent to which they promoted any strong social attitudes for participants and were asked to rate this between 0 and 5, with 5 being a high feature. Overall, the active living-type features were rated 3.95 out of 5 (2.95), which means a high proportion of organizers in the UK focused on promotion of healthy lifestyles, respect for the environment, personal challenge, camaraderie and participating. The much lower figure for the USA is surprising but may be explained by the choice and wealth of terrain available for recreational riding in comparison to the UK, hence organized race events have a more competitive edge whereas UK races tend to be a focus for gathering and the opportunity to ride otherwise out-of-bounds trails and areas. The status symbol features of the event reflected through ultra-competition, fashion and trend setting was rated 2.25 (4.75). There are some clear differences between events, and the underlying values of behaviour and attitude are emphasized here with a much stronger win-ethic in the USA than the UK and a much stronger trend element, perhaps a reflection of the market situation and the USA's preponderance of small manufacturers looking to promote themselves at race events.

Responses to the principle relating to *equity and access*, which asked organizers if they encouraged a wide range of social groups to participate, produced expected results. Whilst very few gave entry concessions, all events had an entry fee structure set according to age and ability with, in some cases, seven different pricing options: 70% (65%) (the remainder did not run races for this group) had reduced entry fees for age groups under 16, 100% (100%) stated they did not tolerate sexist commentary or behaviour, 100% (100%) held specific races for novices and women whilst 55% (45%) also ran under 12s races which were on a shorter version of the main course. Spot prizes were handed out at 60% (25%) of events, a prize given on a whim to any rider deemed worthy of merit. This can be for colour of shirt/bike, name, style etc. and seeks to award random participants, not only those who are successful in competition.

Overall the results for this section highlight the fact that organizers do attempt to make their events accessible to all, up to a certain point. Whilst all events had age and ability categories for both male and female riders, there were significant differences in how this was implemented, often reflected in the status of the event. Although not specifically the result of the data collected here, it is common practice at mountain bike events to have age range categories from under 12s up to over 55s and ability categories within those.

Answers to the question of using and recycling materials for the event gave an indication of the *eco-efficiency* principle. This was well supported with 85% (90%) recycling materials in one form or another, suggesting an awareness of the need not to unnecessarily waste resources in endlessly creating from scratch. However, racing materials such as race numbers 57% (28%) and number ties 42% (25%) are not so efficiently recycled, indicating that the major area of recycle usage is in paper materials, for example for publicity, entry forms and more physical course marking such as route tape and directional stakes. This view of *eco-efficiency* is also supported by organizers of regional events, for example a group in the south of England cooperated to reuse central event supplies such as podiums, directional course marking and banners. This was also apparent in eastern US events. The British Cycling governing body also assisted in this process by supplying similar centrally based materials that any organizer could use. This is a practice that most regional status series events would be likely to adopt.

One issue that has plagued mountain biking both competitively and recreationally is that of land erosion and terrain damage, where the perception by other land users is that mountain bikers cause extensive erosion and damage compared to other users although evidence and research on this topic is minimal. The idea behind the principle of *stewardship* therefore is that organizers act effectively to prevent long-term or permanent damage. Asked whether or not they caused damage to terrain in building a course, 100% (50%) of organizers admitted that putting on the event did result in damage to terrain. The reasons why US event organizers expressed a much lower level of damage are not clear, although it appears to be reflective of the type of terrain often used, such as already built fire-roads. UK events are often sited in parkland and require course shaping as fire-road presence is much less of a feature. Erosive impact itself can be further qualified with 85% (50%) noting that this was occasional and only 15% (15%) saying damage was frequent. Their response to such damage provides a key to organizer attitudes, with 70% (50%) indicating they made some effort to repair this damage, and of those 42% (30%) cited rebuilding of a specific area, 28% (15%) tree planting and 30% (35%) general repair work. This indicates that effective stewardship is a concern although the evidence is inconclusive that practice on preservation of the terrain is wholeheartedly applied.

Preservation for the future is also reflected through the principles *investing in the future* and *democratization*. For the former, organizers were asked if they made any kind of return, financial or otherwise, to the area where the event took place and responses showed a strong awareness of the impact on the host community, with all making at least one worthy return to the immediate area and 84% making more than one. Donations to charity, 56% (25%), was the most preferred method but other options included controlling access to the site, 42% (100%), and involvement in any clean up of the area surrounding the race site, 58% (100%).

Linked to this is the idea of *democratization*, which offers some insight into how an event's future may be shaped. In response to the question of consultation with stakeholders, 85% (78%) directly consulted stakeholders of one type or another and of these over 50% (85%) consulted with more than one group: 42% (50%) directly consulted riders, 18% (0%) spectators, 30% (20%) other event organizers, 85% (82%) local landowners, 15% (20%) the local community, 42% (20%) volunteers and 12% (50%) other agencies (mainly service support). Asked if they considered riders' needs specifically only 54% (75%) said they did. Of these 44% (55%) provided drinks stations, 28% (80%) advice on sun exposure and 42% (55%) attempted to avoid river crossings (land layout permitting). All events, as is common practice, varied the start times of racing. So whilst stakeholders were generally consulted this was mostly a reference to the landowner not the host community and there were clear gaps in approach to dealing with and looking after riders. The issue of land used for races being off-limits to recreational riding is a factor and, historically, some landowners in the UK have discontinued events because riders have attempted to access a site post-event. A clear and active working relationship with the immediate area, both landowners and community, is crucial to this, as is the support of those who participate in and service an event. In this respect organizers demonstrated a number of ways of achieving this, such as donations to local youth groups or ambulance services, which undoubtedly reflected the local context.

As stated above, riders were directly consulted and, whilst not part of the data collected, it is likely that this consultation had more to do with the actual course design rather than race operations. This last point can be linked to the principle of *diversity*, which was addressed through the question of changing course design: 85% (75%) of event organizers consistently made efforts to re-design race course layouts on sites that were used more than once, averting criticism of adopting a monoculture towards race conditions and courses and of providing a sterile racing environment.

Concerning overall *conservation* principles there were some inconsistencies in organizers' practice, both between different events and within the same event. Much of this can perhaps be put down to the poorly documented aspects of practice amongst organizers since only 14% (52%) stated they had a written policy on general conservation. What is also clear is that reference points for good practice were almost invisible as codes of practice for organizers were primarily concerned with how to put the event on. The governing body, British Cycling, had extremely limited input on green practice other than very general and basic guidelines. It is interesting to note here that due to political circumstances the access network of mountain biking is no longer a part of the governing body but resides in a separate, more recreationally based organization, the Cycle Touring Club. The access network is a regionally organized, voluntary-run grouping and represents mountain biking on the issues of land access with landowners and managing agencies. Its separation may explain why written policy is so sparse and why there is emphasis, by British Cycling, on race organization but not equally on land conservation and green practice. A similar situation existed in the USA with the United States Cycling Federation (USCF), North American Off-Road Biking Organization (NORBA) and the International Mountain Biking Association (IMBA). Each of these organizations has interests in mountain biking in one form or another, with event organizers often being committed to supporting one or other body.

The anomalies in this principle between policy and practice are further exemplified in the *leadership* principle. Although clearly strong in some areas leadership was weak in others, sometimes due to the above-mentioned duplicity of interest, other times through poor direction and leadership. In this instance organizers were asked if they made riders aware of good environmental practice and some, who had highly effective green features elsewhere, failed to consistently make riders aware of how they could adopt green practices. All organizers indicated that they made some effort to tell riders of certain good practice. This was mainly to use litter bins (in the car park and in pre-race areas) but the nature of this varied considerably between them. Only 57% (25%) said they made riders aware by advising them not to discard air canisters, 60% (55%) not to discard replaced inner tubes and 14% (20%) advised on using environmentally friendly lube. This could be seen as a contradiction since support for self-sufficiency is a race rule but advice on safe disposal is not strongly applied.

The last principle to be considered is that of *partnerships* and in this respect organizers at this level in the UK were not willing to compromise potential sponsorship whereas US ones were. Asked if they vetted or refused sponsors on ethical grounds, of the 85% (78%) who had sponsors, none (70%) vetted a sponsor on green principles (this being the actual practice of the company). Such a difference is interesting and certainly points again to evidence of the failure of a UK written policy and the probable historical strength of IMBA. No (50%) UK organizer had ever rejected a sponsor on ethical grounds whereas a significant number had done so in the USA. Some explanation for this in the UK is that organizers did not chase sponsorship in certain areas (tobacco and alcohol) although this only accounted for 20% of responses. Notably, and this information was given informally but there is no reason to doubt its authenticity, British Cycling itself had rejected sponsorship offers in the past with products that it felt were not appropriate (notably alcohol), which suggests it is taking the lead in some areas if not others. Reasons for US rejections were unfortunately not documented in many cases but those who did respond pointed out that they had rejected tobacco, alcohol, car dealerships and, in one case, a pesticide company.

Conclusions

The results outlined above are directly related to 11 out of 12 of Chernushenko's principles. The missing one, that of *quality*, has been evaluated as an indication of the overall extent to which all organizers and events could be said to be incorporating sustainable practice. This is an assessment of quality of practice overall using a simple scale of very poor – poor – mixed – good – very good – excellent. Analysing the answers to the survey in relation to the principles, the question is: to what extent are the principles met? Using this overall assessment of *quality* suggests that for the UK, in seven out of the 11 (eight out of 11) headings, event practice was rated as good to very good. What does this mean? It would suggest that mountain bike events are not pre-occupied with the 'higher, faster, stronger' motto of the Olympic Games as the sole driving force behind their events but are, in fact, incorporating values that Lenk has called 'smaller, more beautiful, more intimate, more participatory, more humane' (Chernushenko, 1994, p. 81).

What conclusions can be drawn from this research? Firstly, in some cases the similarity between the UK and the USA is clear and suggests a clear ethical creed and underpinning on the part of organizers. Is it reasonable to suggest that there is a globalization of ethical practice based on the founding principles of mountain biking itself, which have been carried over from the USA to the UK? Many of these have since been officialized via the role of the UCI Mountain Bike Commission. Out of what is still, essentially, volunteer organizing groups (including cycling clubs) there is a strand of practice that is resourceful, applies organizational and participation ethics, and demonstrates evidence of sustainability that would fit into Chernushenko's criteria. A number of his identified principles are operationalized by organizers, albeit sometimes with different methods, as every single organizer surveyed demonstrated. This is clearly a result of mountain biking's immediate real and perceived conflicts with other outdoor users (Cessford, 1995). Mountain bike participation and market strength (as a percentage of all bicycle sales) matured very quickly (Berridge, 1996) in both countries and this raised immediate conflict concerns from ramblers, countryside and outdoor wilderness agencies, local authorities and municipalities, and land management agencies (Ramthun, 1995; Schneider and Hammitt, 1995).

In summary, mountain bike organizers appear to have a commendable approach to green event organizing albeit with self-preservation evident. It is clear though that there are aspects of practice that need developing and, crucially, further guidance since poor environmental management of a racing site could lead to any further events being banned on that site or permission for its use withdrawn. Certainly in the UK, and despite the best efforts of organizers, race site venues have been lost for many reasons. What this ultimately has led to is a lack of diversification of sites as a whole, with many locations now being used repeatedly and with fewer and fewer new venues appearing.

Of course this also suggests some considerable success on the part of organizers to be able to manage a site successfully in order to have repeated use. Their efforts warrant further praise due to the poor leadership offered by the governing body.[1] In effect the leadership on sustainable practice comes from within the sport itself, consisting of riders, the organizers and their regional groupings. The reasons behind this are primarily to do with the conditions in which mountain biking has emerged, whereby in order to be accepted as a viable user of the countryside by managing agencies (on a par particularly with ramblers and horse riders), it has had to show due respect for the land through its practice in organized events and application through recreational riding. In the majority of cases surveyed here it appears to be doing this but despite some regional exceptions this is being done mostly in isolation rather than as part of a coordinated national strategy. Mountain bike event organizers are practising the principles of sustainable events, up to a point, and are doing so primarily through their own good faith and need to preserve future usage of any areas they use. What is missing is a much clearer organizational structure to make green practice consistent at all events and this is where the governing body has a role to play in adopting these principles in a more formulated policy so as to assist in disseminating information more effectively than it is currently doing, a process which Chernushenko would strongly advocate.

Note

[1] As at 2002 the UK governing body had all but abdicated its role of directly supporting a UK National Mountain Bike series and it was left to a group of volunteer organizers to run the series on their own.

References

Anderson, J. and Johnson, D. (1998) As charmless as chain-saws?: managing jet ski use in the UK. In: Merkel, U., Lines, G. and McDonald, I. (eds) *The Production and Consumption of Sport Cultures: Leisure Culture and Commerce*. Leisure Studies Association, Eastbourne, pp. 75–86.

Argyle, M. (1996) *The Social Psychology of Leisure*. Penguin, London.

Barber, A. (1996) Sustainable leisure in the international city. Paper presented to WLRA 4th World Congress, Cardiff, UK.

Berridge, G. (1996) Mountain bike access to the countryside. In: Collins, M.F. (ed.) *Time, Space and Planning; Leisure in Transitory Societies.* Leisure Studies Association, Eastbourne, pp. 51–67.

Boo, E. (1990) *Ecotourism: the Potentials and Pitfalls,* Vols 1 and 2. World Wildlife Fund, Washington, DC.

Brockleman, W.Y. and Dearden, P. (1992) The role of nature trekking in conservation: a case study in Thailand. *Environmental Conservation* 17, 141–148.

Cater, E. and Lowman, G. (1994) *Ecotourism: a Sustainable Option?* John Wiley & Sons, London.

Cessford, G.R. (1995) *Off-road Impacts of Mountain Bikes: a Review and Discussion.* Science and Research Series no. 92. Department of Conservation, Wellington, New Zealand.

Chernushenko, D. (1994) *Greening Our Games: Running Sports Events and Facilities that Won't Cost the Earth.* Centurion Publishing, Ottawa.

Department of the Environment, Transport and the Regions (DETR) (1997) Indicators of sustainable development for the UK: leisure and tourism indicator family (11 December), http://environment.detr.gov.uk/epsim/indics/isdc.htm (accessed 10 June, 1999).

Department of the Environment, Transport and the Regions (DETR) (1999) Code of practice on conservation, access and recreation consultation, draft, chapter 5, recreation (6 May), http://environment.detr.gov.uk/consult/copcar/chap5.htm (accessed 10 June, 1999).

Harris, D. (1997) *Sustainable Tourism: Examples of Best Practice for the London Borough of Hounslow.* Consultant publication.

Kaplan, M. (1975) *Leisure: Theory and Policy.* John Wiley & Sons, New York.

Kelly, J. (1982) *Leisure.* Prentice Hall, Englewood Cliffs, New Jersey.

Lipman, G.H., Savignac, A.E. and Strong, M.F. (1995) *Agenda 21 for the Travel and Tourism Industry: Towards Environmentally Sustainable Development.* WTTC/WTO, London.

Neulinger, J. (1974) *The Psychology of Leisure.* Charles C. Thomas, Springfield, Illinois.

Parker, S. (1999) Volunteering: altruism, markets, causes and leisure. *World Leisure and Recreation* 39(3), 4–5.

Ramthun, R. (1995) Factors in user group conflict between hikers and mountain bikers. *Leisure Sciences* 17, 159–169.

Roberts, K. (1970) *Leisure.* Longman, London.

Rossman, J.R. (1989) *Recreation Programming: Designing Leisure Experiences.* Sagamore Publishing, Champaign, Illinois.

Schneider, I.E. and Hammitt, W.E. (1995) Visitor response to outdoor recreation conflict: a conceptual approach. *Leisure Sciences* 17, 223–233.

Sports Council (1993) *Planning and Provision for Sport Factfile.* Sports Council, London.

Tomlinson, A. (1979) *Leisure and the Role of Voluntary Clubs and Voluntary Groups.* Sports Council/SSRC, London.

Torkildsen, G. (1999) *Leisure and Recreation Management,* 4th edn. E&FN Spon, London.

Travis, A.S. (1982) Managing the environmental and cultural impacts of tourism and leisure development. *Tourism Management* 3, 256–262.

Watt, D.C. (1998) *Sports Management and Administration.* E&FN Spon, London.

Western, D. (1993) Defining ecotourism. In: Lindberg, K. and Hawkins, D.E. (eds)
    Ecotourism: a Guide for Planners and Managers. The Ecotourism Society,
    North Bennington, Vermont, pp. 7–11.
Wight, P. (1993) Ecotourism: ethics or eco-sell? *Journal of Travel Research* 31(3),
    3–9.
Williams, P.W. (1993) Environmental business practice; ethical codes of conduct for
    tourism. *Hospitality Trends* 7(1), 8–11.

Paths to Volunteer Commitment: Lessons from the Sydney Olympic Games

B. Christine Green and Laurence Chalip

The University of Texas at Austin

Introduction

Volunteers have become essential to the delivery of sport and recreation services, adding several hundred dollars of value *per capita* to the contribution that sport and recreation make to gross domestic product (Taylor *et al.*, 1996; Gerson, 1997; Davies, 1998). Volunteers have become particularly vital for the delivery of special events, as most events now depend to some degree on volunteers for event planning and operations (Allen, 2000; van der Wagen, 2001; McDonnell *et al.*, 2002). The growing dependence of the event industry on volunteers is aptly illustrated by the substantial growth of volunteering at the Olympic Games (Moragas *et al.*, 2000). Volunteers were used sparingly until the 1980s. However, the 1980 Winter Olympic Games in Lake Placid made use of 6703 volunteers and the 1984 Summer Olympic Games in Los Angeles made use of 28,742 volunteers. Volunteer numbers rose dramatically during the 1980s and 1990s. The 1998 Winter Olympic Games in Nagano required 32,579 volunteers and the 2000 Summer Olympic Games in Sydney accredited 40,917 volunteers. Chalip (2000) calculated that volunteer labour in Sydney would contribute over Aus$109 million in comparable worth – over Aus$21 for every dollar expended to secure and support the volunteers' work. Without the volunteers, the Games could not have been produced.

The growing importance of volunteers to events has been paralleled by a substantial growth in the use of events in the economic and social development strategies of cities, regions and countries (Mules and Faulkner, 1996; Getz, 1998; Jago *et al.*, 2003). Thus, just as events are becoming increasingly dependent on volunteers, community and national development are becoming increasingly reliant on events as a component of the strategic development mix. Consequently, event volunteers have become vital, not merely to the success of the events at which they volunteer; they have become pivotal to the economic and social development to which events are expected to contribute.

As a result of the increasingly significant role that event volunteers are expected to play, there has been an elevated interest in the means to build and maintain an event volunteer workforce (Williams *et al.*, 1995; Andrew, 1996; Elstad, 1996; Farrell *et al.*, 1998). This is thought to be important, not merely to obtain and retain volunteers during an event, but also to cultivate a volunteer workforce that will work at events from one year to the next. For example, Coyne and Coyne (2001) found that 79% of volunteers at a golf event had volunteered at previous events.

There has been a substantial volume of didactic writing about volunteers and volunteer management, most of which has been derived from models of human resource management that are intended to describe the selection, training and management of paid workers (Brudney, 1990; Fisher and Cole, 1993; Connors, 1995). Although these texts are useful, they are not informed by analyses which suggest that volunteering, particularly in sport and recreation, should be understood as a leisure choice, rather than as a work choice (Stebbins, 1996; Green and Chalip, 1998a). In other words, the factors which prompt and maintain volunteers' commitment to an event may not be well represented by those factors which are associated with commitment to an employer.

Satisfaction

It is commonly assumed that volunteers' commitment to an event organization will be driven, at least in part, by their satisfaction with the volunteer experience (Elstad, 1996; Farrell *et al.*, 1998). This notion derives from studies of workers' job performance (Iaffaldano and Muchinsky, 1985; Meyer and Allen, 1997) which find that satisfied workers are more productive and evidence lower levels of absenteeism. Although the effects of volunteers' satisfaction on commitment to an event organization have not been directly tested, the expectation that satisfaction drives commitment has obvious intuitive appeal.

However, from both a practical and a theoretical standpoint, any finding that satisfaction drives commitment is unsatisfying insomuch as it tells us little about what causes volunteers' satisfaction. If we want to understand event volunteers' satisfaction and commitment, then we need to know what the sources of their satisfaction and commitment are. So doing can help to build a model of volunteer motivation, and can provide insight into the best means to build and maintain volunteer commitment.

Benefits

Research on volunteers finds that commitment and satisfaction are a function of the benefits that volunteers obtain from their volunteer experience. A number of different benefits have been identified. One of the most commonly identified motivations for volunteering is to be helpful to the community (Wymer *et al.*, 1996; Bussell and Forbes, 2002). This is also true for event volunteers. Farrell *et al.* (1998) found that the four items most highly rated (out of 23) for volunteering at an event each had to do with helping the community or the event. Coyne and Coyne (2001) found that 'community spirit' ranked third of 21 reasons for volunteering at an event.

Although volunteering seems inherently altruistic, the claim that volunteers are motivated primarily by the desire to be helpful has been widely criticized (Green and Chalip, 1998a; Knox, 1999; Bussell and Forbes, 2002). When respondents complete a survey instrument that includes measures of the motive to be helpful, social norms dictate that they rate helpfulness highly, even if they have other (less altruistic) reasons for volunteering (Shiarella *et al.*, 2000). Even when there is a genuine desire to be helpful, the motivational value of helping may be mediated by other rewards. In a laboratory and a field experiment, Fisher and Ackerman (1998) found that the desire to be helpful prompted volunteerism primarily when social reward was also promised. The importance of social benefits has also emerged in studies of event volunteers. Williams *et al.* (1995) found that the opportunity to socialize with people sharing common interests was the number one motivation for volunteers at a men's world cup skiing event. Elstad (1996) found that meeting new people and becoming friends with other volunteers was the primary source of satisfaction for volunteers at the 1994 Winter Olympics in Lillehammer.

Learning has also been identified as a vital motivation for event volunteers. Farrell *et al.* (1998) found that a factor represented by obtaining 'an educational experience' and 'broaden my horizons' accounted for over 10% of the variance in the overall motivation to volunteer at a national curling championship. Elstad (1996) found that learning about the event and about other people were significant sources of satisfaction for volunteers at the Lillehammer Olympics.

Events can also be exciting. The opportunity to become part of event production can provide a sense of excitement when volunteering (Green and Chalip, 1998a). Volunteers at a skiing event rated being 'part of the action' as a significant basis for their motivation to volunteer (Williams *et al.*, 1995), while volunteers at a curling event described their participation as 'a chance of a lifetime' (Farrell *et al.*, 1998).

Volunteering can engender contacts and experience that can be professionally useful (Gora and Nemerowicz, 1991; Phillips and Phillips, 2000). Andrew (1996) found that gaining 'more skills and experience' was the second most important reason that his Australian sample volunteered at an event. On the other hand, Williams *et al*. (1995) found that volunteering in order to make job contacts was not a significant motivation for his Canadian sample.

Finally, volunteering at an event can be a source of personal prestige (Green and Chalip, 1998a). Fisher and Ackerman (1998) found that recognition for volunteering enhances the likelihood that people will commit to a volunteer role. Coyne and Coyne (2001) found that the bragging rights associated with meeting celebrities and helping to put on the event were important motivations for volunteers at a golf tournament. Elstad (1996) found the celebrity atmosphere of the Olympics to be the second largest source of satisfaction (after social benefits) for volunteers at Lillehammer.

Sense of Community at the Event

Green (2001) has shown that event spectating and participating are strongly motivated by the sense of community that can be obtained. Green and Chalip (1998a) argue that the same should be true for event volunteers. Sense of community is distinct from social benefits insomuch as it represents a recognition of shared purpose and a common identity. It is a quality of the event experience.

Sense of community has not been incorporated into previous studies of event volunteers, although Elstad (1996) did find that cooperation with other volunteers during the Lillehammer Olympics was a significant source of volunteers' satisfaction. Stronger evidence comes from Omoto and Snyder (2002), who have shown that a psychological sense of community among volunteers and those being served by volunteers can foster and maintain volunteering for service to people living with AIDS.

Commitment as an Evolving Process

Although commitment is expected to be a consequence of satisfaction, benefits obtained and the sense of community that volunteers experience at the event, commitment begins before the event has been experienced. Commitment is an evolving process that begins with expectations, and that is carried forward by the nature of experiences that are obtained along the way (Meyer and Allen, 1997; Cuskelly *et al*., 1998). Initial commitment is affected by the nature of benefits that the volunteer expects to obtain from volunteering (Bussell and Forbes, 2002) and by the volunteer's sense of efficacy regarding the jobs to which he or she is assigned (Wymer *et al*., 1996). In other words, commitment is thought to be grounded in the benefits that the volunteer expects from volunteering, and the volunteer's confidence in his or her ability to mobilize the skills and resources necessary to complete assigned tasks competently.

Research Questions

The Olympic Games provide an ideal context for studying the evolution of commitment in an event context. As a one-time event in the host country, volunteers at the Games bring no experience of the event – at least not as it is organized and executed at its host site. As a 17-day mega-event, the Olympic Games are sufficiently long and sufficiently intense for there to be some observable evolution of volunteers' commitment. On the basis of the foregoing review of the literature, the following hypotheses were formulated, and are illustrated in Fig. 3.1.

H1. Volunteers' sense of commitment to the event at the end of the event is a function of their satisfaction with the event experience.

H2A. Volunteers' sense of commitment to the event at the end of the event is a function of the benefits (prestige, learning, excitement, helping, social benefits and professional benefits) that they feel they obtain.

H2B. The effect of benefits on commitment is both direct and indirect (through their effect on satisfaction).

H3A. Sense of community at the event enhances volunteers' satisfaction and commitment.

H3B. The effect of a sense of community is over and above that engendered by benefits obtained.

H4. Initial commitment to the event has a measurable impact on commitment at the end of the event.

H5. Initial commitment to the event is a function of volunteers' sense of efficacy at the beginning of the event and benefits (prestige, learning, excitement, helping, social benefits and professional benefits) that the volunteer expects to obtain.

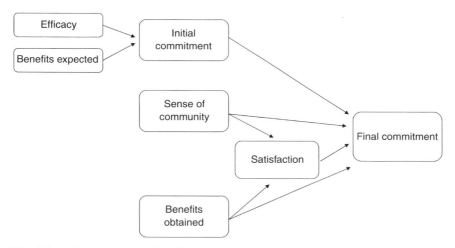

Fig. 3.1. Conceptual model of volunteer commitment.

Method

Sample

The sample consisted of 1702 volunteers at the Sydney Olympic Games. They ranged in age from 15 to 88 years, with a mean age of 46.6 years and a standard deviation of 15.44. Sixty-two per cent of respondents were women. These represented a cross-section of divisions and venues. There were 942 volunteers who responded to both surveys. This sub-sample was nearly identical to the overall sample. Age ranged from 15 to 88 years with a mean age of 49 and a standard deviation of 14.88. Sixty-three per cent of the sample was female.

Procedure

Volunteers were recruited to the project via their work site. Seventeen work sites were selected to provide a cross-section of Olympic volunteer experiences. Four sites (tennis venue, gymnastics venue, sponsor marquee and four regions of the common domain) from within Olympic Park were included. The other sites included single-sport venues (softball, cycling, equestrian, shooting, mountain biking, rowing and beach volleyball), multi-sport venues (Darling Harbour Olympic precinct) and non-competition sites (Olympic village, airport, Olympic family hotels, a volunteer residence hall, and the Uniform Distribution and Accreditation Centre (UDAC)).

Survey packets were distributed to volunteers at the sign-in desks or in the break rooms. Each packet contained a cover letter, a consent form requesting contact details for the follow-up survey, the survey and a return envelope. All forms were numbered for matching purposes. Volunteers were asked to complete the survey provided, to provide contact information on a separate form, to seal both completed forms in the envelope provided and to return the survey to the drop box provided in their venue. A database of contact information and survey number was created and then destroyed after posting the final surveys.

A total of 2800 surveys were distributed to venues. Although it is unclear how many surveys reached volunteers, 1702 usable surveys were returned. This represents a minimum response rate of 61% for the first survey. A second survey was mailed to every volunteer who provided his or her mailing address when responding to the initial survey (1683 volunteers); 118 surveys were returned undeliverable. Of the remaining 1584, 942 usable surveys were returned for a response rate of 60%.

Following the Games, focus groups with Olympic volunteers were conducted in seven cities throughout Australia. Participants were selected from the pool of respondents to the initial survey. Equal numbers of men and women were recruited for each group. The report which follows draws on the focus group findings only for purposes of constructing the satisfaction measure and to illustrate insights derived from the surveys.

Measures – survey 1

Commitment
Commitment was measured using four items from the Mowday, Steers and Porter (1979) measure of organizational commitment (Organizational Commitment Questionnaire (OCQ)). Volunteers responded to each item on a six-point scale ranging from 'strongly disagree' to 'strongly agree'. Mowday *et al.* report test–retest reliabilities for the original scale ranging from 0.62 to 0.072 over 2 and 3 months. The scale predicts turnover, tenure, absenteeism and performance in work settings, with convergent validity coefficients ranging from 0.63 to 0.74 (Mowday *et al.*, 1979). The original nine-item short form includes items that are specific to work settings, but that do not apply to voluntary associations. A modified version of the OCQ has been used in a voluntary sport setting to predict parents' enduring involvement with soccer (Green and Chalip, 1997), and has been associated with programme satisfaction (Green and Chalip, 1998b). Shorter versions of the OCQ provide internal consistency measures of at least 0.79 in voluntary sport settings (Green, 1997; Green and Chalip, 1998b). Four items were selected to measure volunteers' commitment to the Sydney Olympic Games: (i) 'I am willing to put in a great deal of effort beyond that normally expected in order to help the Sydney Olympic Games be successful'; (ii) 'Deciding to work for the Sydney Olympic Games was a definite mistake on my part'; (iii) 'I would accept almost any type of job assignment in order to keep working for the Sydney Olympic Games'; and (iv) 'I really care about the fate of the Sydney Olympic Games'. The four items were averaged and the data centred on zero (a neutral point). Thus positive responses indicate commitment to the Sydney Olympic Games and negative responses indicate a lack of commitment to the Sydney Olympic Games.

Benefits expected
An initial pool of 24 items was generated to represent six common benefits identified from previous research (Clary *et al.*, 1992; Williams *et al.*, 1995; Andrew, 1996; Elstad, 1996; Wymer *et al.*, 1996; Farrell *et al.*, 1998). Respondents were asked to rate the likelihood that their volunteer experience would provide them with each of the benefits listed. Items were scaled on an eight-point Likert-type scale ranging from very unlikely (1) to very likely (8). The 24-item questionnaire was given to 200 volunteers at the British Olympic Association's Pre-Olympic Holding Camp held on the Gold Coast of Australia; 164 usable surveys were returned. LISREL was used to test and develop a reduced (12-item) scale. Multi-dimensional items were first eliminated, as were items with weak loadings. Items were eliminated in successive

iterations resulting in six two-item subscales (one for each of the original benefits). The final model fits the data well ($\chi^2/df = 2.18$, RMSEA $= 0.085$, GFI $= 0.92$, NFI $= 0.90$), indicating that the six dimensions were independent (though correlated), and well represented by the 12 variables.

Olympic volunteers completed the 12-item scale using the following stem: 'How likely is it that your volunteer experience at the Sydney Olympic Games will provide the following opportunities?' Prestige was represented by the items 'to be a part of a prestigious event' and 'to participate in a once-in-a-lifetime opportunity'. Learning was measured by the items 'to gain some useful experience' and 'to see something of how the event is run'. Excitement was represented by the items 'to do something stimulating' and 'to encounter exciting things'. Helping was represented by the items 'to put something back into the community' and 'to be helping out'. Social benefits were measured via the items 'to meet new people' and 'to enjoy the company of others', and professional benefits by the items 'to make useful contacts for my career' and 'to develop skills I can use in my job'. The two items in each subscale were averaged to provide an overall indicator of volunteers' perceptions of the likelihood of obtaining each benefit. Data were also transformed by centring the data on a neutral point (neither likely nor unlikely). Thus positive responses indicate positive expectations (i.e. at least somewhat likely) and negative responses indicate negative expectations (i.e. at least somewhat unlikely).

Efficacy
Volunteers were asked to indicate their level of agreement with two statements measuring their perceptions of their own efficacy: (i) 'I have the skills needed to work effectively in my role as a volunteer' and (ii) 'I have the confidence needed to be an effective volunteer'. The alpha for this scale was 0.72. Items were measured on a six-point Likert-type scale ranging from 'strongly disagree' to 'strongly agree'. Responses to the items were averaged and centred on zero (neutral point). Thus, positive responses indicate agreement and negative responses indicate disagreement.

Measures – survey 2

Commitment
The four-item modified OCQ (Mowday *et al.*, 1979) included in the first survey was repeated in the second survey. Since the instrument was completed after the Games, items were phrased in the past tense. Items were averaged and the overall measure was centred on zero.

Satisfaction
Focus groups with Olympic volunteers after the Games were over suggested eight key aspects of volunteers' satisfaction with their experience: training, job assignment, rewards earned, distribution of rewards, recognition,

support, equality, and the relationship between paid staff and volunteers. Items were written to reflect each of these dimensions. Volunteers were asked to rate how satisfied they were with each aspect of their experience. Items were scaled on a six-point Likert-type scale ranging from 'very dissatisfied' to 'very satisfied'.

The items were factor analysed to uncover any underlying dimensions of satisfaction. A principal components analysis extracted a single component (eigenvalue = 4.66; all others were below unity) which explained 58.3% of the variance. Factor loadings ranged from 0.68 to 0.85. The eight-item scale shows strong internal consistency ($\alpha = 0.90$). The items were averaged and then centred on zero for further analysis. Consequently, positive scores indicate satisfaction and negative scores indicate dissatisfaction with the experience.

Benefits obtained

The expected benefits scale used in the initial questionnaire was reworded to measure volunteers' perceptions of the benefits that were obtained through their experience. Thus, the question stem was changed to, 'thinking back on your experience as an Olympic volunteer, please indicate your level of agreement or disagreement with each of the following statements'. As before, items in each subscale were averaged and centred on zero.

Community

Volunteers' psychological sense of community at the Games was measured using a four-item scale adapted from Nasar and Julian's (1995) 11-item sense of community scale. Nasar and Julian's scale was developed to measure psychological sense of community in neighbourhoods. They report a Cronbach alpha reliability score of 0.87, and show both discriminant and convergent validity.

Four items were adapted for this study: (i) 'People working at the Games knew they could get help from others in our work group if they needed it'; (ii) 'Being a member of my work group was like being a member of a group of friends'; (iii) 'I had no friends in my work group on whom I could depend' (reverse scored); and (iv) 'The volunteers in my work group were people you could trust'. Items were measured on a six-point Likert-type scale ranging from 1 (strongly disagree) to 6 (strongly agree). Items were averaged and centred on zero for further analysis.

Results

Descriptive statistics for the variables are presented in Table 3.1. Examination of Table 3.1 shows that, on average, commitment at the beginning and end of the Games was positive. At the beginning of the Games, efficacy and all the expectations for benefits from volunteering were also positive on average, except for the expectation of professionally relevant benefits. At the

Table 3.1. Means, standard deviations and correlations of variables.

Variable	Mean	SD	Cmt1	Prest1	Learn1	Excit1	Help1	Soc1	Prof1	Effic	Cmt2	Satisf	Prest2	Learn2	Excit2	Help2	Soc2	Prof2
Cmt1	1.84	0.66																
Prest1	2.91	1.10	0.368															
Learn1	1.65	1.68	0.260	0.431														
Excit1	2.07	1.56	0.379	0.520	0.622													
Help1	2.66	1.16	0.500	0.511	0.399	0.495												
Soc1	2.29	1.39	0.341	0.453	0.517	0.583	0.531											
Prof1	-0.91	2.33	0.030	0.165	0.521	0.330	0.108	0.308										
Effic	2.01	0.62	0.340	0.198	0.166	0.228	0.322	0.234	0.054									
Cmt2	1.91	0.58	0.581	0.292	0.211	0.291	0.377	0.321	0.026	0.188								
Satisf	1.24	0.96	0.376	0.208	0.346	0.369	0.298	0.328	0.116	0.099	0.423							
Prest2	3.11	0.90	0.193	0.263	0.204	0.250	0.206	0.221	0.090	0.115	0.264	0.279						
Learn2	1.78	1.58	0.247	0.251	0.495	0.415	0.266	0.386	0.321	0.119	0.337	0.505	0.368					
Excit2	2.19	1.44	0.288	0.236	0.360	0.444	0.293	0.367	0.178	0.178	0.431	0.488	0.453	0.683				
Help2	2.75	1.07	0.280	0.239	0.250	0.304	0.377	0.300	0.077	0.208	0.388	0.404	0.652	0.479	0.536			
Soc2	2.69	1.11	0.287	0.196	0.284	0.315	0.240	0.425	0.170	0.134	0.359	0.453	0.539	0.541	0.614	0.631		
Prof2	-1.12	1.97	0.061	0.164	0.369	0.283	0.126	0.263	0.564	0.074	0.131	0.268	0.048	0.452	0.318	0.125	0.213	
Commun	1.66	0.80	0.391	0.224	0.311	0.366	0.347	0.448	0.149	0.199	0.448	0.636	0.460	0.460	0.487	0.399	0.536	0.279

Sample size at the beginning of the Games (time 1) = 1702; sample size at the end of the Games (time 2) = 942. Cmt1, commitment time 1. Expectations for benefits from volunteer experience: Prest1, prestige benefits; Learn1, learning benefits; Excit1, excitement benefits; Help1, helping benefits; Soc1, social benefits; Prof1, professional benefits. Effic, efficacy; Cmt2, commitment time 2; Satisf, satisfaction. Benefits obtained from volunteer experience: Prest2, prestige benefits; Learn2, learning benefits; Excit2, excitement benefits; Help2, helping benefits; Soc2, social benefits; Prof2, professional benefits. Commun, sense of community end of the Games, satisfaction, the sense of community and the sense that benefits were obtained were also positive on average, with the exception of professionally relevant benefits, which were again negatively rated. At the beginning of the Games, expectations for benefits are moderately correlated, with correlations ranging from 0.108 to 0.622. The same is true at the end of the Games, when correlations among benefits obtained range from 0.048 to 0.683. Interestingly, both before and after the Games, the highest correlation is between excitement and learning. Ratings for benefits expected (at the beginning of the Games) and those obtained (by the end of the Games) are also moderately correlated, ranging from 0.263 to 0.564. Commitment at the beginning of the Games was also moderately correlated with commitment at the end of the Games, with almost 34% shared variance.

Paths to final commitment

In order to determine whether satisfaction, benefits and sense of community enhance prediction of volunteers' final sense of commitment to the event organization, a hierarchical regression was calculated for which organizational commitment at the end of the Games was the dependent variable, and for which the independent variables were organizational commitment at the beginning of the Games, satisfaction, the six dimensions of benefits obtained and sense of community. Commitment at the beginning of the Games was entered in the first block; satisfaction was entered in the second block; the six dimensions of benefits obtained were entered as the third block; and sense of community was entered in the final block. Hierarchical regression provides an F-ratio test of whether each successive block improves prediction of the independent variable. Thus, the second block tested whether satisfaction improved prediction of end-of-Games commitment beyond prediction obtained from commitment at the beginning of the Games. The third block tested whether the six benefits (as a whole) improved prediction beyond that obtained by commitment at the beginning of the Games and satisfaction. The final block tested whether sense of community improved prediction beyond that obtained using beginning commitment, satisfaction and benefits. All four blocks were statistically significant: for the effect of commitment at the beginning of the Games, $\Delta R^2 = 0.340$, $F(1,846) = 436.62$, $P < 0.001$; for the incremental prediction by satisfaction, $\Delta R^2 = 0.048$, $F(1,845) = 66.33$, $P < 0.001$; for the incremental prediction by benefits obtained, $\Delta R^2 = 0.047$, $F(6,839) = 11.77$, $P < 0.001$; for the incremental prediction by sense of community, $\Delta R^2 = 0.009$, $F(1,838) = 13.81$, $P < 0.001$. It is concluded that commitment at the end of the Games is, in part, a function of commitment at the beginning of the Games. Satisfaction improves prediction of final commitment; benefits obtained further improve prediction; and sense of community improves prediction still further.

Examination of the parameter estimates for the final model showed that only some of the benefits significantly improved prediction of commitment.

Table 3.2. Regression of best fit for variables predicting volunteers' commitment at the end of the games ($N = 848$).

Variable	B	$SE\ B$	β
Commitment (at beginning)	0.408	0.027	0.437***
Satisfaction	0.037	0.021	0.062*
Excitement	0.057	0.013	0.142***
Helping	0.061	0.017	0.112***
Sense of community	0.095	0.026	0.132***

$R^2 = 0.448$, adjusted $R^2 = 0.445$. ***$P < 0.001$, *$P < 0.05$ (one tailed).

Those that did not contribute significantly to prediction were removed from the model one at a time in order to obtain a final model of best fit. Four of the benefits were removed: prestige, learning, social benefits and professional benefits. The final model is presented in Table 3.2. Examination of Table 3.2 shows that the model predicts over 44% of the variance in final commitment. Commitment at the beginning of the event provides the highest level of prediction; excitement, helping and sense of community provide comparable levels of prediction; satisfaction contributes least (though significantly) to prediction.

Paths to satisfaction

In order to determine whether satisfaction was a function of benefits obtained and/or sense of community, a regression analysis was conducted for which satisfaction was the dependent variable, and for which benefits and sense of community were independent variables. The regression was statistically significant; $F(7,876) = 109.61, P < 0.001$. Examination of the parameter estimates showed that several of the benefits did not contribute significantly to prediction. In order to obtain a model of best fit, independent variables not providing significant prediction were eliminated one at a time. Three benefits were eliminated: prestige, social benefits and professional benefits. The resulting regression is presented in Table 3.3. Examination of Table 3.3 shows that the model predicts 47% of the variance in satisfaction. Sense of community is the strongest predictor. Learning provides the next highest level of prediction, with excitement and helping rendering small but significant added prediction.

Paths to initial commitment

Finally, a regression was calculated for which commitment at the beginning of the event was the independent variable, and for which respondents' effi-

Table 3.3. Regression of best fit for variables predicting volunteers' satisfaction ($N=884$).

Variable	B	SE B	β
Learning	0.118	0.022	0.192***
Excitement	0.048	0.025	0.072*
Helping	0.064	0.027	0.071*
Sense of community	0.573	0.035	0.482**

$R^2=0.470$, adjusted $R^2=0.467$. ***$P<0.001$, *$P\leq0.05$.

Table 3.4. Regression of best fit for variables predicting volunteers' commitment at the beginning of the games ($N=1565$).

Variable	B	SE B	β
Prestige	0.058	0.016	0.095***
Excitement	0.051	0.011	0.120***
Helping	0.192	0.015	0.338***
Efficacy	0.192	0.023	0.183***

$R^2=0.312$, adjusted $R^2=0.310$. ***$P<0.001$.

cacy and their level of expectation (at the beginning of the Games) that they would obtain each benefit were the independent variables. The regression was statistically significant; $F(7,1557)=104.69$, $P<0.001$. Examination of the parameter estimates showed that not all were significant predictors. In order to obtain a model of best fit, non-significant predictors were eliminated one at a time. Three expectations of benefit were eliminated: learning, social benefits and professional benefits. The resulting regression is presented in Table 3.4. Examination of Table 3.4 shows that the model predicts over 31% of the variance in commitment at the beginning of the Games. The volunteers' expectation that the work would be helpful is the strongest predictor, with efficacy being the next strongest. Expectations for prestige and excitement rendered small but significant added prediction.

The resulting model is illustrated in Fig. 3.2. As examination of the model shows, efficacy and three expected benefits (prestige, helping and excitement) had indirect effects on final commitment, through their effect on initial commitment. Sense of community had direct and indirect (through satisfaction) effects on final commitment. Excitement and helping had both direct and indirect (through satisfaction) effects on final commitment, but learning had only an indirect effect (through its effect on satisfaction).

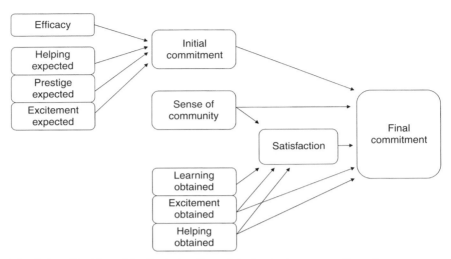

Fig. 3.2. Final (empirically derived) model of volunteer commitment.

Discussion

Findings here are generally consistent with hypotheses derived from the literature. As expected, volunteers' sense of commitment to the event develops as a function of their experience with the event. Although final commitment is, in part, a consequence of the volunteers' initial commitment, there is also significant change in commitment over time, as initial commitment and final commitment share only one-third common variance. Satisfaction with their event experience is an important driver of volunteers' eventual commitment, and satisfaction is itself driven by benefits and the sense of community that volunteers obtain at the event. The effect of benefits and community do not accrue strictly through their effect on satisfaction, as there are also direct effects on final commitment.

The experience of the event also modifies, to some degree, volunteers' perceptions of benefits. Whereas expected benefits affected initial commitment, the sense of benefits ultimately obtained were correlated only moderately with benefits that were expected, sharing only between 7% and 32% of their variance in common. When one looks at the two benefits that had a consistent impact on commitment, excitement and helping, the shared variance between the benefit expected at the beginning and what was obtained is only 20% and 14%, respectively.

The effect of event experience on volunteers' perceptions is also reflected in the change of benefit effects. Whereas expected prestige had a significant effect on initial commitment, it had no effect on final commitment. On the other hand, whereas expected learning had no effect on initial commitment, it had an indirect effect on final commitment. The effect of expectations for prestige on initial commitment is consistent with Fisher and Ackerman's (1998) finding that group need attracts volunteers only when they also expect social approval for volunteering. What is interesting here is that volunteers' eventual commitment does not seem to require that social approval. Rather, the experience of community with other volunteers at the event, and the learning that they accrue, seem to have displaced prestige as a motivator.

It is certainly true, however, that volunteers at the Sydney Olympics received substantial accolades in the domestic and international press, including a post-Games parade through Sydney. Nevertheless, volunteers who took part in our post-Games focus groups were unanimous in their claims that the accolades were 'over the top' and 'unnecessary'. Whether the demise of the prestige effect in our data is a function of some saturation due to all the accolades is unclear, and is untestable in these data. However, the data do clearly indicate that volunteers' eventual commitment to an event changes as they obtain first-hand experience of the event, and the emergent drivers of commitment and satisfaction (i.e. sense of community and learning) are intrinsic to the event experience itself. This is consistent with Ryan *et al.*'s (2001) finding that the motives of environmental volunteers change as a consequence of their experience with the programmes in which they volunteer, and with Coyne and Coyne's (2001) finding that first-time and veteran event volunteers differ in their rank ordering of reasons for volunteering. It is also consistent with the fact that benefits which are intrinsic to the event experience, excitement and helping, were consistently important, while extrinsic gains, such as professional benefits, never had a significant impact.

These findings suggest that event volunteer managers need to give detailed consideration to the nature of the volunteer experience itself, rather than to the nature of rewards that volunteers will receive. Whereas texts on volunteer management (Tedrick and Henderson, 1989; Brudney, 1990) give some attention to volunteer recognition and reward, they do not develop a considered analysis of the management of the volunteer experience. This was reflected at the Sydney Olympics, where a complex system of rewards was implemented, including a special volunteer passport that was stamped at each shift so that the volunteer could qualify for particular prizes. Olympic organizers did not give comparable attention to the nature of the volunteer's lived experience while on station as a volunteer. To some degree, this was a function of the different challenges posed by different volunteer sites and different volunteer duties. Site managers were trained to execute team-building initiatives, including volunteer meetings, publication of a newsletter and contests. It was their job to find the best means to use these tactics to build and maintain their volunteer teams.

Our post-Games focus groups found that most volunteers felt that these exercises helped to build their sense of community with the organization and with other volunteers. The focus groups also found that volunteers felt that these

tactics were not key to their sense of identification with their volunteer assignment. It was the sense of camaraderie, shared purpose and pulling together that
made their experience worthwhile. This is consistent with the dominating effect
that sense of community had on volunteers' satisfaction in the data reported
here. It suggests the value of future work examining volunteers' lived experience
of volunteering, and it recommends work that moves from motives and benefits
to the factors and processes that build a sense of community among those
working at an event – whether they are paid or volunteer.

Two findings provide useful starting points. The important role of efficacy on initial commitment is consistent with other findings showing that efficacy plays an important role in motivation and performance (Bandura,
1997). The standard means for building efficacy among volunteers is to
implement a training programme. During volunteer training, volunteers first
come into contact with other volunteers and/or with paid staff. It is a potential occasion to begin the process of building the volunteers' sense of community in association with the event. If training is viewed in this way, it
becomes more than a time to introduce procedures and policies; it becomes
a time for volunteers to build relationships and to strengthen their joint sense
of purpose. Further work is needed to identify training methods and styles
that foster and nurture volunteers' sense of community.

The consistently high relationship between excitement and learning is
also relevant here. The two shared 39% of their variance in common at the
beginning of the Games and 47% of their variance in common at the Games'
end. Yet, despite their high association at the end of the event, learning has
an independent impact (along with excitement) on satisfaction. It seems that
the two function in tandem – that learning something of how the event runs
is itself a source of excitement and satisfaction, at least for some volunteers.
This would be consistent with Elstad's (1996) finding that learning was a key
element of the excitement and satisfaction that volunteers obtained at the
Lillehammer Olympics. It suggests that volunteer managers need to help volunteers see how their role fits into the overall operation of the event, no
matter how seemingly trivial the volunteer's task. It also suggests the value
of future research that explores the factors that drive and sustain a relationship between the learning and sense of excitement that volunteers obtain.

Just as volunteers are becoming more essential to the planning and execution of events, it is becoming increasingly challenging to recruit and retain
volunteers (Gaskin, 1998; Putnam, 2000; Warburton and Crosier, 2001).
For that reason, their commitment to an event is important not merely for
the duration of the event, but also as a means to build a pool of volunteers
who will be available for future events. If commitment develops as a function
of the volunteer's experience at an event, it will also develop as a function of
experience across an array of events or at an event as it is staged in subsequent years. By examining the ways that event experiences accrue during
and across events, the study of event volunteers will develop a more fully
articulated understanding of volunteering as a leisure choice.

Acknowledgements

This research was supported by the Sydney Organizing Committee for the Olympic Games and the Australian Research Council. The authors extend their appreciation to the six other members of the research team, whose work made collection of these data possible: Graham Cuskelly, Deborah Edwards, Sheranne Fairley, Pamm Kellett, Jenny Moore and Michael Pattishall.

References

Allen, J. (2000) *Event Planning*. John Wiley & Sons, Toronto.

Andrew, J. (1996) Motivations and expectations of volunteers involved in a large scale sports event – a pilot study. *Australian Leisure* March, 21–25.

Bandura, A. (1997) *Self-efficacy: the Exercise of Control*. W.H. Freeman, New York.

Brudney, J.L. (1990) *Fostering Volunteer Programs in the Public Sector*. Jossey-Bass, San Francisco.

Bussell, H. and Forbes, D. (2002) Understanding the volunteer market: the what, where, who and why of volunteering. *International Journal of Nonprofit and Voluntary Sector Marketing* 7, 244–257.

Chalip, L. (2000) Sydney 2000: volunteers and the organization of the Olympic Games: economic and formative aspects. In: Moragas, M. de, Moreno, A.B. and Puig, N. (eds) *Volunteers, Global Society and the Olympic Movement*. International Olympic Committee, Lausanne, pp. 205–214.

Clary, E.G., Snyder, M. and Ridge, R. (1992) Volunteers motivations. *Nonprofit Management and Leadership* 2(4), 28–40.

Connors, T.D. (1995) *The Volunteer Management Handbook*. John Wiley & Sons, New York.

Coyne, B.S. and Coyne, E.J. Sr (2001) Getting, keeping and caring for unpaid volunteers for professional golf tournament events. *Human Resource Development International* 4, 199–214.

Cuskelly, G., McIntyre, N. and Boag, A. (1998) A longitudinal study of the development of organizational commitment amongst volunteer sport administrators. *Journal of Sport Management* 12, 181–202.

Davies, J. (1998) The value of volunteers. *Australian Parks and Recreation* 34(1), 33–35.

Elstad, B. (1996) Volunteer perception of learning and satisfaction in a mega-event: the case of the XVII Olympic Winter Games in Lillehammer. *Festival Management and Event Tourism* 4, 75–86.

Farrell, J.M., Johnston, M.E. and Twynam, G.D. (1998) Volunteer motivation, satisfaction, and management at an elite sporting competition. *Journal of Sport Management* 12, 288–300.

Fisher, J.C. and Cole, K.M. (1993) *Leadership and Management of Volunteer Programs*. Jossey-Bass, San Francisco.

Fisher, R.J. and Ackerman, D. (1998) The effects of recognition and group need on volunteerism: a social norm perspective. *Journal of Consumer Research* 25, 262–275.

Gaskin, K. (1998) Vanishing volunteers: are young people losing interest in volunteering? *Voluntary Action* 1, 33–43.

Gerson, M.J. (1997) Do do-gooders do much good; most volunteers don't solve core problems. *US News and World Report* 122(16), 26.

Getz, D. (1998) Trends, strategies, and issues in sport-event tourism. *Sport Marketing Quarterly* 7(2), 8–13.

Gora, J.A. and Nemerowicz, G. (1991) Volunteers: initial and sustaining motivations in service to the community. *Research in the Sociology of Health Care* 9, 233–246.

Green, B.C. (1997) Action research in youth soccer: assessing the acceptability of an alternative program. *Journal of Sport Management* 11, 29–44.

Green, B.C. (2001) Leveraging subculture and identity to promote sport events. *Sport Management Review* 4, 1–20.

Green, B.C. and Chalip, L. (1997) Enduring involvement in youth soccer: the socialization of parent and child. *Journal of Leisure Research* 29, 61–77.

Green, B.C. and Chalip, L. (1998a) Sport volunteers: research agenda and application. *Sport Marketing Quarterly* 7(2), 14–23.

Green, B.C. and Chalip, L. (1998b) Antecedents and consequences of parental purchase decision involvement in youth sport. *Leisure Sciences* 20, 95–109.

Iaffaldano, M.T. and Muchinsky, P.M. (1985) Job satisfaction and job performance: a meta-analysis. *Psychological Bulletin* 97, 251–273.

Jago, L., Chalip, L., Brown, G., Mules, T. and Ali, S. (2003) Building events into destination branding: insights from experts. *Event Management* 8, 3–14.

Knox, T.M. (1999) The volunteer's folly and socio-economic man; some thoughts on altruism, rationality, and community. *Journal of Socio-economics* 28, 475–493.

McDonnell, I., Allen, J. and O'Toole, W. (2002) *Festival and Special Event Management*, 2nd edn. Wiley, Brisbane.

Meyer, J.P. and Allen, N.J. (1997) *Commitment in the Workplace: Theory, Research, and Application*. Sage, Thousand Oaks, California.

Moragas, M. de, Moreno, A.B. and Paniagua, R. (2000) The evolution of volunteers at the Olympic Games. In: Moragas, M. de, Moreno, A.B. and Puig, N. (eds) *Volunteers, Global Society and the Olympic Movement*. International Olympic Committee, Lausanne, pp. 133–154.

Mowday, R.T., Steers, R.M. and Porter, L.W. (1979) Measurement of organizational commitment. *Journal of Vocational Behavior* 14, 224–227.

Mules, T. and Faulkner, B. (1996) An economic perspective on special events. *Tourism Economics* 14, 314–329.

Nasar, J.L. and Julian, D.A. (1995) The psychological sense of community in the neighborhood. *Journal of the American Planning Association* 61, 178–184.

Omoto, A.M. and Snyder, M. (2002) Considerations of community: the context and process of volunteerism. *American Behavioral Scientist* 5, 846–867.

Phillips, A.S. and Phillips, C.R. (2000) Using skills gained through volunteerism in job searches: a workable strategy. *Journal of Business and Psychology* 14, 573–575.

Putnam, R.D. (2000) *Bowling Alone: the Collapse and Revival of American Community*. Simon and Schuster, New York.

Ryan, R.L., Kaplan, R. and Grese, R.E. (2001) Predicting volunteer commitment in environmental stewardship programmes. *Journal of Environmental Planning and Management* 44, 629–648.

Shiarella, A.H., McCarthy, A.M. and Tucker, M.L. (2000) Development and construct validity of scores on the community service attitudes scale. *Educational and Psychological Measurement* 60, 286–300.

Stebbins, R.A. (1996) Volunteering: a serious leisure perspective. *Nonprofit and Voluntary Sector Quarterly* 25, 211–224.

Taylor, P., Shibli, S., Gratton, C. and Nichols, G. (1996) *Valuing Volunteers in UK Sport: a Sports Council Survey into the Voluntary Sector in UK Sport.* Sports Council, London.

Tedrick, T. and Henderson, K. (1989) *Volunteers in Leisure.* AAHPERD, Reston, Virginia.

van der Wagen, L. (2001) *Event Management.* Hospitality Press, Melbourne.

Warburton, J. and Crosier, T. (2001) Are we too busy to volunteer? The relationship between time and volunteering using the 1997 ABS time use data. *Australian Journal of Social Issues* 36, 295–314.

Williams, P.W., Dossa, K.B. and Tompkins, L. (1995) Volunteerism and special event management: a case study of Whistler's Men's World Cup of Skiing. *Festival Management and Event Tourism* 3, 83–95.

Wymer, W., Riecken, G. and Yavas, U. (1996) Determinants of volunteerism: a cross-disciplinary review and research agenda. *Journal of Nonprofit and Public Sector Marketing* 4(4), 3–26.

Changing Volunteer Lifestyles: Motivation and Satisfaction

The three chapters in this section discuss serious leisure volunteers and their motivation to volunteer as well as the fulfilment they derive from their diverse pursuits. Motivation to volunteer remains a difficult question, in part because motives vary substantially from one volunteer activity to another, and, in part, because we have yet to examine carefully many of the activities comprising the field of volunteerism. These chapters contain data from research conducted in Canada, Great Britain and the USA.

Kenneth B. Perkins and John Benoit open this section of the book with an analysis of volunteer firefighters, employing the conceptual frameworks of serious leisure and human and social capital. They learned from their exploratory study that career changes during a volunteer's membership in a firefighting unit generate fulfilment sufficient to enable this person to tolerate the various disagreeable tasks occasionally encountered in this endeavour and to gain experiences that translate into human capital. There is also some evidence that the social relationships formed in this genre of serious leisure also facilitate acquisition of social capital. Perkins and Benoit surveyed firefighters in 15 volunteer rural fire departments in Canada, concentrating on several variables, including satisfaction with volunteering and human capital acquisition.

Kenneth E. Silverberg reports in Chapter 5 that, according to the United States Bureau of the Census, approximately 50% of American adults volunteer their time to serve the public good. As volunteers have become an integral part of public-service provision, need has grown among people who manage these volunteers for greater understanding of volunteer motives. Working from a psychological functionalist perspective of volunteerism, Silverberg assesses whether a relationship exists between volunteer function, volunteer job setting and volunteer job satisfaction. Using a sample of parks and recreation volunteers, he also examines the relationship between volunteer function and sociodemographic characteristics. Results of this study show that the psychological functions of volunteering vary across volunteer job settings as well as according to specific sociodemographic variables that could be expected to be related to shared meanings. Further, the results suggest that volunteer job satisfaction is, in part, a product of the interaction of job setting and psychological function served by the job setting.

In Chapter 6, Brian E. Wilson notes that amateur sport in the UK is based on a network of clubs run by volunteers. Volunteer coaches in these clubs devote much of their leisure time to developing the sporting abilities of young people. The coaches further ensure that public and private investments in sports facilities are effectively used and that athletes experience a safe and healthy life in the community. Many an international sporting star has been nurtured in this milieu. Despite the large number of people involved, the financial investment made and the amount of youth development that occurs, very little is known about decision making among these volunteers.

Starting from social exchange theory and Brandenburg's work on the recreational activity adoption process, Wilson develops a conceptual model of decisional processes in volunteer sport. Then, using a logistic regression model, he expresses mathematically his conceptual model. Unlike other regression methods, logistic regression can handle the binary nature of an individual's decision whether to volunteer. It can also handle binary, categorical and non-normally distributed variables such as gender, number of children and distance travelled. Wilson collected his data through personal interviews with 112 individuals involved in athletics (track and field). They included qualified athletic coaches, adult athletes and parents of junior athletes, all of them unpaid volunteers. The object of the research was to test a substantive model of the decision to become a volunteer coach.

Volunteer Satisfaction and Serious Leisure in Rural Fire Departments: Implications for Human Capital and Social Capital[1]

4

Kenneth B. Perkins[1] and John Benoit[2]

[1]Longwood University, Farmville, Virginia, USA; [2]Dalhousie University, Halifax, Nova Scotia, Canada

Introduction

This chapter seeks to analyse the phenomenon of volunteer firefighting within the conceptual framework of serious leisure, human capital and social capital. We have found in this exploratory study that career changes during the volunteer's membership allow the member sufficient satisfaction to tolerate the disagreeable tasks, to gain experiences that translate into human capital. There is also some evidence that the social relationships involved in this form of serious leisure can allow for the acquisition of social capital.

Our main subjects were 217 volunteer firefighters in volunteer fire departments in Canada who were surveyed on several variables including satisfaction with volunteering and human capital acquisition. Additionally, both co-authors have a considerable number of years working in the volunteer fire service. The lead author has been a member of a volunteer fire department for 17 years. The second author has built a continuing education programme for leadership training of fire officers in Canada.

The relevance of a study of volunteer firefighters and their departments might not be readily apparent. However, when we consider that in the USA and Canada there are over 40,000 departments in as many separate communities with over 1.1 million volunteer firefighters, the value of this service is considerable (Penwell Publications, 1993). That value is large not only in dollars of labour costs saved by the localities, but also in terms of volunteer fire departments' contribution to community life.[2]

This chapter will be organized in the following manner. First, we will present what we have called a paradox. What is paradoxical is the question

© 2004 CAB International. Volunteering as Leisure/Leisure as Volunteering: an International Assessment (eds R.A. Stebbins and M. Graham)

71

of why anyone would continue to volunteer for years in something that actually turns out not to be a terribly exciting activity, but one that has a number of potentially monotonous and disagreeable features (Perkins and Benoit, 1997). Second, we will offer a short overview of the difference between rural and urban firefighting. This will be important partly because most of the thousands of fire departments are rural, and partly because there are some crucial sociological differences, which provide the foundation for seeing the serious leisure concept in operation. Third, we will present the methods and findings from our ongoing study of volunteer satisfaction and where we used a factor analysis to find some intriguing patterns in the 'career path' of volunteer firefighters. We conclude with possible policy implications as well as some speculation about the potential for serious leisure to be linked with not just human capital acquisition but with social capital development as well.

The Paradox

As noted earlier, there are over 1.1 million volunteer firefighters in over 40,000 fire departments in the USA and Canada; thus, the volunteer fire service is quite large. The average volunteer contributes about 5 hours per week. If the volunteer's labour is valued at $8.00 per hour (a common estimate of its value in the USA), then these volunteers provide (1,100,000 persons × 5 hours × 52 weeks × $8.00 per hour) about $2.29 billion of service per year; thus, the monetary value of the volunteer fire service is quite significant. In eastern North America, many rural volunteer fire departments trace their histories to the early 19th century. Moreover, these services have been provided continuously from the point of founding to the present; thus, the volunteer fire service is old.

Having said all this, the volunteer fire service would seem to be one that is very busy fighting fires. Yet appearances are deceiving. The great majority of these 40,000 fire departments have only about one emergency call *per week*. The great majority of these fire departments fight only about one building or structural fire *per year*. If volunteers join to fight fires, and if they fight so few fires, why do they remain volunteers? Now let us consider another fact. Few volunteer fire departments can realistically offer a firefighting service unless they can purchase a pumper fire engine (cost: $250,000) that can be housed in a fire station (cost: at least $500,000). The debt servicing on these capital expenditures and the operating cost of heat, fuel, utilities, insurance and licences will require a minimum of $50,000 per year. The money to pay these costs is typically obtained mainly from fund-raising by the volunteers and to a smaller degree by grants from the community's local government.

Unfortunately, these forms of financing create two general problems for the volunteers. First, most volunteers dislike fund-raising and see it as a necessary evil. Second, many volunteers also dislike having to deal with local politicians. The disagreeable nature of fund-raising (e.g. selling raffle tickets, running bingo games, canvassing door-to-door for money, collecting items for a rummage sale) is fairly obvious. The dislike of local politicians stems from an organizational culture that values autonomy from government and sees government as a potentially meddlesome outside (and non-expert) authority intruding into the often club-like affairs of the department. The young adult rural males who are looking for a hot fire to attack typically have little regard for the middle-aged people who may know nothing about firefighting but who run the local council meetings where funding decisions are made. If rural volunteer firefighters do not like politicians, and if rural volunteer fire departments fight so few fires, why do local governments grant money to fire departments? Why even do citizens give money to such reluctant fund-raisers? The two crucial contingencies that maintain a rural volunteer fire department (that is volunteer labour and money) would seem to be in jeopardy.

Why does the rural fire service seem to thrive, despite the fact that so few fires are fought? Why do most volunteers continue for years, despite so few fires? Why do most volunteers stay in a department when they have to go out into the community and raise money in time-consuming ways? Why do they not quit when they must rely on disliked politicians for some of their vital funding? Collectively, these questions suggest a paradox. Before we turn to our data analysis we need to describe typical rural firefighting as it contrasts with that in urban areas.

Rural and Urban Firefighting

Two of the major differences between urban and rural areas in the USA and Canada are how fire departments are organized and how fires are fought. Fire departments in urban areas tend to be organized and managed like most other government bureaux. These departments are heavily bureaucratized and almost solely rely on paid labour. It is not unusual to find union locals in most urbanized fire departments. Fire departments in rural areas are quite different. First, most departments completely rely on volunteers. Second, while there is variation in how volunteer departments are constituted, the typical situation is for fire departments to be non-profit organizations. Here members are represented by boards of directors that own the property, firefighting apparatus and equipment. Third, rural departments are community-based, grassroots organizations and are often one of the main providers of community identity (Smith, 1997). Fourth, the ties between departments and local governments are often weak. Departments wish to be left alone, and governments, often due to a misunderstanding of legal risks, are more than happy to oblige.

Regarding the actual emergency response and suppression of fire, in urban areas a person or a smoke detector sends an alarm to an emergency dispatch centre. The alarm is sent to nearby fire stations, from which paid firefighters respond, usually arriving at the fire in about 7–10 minutes after the initial alarm. Usually citizens will have evacuated the building on fire, and firefighters will proceed to extinguish the fire.

In rural areas, a person sends the alarm to the same type of emergency dispatch centre, from which the alarm is sent to the fire station and to the pagers that are worn by the volunteer firefighters. Typically the volunteers will travel from their homes or work to the fire station; they will board the fire engine and travel to the location of the fire, usually arriving 15–20 minutes after the initial alarm. Citizens, or livestock in the case of a barn, will hopefully have evacuated the burning building, and the volunteers will proceed to attempt to extinguish the fire. Unfortunately, since the fire has progressed for about 8–10 minutes longer than in an urban area, the fire will be larger, requiring more water to extinguish it. In a rural area this will be a problem because the amount of water that can be applied will be limited to what the volunteers can carry on their fire trucks.

Why do urban and rural areas fight fires so differently? The principal and obvious explanation has to do with economics. A large urban area has a tax base that can afford to pay for firefighters to occupy fire stations 24 hours a day, 7 days a week. These fire stations are no more than about 5 km from the average fire; thus, response time can be rapid and success reasonably assured. The urban area has sufficient demand for a fire service, and sufficient funds to justify paying firefighters to respond instantly to any alarm. In rural areas, however, the small tax base and the scarcity of fires make paying for firefighters cost-prohibitive. Nevertheless, since many citizens want some protection from fire, these citizens encourage their neighbours to organize fire departments and to volunteer to fight fires. The community's citizens also are willing to undergo modest taxation to pay for a fire station, and maybe even some of the costs of fire engines and the equipment that the volunteer firefighters will need, but not any salaries.

Despite this admirable response by volunteers, the rural volunteer fire department confronts a considerable problem that, oddly enough, is a good thing for the community. Many rural volunteer fire departments fight only about one structural fire a year – clearly not enough to keep volunteers busy at firefighting. A scarcity of fires is good news for the community but bad news for volunteer firefighters. This scarcity can lead to volunteer apathy and can even lead to decisions to resign from the fire department.

Fighting fires is perceived to be (and often is) dangerous, exciting and complex work. As a consequence, significant training is necessary to fight fires. The volunteers will have to learn how to drive fire engines, pump water, advance hoselines, wear self-contained breathing apparatus, ventilate buildings, search smoke-filled rooms for victims, and, of course, extinguish fires. Many rural volunteer fire departments will train their volunteers one evening each week for a year or two to gain the expertise needed to carry out these tasks safely. Furthermore, because fire suppression is a team effort, the volunteer firefighters will participate in dozens of practice drills commanded by the volunteer fire officers who assume responsibility for firefighter safety. Initially this training is highly motivating as the volunteers are learning new skills and sharing anxiety-provoking experiences. Over time, however, volunteers begin to wonder when their skills will be put to use. Boredom can arise.

The situation above does not mean that volunteers are idle all the time. Once or twice a week they may respond to such events as emergency medical calls, brush fires, chimney fires, false alarms and the occasional motor vehicle accident. Useful though these responses are, many volunteers can be frustrated because these types of calls do not match their skills, and these calls do not provide the peak emotional experiences that led them into the fire department in the first place. Again, the result could be a decision to resign from the volunteer fire department, creating a volunteer shortage. Despite this, many of the volunteers persevere.

Serious Leisure, Human Capital and Social Capital

One way to begin to understand why volunteer firefighters persevere despite the lack of structural fires is to consider the concept of serious leisure (Stebbins, 1992, 1996). Serious leisure is defined as the '[s]ystematic pursuit of an amateur, hobbyist, or volunteer activity sufficiently substantial and interesting in nature for the participants to find a career there in the acquisition and expression of a combination of its special skills, knowledge and experience' (Stebbins, 1992, p. 3). Stebbins argues that the *career aspects* (italics ours) of serious leisure provide the social and psychological support necessary to cope with the inevitable frustrations that arise in practising and performing the volunteer skills. It may well be that this aspect of serious leisure will help us to address the paradox whereby firefighters continue to volunteer despite the lack of structural fires.

It is worth quoting Stebbins at greater length regarding the role played by perseverance in volunteering:

> [A]s with other types of serious leisure, career volunteering brings on the
> occasional need to persevere. Participants who want to continue experiencing
> the same level of satisfaction in the activity have to meet certain challenges
> from time to time . . . Thus . . . musicians must practice assiduously to master
> difficult musical passages, the baseball players must throw repeatedly to
> perfect their favorite pitches, and the volunteers must search their
> imaginations for new approaches with which to help children with reading
> problems. Perseverance can also lead to the realization of rewards such as self-
> actualization and self-expression. At times, in all three types of serious leisure,
> the deepest satisfaction comes from the end of the activity rather than during
> it. To repeat, all participants experience their serious leisure as a substantially
> favorable balance of costs and rewards, where the second substantially
> outweigh the first.
>
> (Stebbins, 1996, p. 218)

From this quotation, it becomes clear that satisfaction is an outcome of engaging in serious leisure. Thus, if we can understand what the various factors of volunteer firefighter satisfaction are, and what determines these factors, we may be able to understand why some volunteers remain within the rural volunteer fire department and perhaps why others do indeed resign.

The concept of human capital is fairly obvious in its application. Volunteer firefighting is serious leisure, and in pursuing this leisure it is not hard to imagine the acquisition of 'special skills, knowledge and experience' that have a durable and enabling effect on the individual volunteer. Training provides skills and credentials. Real firefighting allows for the acquisition of transferable skills as well. Stebbins has already made this link between serious leisure and human capital.[3]

The social capital connection may not yet have been established. Social capital is quite a popular concept in sociology, anthropology and political science. Social capital is a form of capital that, as is the case with any type of capital, is enabling and somewhat enduring, but it is distinct in that it originates in and is dependent upon *social relationships*. Most scholars agree that high levels of trust, expectations of reciprocity and clarity of social norms characterize such relationships. Woolcock (1997, p. 13) defined it as 'the norms and networks that facilitate collective action'. Castle (2002, p. 336) defined it similarly as 'those group relations, or norms and networks, which facilitate accomplishments by social and economic systems'. Thus, from these definitions, social capital is not the same thing as human capital but something like an engine for moving groups (teams, a new cohort of recruits or officers in a volunteer fire department) and larger social structures (local communities, for example) toward positive goals. It may be that, as Coleman (1988) has argued, human capital is one result of social capital, but we will limit our ventures into the theory behind the concept.

An important analytical distinction in the concept should be mentioned here. Narayan (1997) noted that social capital can be bonding or bridging. Bonding social capital functions 'horizontally' as persons with homogeneous social characteristics interact, and bridging social capital functions 'vertically' as persons with more heterogeneous characteristics interact.

Relationships with other volunteer fire departments might be considered as producing bonding social capital, a form of capital that enables goodwill, more efficiency at the fire scene, reciprocity in providing mutual aid, increased training opportunities. Relationships between a fire department and, for example, local government, the police department, the local school system could be considered as bridging social capital and produce benefits as well. The potential benefits would include increased funding, more youth involvement in the honourable fire service, or in terms of the early French sociologist, Emile Durkheim, greater community integration.

The quantitative data for this chapter allow only a limited base from which to speculate about the interaction of serious leisure and social capital formation because our unit of analysis is the individual, not the department nor the community. Human capital acquisition can be seen more easily. Conversely, an analysis of social capital requires data on how social structures interact. However, we will use, along with our limited quantitative data, our observations over the past 15 years in studying volunteers and their departments to suggest some paths for further research about serious leisure and social capital (Perkins and Benoit, 1996; Benoit and Perkins, 2001).

Method

Our research seeks to answer the following questions: What are the components of volunteer satisfaction in rural volunteer fire departments? What are the explanatory variables that underlie these component factors of satisfaction? And, bringing to bear our qualitative experiences over the years on this data, this question: What conceptual and policy implications stem from this research?

In the spring of 2002 we conducted an exploratory survey of volunteer officers and firefighters that addressed such concepts as volunteer satisfaction and human capital acquisition. Many of the questions we used were adapted from the United States Social Capital Community Benchmark Survey conducted in 2001 (Saguaro Seminar, 2001).

The sample of the survey was opportunistic, so no claims are made about its generalizability to the population of departments or members. However, there are possibilities for hypothesis development. At the time of writing, this survey remains ongoing; nevertheless, we are able to report on 217 volunteer firefighters, collected from 15 rural volunteer fire departments, the majority of which are from south-western New Brunswick. The survey research instrument is a questionnaire requiring an average of 17 minutes of a respondent's time. Most often the volunteer firefighters completed the questionnaire at their monthly meeting held in the fire hall. Past experience indicates that this method maximizes response rates.

Results

First it must be understood that just as the volunteer's job as a member of a fire department is multidimensional, so the volunteer's satisfaction with the job should be multidimensional as well. Our survey asked respondents to assess satisfaction using a five-point Likert scale on 32 aspects of volunteer work in fire departments. A factor analysis of these 32 variables was conducted to extract the underlying dimensions of satisfaction. An oblique rather than a varimax rotation of axes was conducted using the OBLIMIN method (Rummel, 1970). An oblique rotation was employed because, although satisfaction is multidimensional, some correlation among the dimensions ought to be expected. For example, it is difficult to imagine

Table 4.1. Factor pattern matrix (factor loadings).

	Factors			
Satisfaction with:	Firefighting	Commanding	Fund-raising	Politicking
Entering a burning building to extinguish	**0.909**	−0.073	−0.088	0.152
Searching a burning building to rescue	**0.905**	−0.050	−0.133	0.094
Operating a pump	0.064	**0.781**	0.079	−0.031
External attack on a fire	**0.712**	0.084	0.124	−0.035
Ventilating a fire	**0.774**	0.120	0.157	−0.030
Water transport	0.227	**0.592**	0.141	0.019
Fire ground command	0.086	**0.709**	0.064	0.216
Sector command	0.070	**0.789**	0.019	0.162
Buying vehicles	−0.072	**0.724**	−0.235	0.062
Buying equipment	−0.080	**0.784**	−0.114	0.017
Training volunteers	0.037	**0.529**	0.327	−0.072
Attending social fund-raisers	0.220	−0.066	**0.621**	0.049
Cleaning after a fire	0.177	0.076	**0.627**	0.008
Station maintenance	0.132	0.172	**0.553**	−0.145
Cleaning after a social event	−0.027	−0.015	**0.626**	0.190
Preparing food or bar-tending	−0.121	−0.108	**0.727**	0.127
Speaking at a fire department meeting	0.182	0.077	0.203	**0.722**
Speaking at a council meeting	0.007	0.032	0.002	**0.854**
Speaking at a public meeting	0.053	−0.018	−0.032	**0.868**
Preparing a report	−0.105	0.138	0.027	**0.673**
Being trained in a new skill	**0.685**	0.036	0.001	−0.029

being satisfied with commanding if there did not previously exist a satisfaction with firefighting. SPSS 11.0 was used to employ the OBLIMIN technique. The loadings of the factor pattern matrix were studied to extract the factors. This factor pattern matrix is presented in Table 4.1. Those loadings above 0.50 are in bold.

The result is the extraction of four factors of volunteer satisfaction. They are satisfaction with: (i) firefighting operations (firefighting); (ii) command operations (command); (iii) fund-raising activities (fund-raising); and (iv) political activities (politicking). Further, Table 4.2 reveals the correlations among these four factors.

Table 4.2.   Correlation matrix among four factors of satisfaction.

Satisfaction type	Firefighting	Commanding	Fund-raising	Politicking
Firefighting				
Commanding	0.38			
Fund-raising	0.55	0.18		
Politicking	0.19	0.46	0.24	

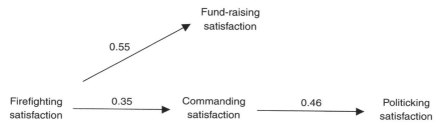

Fig. 4.1.   Correlation among dimensions of satisfaction.

Figure 4.1 is particularly instructive on the time order of the factors of satisfaction. It demonstrates what might be seen as a career. Volunteers first learn how to fight fires, expressing satisfaction with firefighting. Then they participate in fund-raising. After several years some volunteers become fire officers and engage in command activities. Senior officers will also engage in political activities with the council of the local government, the mayor and the chief administrative officer of the local government in order to maximize the fire department's operating and capital grants from local government. This time order of the factors is further supported by the higher satisfaction that officers have with commanding and politicking, as Table 4.3 indicates. Further support for the time order is the correlation between tenure as a volunteer and the various factors, as Table 4.4 indicates.

Table 4.3.   The effect of officer status on satisfaction with commanding and satisfaction with politicking.

	Mean score	
Satisfaction type	Firefighter	Officer
Commanding[a]	2.46	2.92
Politicking	2.35	2.73

[a]See Table 4.1 to examine the relevant factor loadings within the battery of satisfaction questions.

Table 4.4. The correlation between tenure in the fire
department and types of satisfaction.

Types of satisfaction	Tenure
Firefighting	−0.128
Fund-raising	−0.036
Commanding	+0.255
Politicking	+0.009

In general there is no relationship between tenure and satisfaction;
however, a modest positive correlation between commanding satisfaction
and tenure is evident ($r = 0.25$). This relationship is attenuated once officer
status is controlled; the partial correlation between tenure and commanding
satisfaction controlling for officer status is 0.14. It is clear that the reason that
tenure is related to commanding satisfaction is essentially mediated by
assuming an officer status.

One way to understand the various dimensions of volunteer satisfaction
and the apparent time order among them is to consider the volunteer career,
the years from joining the department to becoming a senior officer. The volunteer firefighter or officer may engage in serious leisure by finding a career
in the acquisition of a 'combination of special skills, knowledge or experience' but not find sufficient opportunity for the expression of this particular
combination owing to the lack of structural fires. Nevertheless, the attainment of officer status allows for the expansion of the range of serious leisure
so that the volunteer is now compensated for the frustration arising from the
lack of real fires. This compensation is the serious leisure of officer duties.

Let us examine the career chronologically. First, a recently recruited volunteer quickly recognizes that fighting fires requires the acquisition of skills;
each training exercise is an illustration of the need to 'do the right thing at
the right time'. The initial training provides satisfaction. However, since so
little time is actually spent fighting fires, training also takes on an important
role in preventing the atrophy of acquired firefighting skills. Unfortunately,
the maintenance of extant skills is not nearly so satisfying as the acquisition
of new skills.

Second, another hurdle in the volunteer career is more daunting, despite
its benign appearance. This is the problem of having to participate in fund-
raising. The majority of rural volunteer fire departments require substantial
infusions of funds beyond the support of local government. There are for-
profit companies that specialize in fund-raising for fire departments and
police organizations (some sell family photographs, others solicit donations
in the name of the fire department). Nevertheless, for the most part the
heaviest load of this task falls on the shoulders of individual firefighters. Fund-
raising may include bake sales, dances, bingos, raffles, suppers, auctions,

junk sales or door-to-door solicitation. Usually, the volunteers regard participation in such activities as boring, if not outright onerous. Some volunteers will suffer burnout at this stage because there is no intrinsic reward. Nevertheless, some volunteers see fund-raising as an instrumental activity that facilitates the acquisition of the treasured fire engine.

After about five years, many firefighters seek to emulate their volunteer fire officers, who direct such activities as water transport, rescue, fire suppression, building ventilation or even incident command. Mastering these operational management skills is highly anxiety provoking but satisfying once accomplished. The role of fire officer, however, is more than just engaging in command. It is also the planning and preparation necessary to ensure that the rural volunteer fire department can effectively respond to an alarm. Part of this planning includes the training of firefighters; part of it includes the planning for and acquisition of fire vehicles such as pumpers, rescue vehicles or safety equipment. Naturally such acquisition requires money, some of which is acquired by fund-raising, some of which is acquired by lobbying local government. Lobbying with local government requires a different skill set. Usually the politicians and the chief administrative officer lack the passion for the fire service that volunteer chief officers have. We mentioned earlier the mutual desire not to know much about the affairs of the other. This places the officers who are asking for money in a relatively powerless position. Nevertheless, the officers must learn to 'sell' the value of the very low-cost, and often low-profile, volunteer fire service to their local government. How this is accomplished will be addressed below.

Officer status is critical to developing satisfaction for officer-related duties such as commanding and politicking. The reasons for this are probably a function of: (i) selection that influences motivation and (ii) human capital acquisition that arises from some training and some experience within the fire department. The differences in perceived skill, with one exception, favour the officers, as Table 4.5 demonstrates. Moreover, most of this skill is gained at the fire department as opposed to elsewhere.

At a general level, in Fig. 4.2 we observe a model whereby the measured variables of perceived skill, officer status and satisfaction mutually reinforce each other. Moreover, the unmeasured variable, serious leisure, intervenes between volunteer satisfaction and perceived skill. As skill increases, selection or election to officer status becomes more likely. Officer status leads to new duties and experiences that allow for the development of new skills such as commanding and politicking. The acquisition of skill results in participating in a form of serious leisure that, in turn, results in the satisfaction of the mastery of the skill, and that satisfaction motivates the officer to participate in more serious leisure by taking on more duties that lead to more skill acquisition. Satisfaction in firefighting leads to motivation to become an officer, and officer status leads to more satisfaction.

This model is reasonably consistent with the data, but it is a general model only. After all, notwithstanding the results of the oblique factor analysis, the

Table 4.5. The effect of officer status on perceived skill.

	Mean perceived skill[a]	
Skill	Firefighters	Officers
Making a speech	0.573	0.600
Writing a report	0.671	0.786
Preparing a budget	0.355	0.482
Presenting a budget	0.261	0.482
Meeting public officials	0.691	0.785
Negotiating a price	0.651	0.607
Selling a service	0.530	0.553
Incident command	0.523	0.767
Sector command	0.463	0.804
Teaching volunteers	0.819	0.929

[a]Skill present = 1; skill absent = 0.

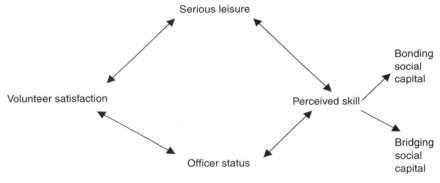

Fig. 4.2. Skill, satisfaction and status. This is a general model with heuristic rather than specific prediction value. Both volunteer satisfaction and perceived skill are multidimensional. Nevertheless, it maybe possible to develop specific predictive models when the various dimensions of volunteer satisfaction and perceived skill are employed.

dimensions of satisfaction are primarily unrelated because satisfaction includes at least four fairly separate factors. Nevertheless, the model shows how the serious leisure of volunteer firefighting induces socialization and selection that lead to officer status. The officers, in turn, interact with local politicians and other public officials to maintain or even enhance the level of financial support for the fire department and its activities. If we consider how the rural volunteer fire department relates to its local government, then a combination of skills and satisfaction lead to an increased skill in the volunteer officers' meeting with public officials. A multiple regression that includes

Table 4.6. Explaining perceived skill in meeting public officials.

	β	t
Skill in report writing	0.310	4.76
Skill in negotiating a price	0.257	4.09
Satisfaction with speaking at a public meeting	0.188	2.93

$R^2 = 0.253$.

skill with meeting public officials as the dependent variable shows the most significant independent variables are: skill in report writing, skill in negotiating a price and satisfaction in speaking at a public meeting. As Table 4.6 shows, these three independent variables explain slightly over 25% of the variance in skill in meeting public officials.

Other volunteer firefighters are relatively less trusting of local government and relatively less satisfied in playing a politicking role; nevertheless, these volunteer firefighters tend to trust their officers, who, in turn, are more trusting of local government. The officers, therefore, play an important mediating role between the firefighters and the politicians or bureaucrats. It may well be that officer socialization and increased satisfaction with politicking each play a role in providing a form of *bridging social capital* between the volunteer firefighters and local government (Putnam, 1993, 2000; Narayan, 1997; Duncan, 2001).

Bonding social capital tends to be high when many of the volunteers' friends are members of the rural volunteer fire department. Similarly, much of the volunteers' time is spent in socializing with each other. These bonds are particularly strengthened by common experience in a stress-producing situation such as an emergency, intensive training for an emergency or in sharing in the hardships of fund-raising. These are precisely the conditions experienced in rural volunteer fire departments and, therefore, this is why these organizations are more than simple rural social clubs. Many of the social events that induce bonding social capital within the department can be fund-raising events that also induce bridging social capital with the more heterogeneous members of the community.

Conclusion

What policy implications arise from these findings? There are several. First, the very fact that fund-raising satisfaction is primarily (but not entirely) independent from firefighting satisfaction suggests that rural volunteer fire departments could recruit those who get more satisfaction from fund-raising, citizens who will tend to be older and include a number of women. These fund-raising volunteers would probably not engage in firefighting.

.d, the fact that training enhances both firefighter satisfaction and
fing satisfaction suggests that more resources for training could very
nance these components of volunteer satisfaction, retention and, on
:casions when a fire occurs, fire suppression performance at a real
m.   .ne. Third, although we have insufficient data for definitive conclusions, our qualitative observations suggest that fund-raising does contribute
to bridging social capital within the community. Perkins (1987) noted that
fund-raising in the department he studied contributed to community integration. Community integration, a concept that can be traced to Emile
Durkheim, may have been the earliest sociological expression of bridging
and bonding social capital. Local governments could provide incentives to
increase fund-raising by rural volunteer fire departments. One way this could
be done would be to establish a formula that assigns the size of the government grant proportionate to the magnitude of fund-raising.

Let us return to our initial questions that generated the paradox and
provide some tentative answers: Why are so many volunteers remaining in
the fire service? They tend to pursue serious leisure by following a career path
that alters what is satisfying. Once initial training leads to satisfaction with
firefighting, many volunteers seek to learn and to practise sector and incident command. Once the challenge of command is frustrated by the lack of
fires, other managerial challenges arise, challenges such as teaching, major
equipment purchasing, and of course, politicking. Conversely, those volunteer firefighters who do not reach officer status maintain a lower commitment to the rural volunteer fire department. This explains why officers
volunteer about 20 hours per week, whereas firefighters give about 5 hours
per week.

Why do volunteers continue to fund-raise when they dislike the process
so much? They are given social support by their spouses in the ladies auxil-
iary and by their fellow firefighters during the fund-raising process. The group
activity, such as a dance or a supper, requires modest conformity, generates
some enthusiasm and at least raises commitment. The fund-raising is the
serious part of serious leisure; the fund-raising *activity* is the *leisure* part of
serious leisure.

Why do volunteers continue to rely on the politicians' financial support
when they do not particularly care for these same politicians? The volunteer
firefighters respect and tend to like their fellow officers. The officers, by selection and learning, demonstrate skill at interacting with the politicians. This
skill reinforces the officers' satisfaction with politicking, preventing the officers from resigning and thus ensuring that their political skills will be put to
good use.

One question remains. Why does the community, through donation or
taxes, contribute to a fire service that hardly ever fights fires? Partly, the
answer is that the public, whether rural or urban, expects some level of fire
service and most state legal codes place the responsibility to provide it, to
varying extents, on the local governments. Yet, these reasons do not explain

why in some rural counties there are volunteer fire departments in nearly every village, each receiving local government and community support. The other part of this answer we believe relates much more to the function of serious leisure to stimulate social capital development. From our qualitative observations and quantitative findings reported here, it would appear that both fund-raising and politicking contribute to the development of bonding social capital within the fire department organization. This bonding social capital supports the fund-raising activity, which attracts other citizens. As a result, *bridging* social capital is created between the department and the community. Similarly, bonding social capital within the department motivates volunteer fire officers to politick with the community's local government thus creating more social capital.

We need to bring our analysis to a close; we are quite confident in saying that human capital is created by the serious leisure of volunteer firefighting. At this point in our research, we are slightly less confident about any hard and fast empirical findings regarding social capital, but this has not caused us to refrain from speculation. At the very least, our research context, rural communities, their local governments, the volunteer fire departments within and member volunteer firefighters, seems to provide a fertile ground for empirical examination of how social capital is created and maintained. We ask the reader to consider the notion of serious leisure in the rural setting and study the conditions under which social capital is created.

Notes

[1] The authors are particularly indebted to Captain John O'Neill of the Saint John Fire Department, who administered the survey in New Brunswick, to Halima Mohamed, who painstakingly coded the survey data and to Bob Aldcorn of the Fire Academy of the Justice Institute of British Columbia, who consulted on questionnaire design.

[2] Volunteer fire departments are generally considered to be grassroots associations in terms of the definition of David Horton Smith. That is '[l]ocally based and basically autonomous, volunteer-run, non-profit groups that have an official membership of volunteers' (Smith, 1997, p. 273). Smith further notes that these volunteers are considered to be *associational* rather than *programme* volunteers, the latter being part of some employment-related volunteer programme. Smith's research outlines a typology of contributions that these kinds of organizations contribute to the volunteer, to the community and to the larger society.

[3] The human capital side of this role career can be illustrated by the application of something called 'empowerment theory'. To quote Arai in her analysis of serious leisure: '[T]hus volunteering is not only connected to psychological empowerment (self-conception, self-efficacy, locus of control), but also to social empowerment (increased access to information, knowledge, skills and resources; increased connections), and political empowerment (access to decision making processes, power of voice and collective action)' (Arai, 1997, p. 22).

References

Arai, S.M. (1997) Volunteers within a changing society: the uses of empowerment theory in understanding serious leisure. *World Leisure and Recreation* 39, 19–22.

Benoit, J. and Perkins, K.B. (2001) *Leading Career and Volunteer Firefighters.* Henson College, Dalhousie University, Halifax, Nova Scotia.

Castle, E.N. (2002) Social capital: an interdisciplinary concept. *Rural Sociology* 67, 331–349.

Coleman, J.S. (1988) Social capital in the creation of human capital. *American Journal of Sociology* 94, 95–120.

Duncan, C.M. (2001) Social capital in America's poor rural communities. In: Saegert, S., Thompson, J.P. and Warren, M.R. (eds) *Social Capital and Poor Communities.* Russell Sage Foundation, New York, pp. 60–86.

Narayan, D. (1997) *Voices of the Poor: Poverty and Social Capital in Tanzania.* World Bank Development Studies and Monographs Series 20. World Bank, Washington, DC.

Penwell Publications (1993) *Directory of Fire Departments.* Penwell Publications, Tulsa, Oklahoma.

Perkins, K.B. (1987) Volunteer fire departments: community integration, solidarity and survival. *Human Organization* 46, 342–348.

Perkins, K.B. and Benoit, J. (1996) *The Future of Volunteer Fire and Rescue Services.* Fire Protection Publications, Stillwater, Oklahoma.

Perkins, K.B. and Benoit, J. (1997) Volunteer firefighting activity in North America as serious leisure. *World Leisure and Recreation* 39, 23–29.

Putnam, R. (1993) *Making Democracy Work.* Princeton, New Jersey.

Putnam, R. (2000) *Bowling Alone: the Collapse and Revival of American Community.* Simon & Schuster, New York.

Rummel, R.J. (1970) *Applied Factor Analysis.* Northwestern University Press, Evanston, Illinois.

Saguaro Seminar (2001) *US Social Capital Community Benchmark Survey.* Roper Center, Storrs, Connecticut.

Smith, D.H. (1997) Grassroots associations are important: some theory and a review of the impact literature. *Nonprofit and Voluntary Sector Quarterly* 26, 269–306.

Stebbins, R.A. (1992) *Amateurs, Professionals and Serious Leisure.* McGill-Queen's University Press, Montreal.

Stebbins, R.A. (1996) Volunteering: a serious leisure perspective. *Non-profit and Volunteer Sector Quarterly* 25, 211–224.

Woolcock, M. (1997) Social capital and economic development. *Theory and Society* 27, 151–208.

Understanding American Parks and Recreation Volunteers Utilizing a Functionalist Perspective

5

Kenneth E. Silverberg

Department of Parks, Recreation, and Tourism, University of Utah, 250 South 1850 East Room 200, Salt Lake City, UT 84112-0920, USA

The Need for Volunteerism in the Provision of Parks and Recreation Services

Doing more with less has been a theme in the parks and recreation profession for the past five decades. Some recent literature has focused on innovative ways to finance and operate parks and recreation agencies through repositioning, partnerships, exactions and support from external sources (Crompton, 1999). However, while there is a high interest among agencies to employ non-traditional methods for service delivery, levels of activity are quite low 'for all but the most traditional alternatives' (Cigler, 1987, p. iv).

David Osborne and Ted Gaebler (1993), in their timely book *Reinventing Government*, discuss government in terms of a new 'entrepreneurial' spirit, where the public sector is giving rise to new public institutions, which are 'lean, decentralized and innovative' (p. 2). According to Osborne and Gaebler, today's governments are flexible and adaptable, using competition, customer choice and other non-bureaucratic mechanisms to get things done. Local governments are being analysed in terms of productivity and quality, as more public-administration literature is discussing new and innovative ways to make local governments more efficient in their provision of public services. A new area within public administration now focuses on alternative approaches to public-service delivery, as communities face service provision problems that require novel ways to 'do more with less'.

Public entrepreneurship is becoming a crucial element in the support of local government services and has led to new business opportunities for the private sector (Silverstein, 1996). Local governments are viewing the private sector as a potential partner as well as a service provider. As local governments continue to downsize, public-service managers are continuing to search for ways to save tax dollars while improving the quality of their services. Public–private partnerships are an important part of the entire government reinvention movement (Holderman, 1996). Ultimately, public entrepreneurship and public–private partnerships will lead to advantages for both the public- and private-service providers. It will be imperative that all public-service agencies examine any and all alternative approaches to the delivery of public services. In an era of fiscal constraints, public-service managers must understand and examine the possibilities associated with the use of private resources in helping with the delivery of public services.

This somewhat recent shift in the provision of public goods and services has led to the debate over the balance between the government's responsibility for and private individuals' willingness to meet needs of local communities. Dialogue over decentralization of governmental power to smaller neighbourhood and community political units has been one factor in this shift (Nanetti, 1980). Certainly another factor has been the post-war taxpayer revolts of the past two decades. While the most widespread of these tax limitations was the voter-endorsed Proposition 13 of California's 1978 election, tax limitations actually started much earlier in the 1970s, with many early reforms aimed at providing property tax relief in the form of property tax caps and limits on property tax revenues. Once again today, California, as many states, is facing the possibility of major tax cuts, and the elimination of numerous parks and recreation services and even entire departments.

During the Clinton Administration, there was the advent of several conferences known as 'Summits for America's Future', and what the President at the time was calling the end of the era of big government and the beginning of the era of the big citizen (Alter, 1997). Volunteerism became the cornerstone for this new American agenda. The particular initiative focused on the fundamental needs of America's youth and looked toward citizens as well as the private and non-profit sectors to become part of an enormous volunteer 'army' to help rescue 'at risk' youth. Interestingly, this was the same agenda that public parks and recreation agencies had developed and implemented for at least 20 years prior to the Clinton Initiative.

The United States Bureau of Census reports that over 50% of American citizens volunteer time to serve the public good (US Census, 1990). Budget challenges over the past quarter century have resulted in a situation in which services that volunteers provide are increasingly crucial especially to the provision of public parks and recreation services. Public parks and recreation agencies of all sizes have relied on the use of volunteers to ensure the continued success of their programmes. Increasingly, local residents have become essential elements in providing recreation programmes and attractive and safe parks. Examples can be found in severely impacted jurisdictions such as New York City, Los Angeles and Atlanta, where many services are not provided until a sufficient 'match' of voluntary effort is forthcoming from the community (Ferris, 1988). Given this increased reliance of public parks and recreation departments upon volunteers, it is vitally important for parks and recreation managers to develop a greater understanding of the motives for volunteerism, or the psychological 'functions' (Clary *et al.*, 1998; Silverberg *et al.*, 1999a) that volunteering serves.

Much of the past management literature emphasizes the responsibility of managers to understand the motives, functions and related needs of workers in order to recruit individuals effectively to jobs for which they are suited and to empower workers to function effectively as individuals and as members of cooperative teams (Crosby, 1979; Deming, 1986; Juran, 1988; Walton, 1990). Existing evidence clearly suggests that public administrators also need guidance in managing the different roles of citizen volunteers. Many managers of public agencies have, in fact, been found to lack the understanding and background necessary to manage their volunteer workforce effectively (Walter, 1987).

In addition, there has been minimal empirical testing accomplished in terms of volunteer effectiveness as a viable alternative delivery approach (Cnaan and Goldberg-Glen, 1991). While the parks and recreation profession as a whole has expressed how much of its success has been based on the enormity of its volunteer labour force, there is essentially very little empirical literature concerning the motivations of and distinctions between these volunteers. Only recently has the parks and recreation literature begun to investigate whether different volunteers are motivated for different reasons (Backman *et al.*, 1997; Silverberg, 1999; Silverberg *et al.*, 1999a).

A Functionalist Perspective to Understanding Volunteers

Building on the earlier work of the functional theorists in psychology who examined the functions of attitudes, more recent psychological research has adopted and expanded a line of reasoning that has been used to answer motivational questions related to volunteerism. This approach 'is explicitly concerned with the reasons and the purposes, the plans and the goals, that underlie and generate psychological phenomena . . . that is the personal and social functions being served by an individual's thoughts, feelings and actions' (Snyder, in Clary *et al.*, 1998, p. 1517). This research has led to the development of a scale to measure the functions of volunteering. This scale, the Volunteer Function Inventory (VFI), is designed to delineate functions comprising the motivations to volunteer. The functionalist research leading to the development of the VFI revealed an identification of generic motivations of volunteerism indicated by six functions identified as values, understanding, social, career, protective and enhancement. The following is a description of each of those six functions:

- Values: individuals who volunteer in service of this function do so in order to express values that are related to altruistic and humanitarian concerns for others.
- Understanding: this function, which may be served through volunteerism, is related to the opportunity for new learning experiences and a potential for the exercise of knowledge and skills that may otherwise not be utilized.
- Social: this function concerns the relationship the volunteer has with others. The volunteer experience has the potential to offer a variety of opportunities for individuals to be with their friends and/or engage in an activity that they perceive as being viewed favourably by others.
- Career: volunteering may also serve a function of career-related benefits. It may be a means of either preparing for a new career or maintaining skills related to a current career.
- Protective: this function is concerned with processes related to the functioning of the ego. An individual may volunteer to reduce guilty feelings of being more fortunate than others and/or confront their own personal problems.
- Enhancement: in contrast with the protective function of trying to eliminate negative feelings related to the volunteer's ego, this function is served by a motivation for the growth of one's ego, through individual, personal development.

In turn, this opened up the possibility for future studies to explore other meaningful variations of functions, based on differences in volunteer activities and settings (Clary et al., 1998).

The core proposition of functionalist theory as it has been used in the analysis of volunteerism is that 'acts of volunteerism that appear to be quite similar on the surface may reflect markedly different underlying motivational processes' (Clary et al., 1998, p. 1517). Simply put, different people can engage in activities that on the surface seem similar, yet they may be doing so for very different reasons and serving very different psychological functions. The underlying meaning behind this theoretical tenet lends itself well to the question of individual motivational differences in relation to the specific volunteer task being performed (situational variables related to the volunteer experience).

Another proposition states, 'the functions served by volunteerism manifest themselves in the unfolding dynamics of this form of helpfulness, influencing critical events associated with the initiation and maintenance of voluntary helping behaviour' (Clary et al., 1998, p. 1517). Consistent with this perspective, the extent to which functions are adequately served (or, equivalently, needs are adequately being met) would clearly influence volunteer job satisfaction. In fact, during the empirical testing of the VFI it was concluded that the level of satisfaction with a person's volunteer experience is positively correlated with the person receiving functionally relevant benefits congruent with their motivations (Clary *et al.*, 1998). In fact, the notion of meeting worker needs has been of central importance to most models of worker satisfaction (McClelland, 1953; Herzberg *et al.*, 1959; Herzberg, 1968, 1971; Spector, 1997).

A final proposition of functionalist theory suggests that objects with shared meanings among members of defined groups may create similarities in terms of psychological functions sought through volunteering (Shavitt, 1989; Snyder, 1993; Clary *et al.*, 1998). Knowledge of the relationships between psychological functions and such variables may provide managers with information needed for effective recruitment, placement and supervision of volunteers. The potential importance of this notion gives credence to an exploratory examination of sociodemographic variables considered as potential objects with socially constructed meanings. It is apparent that these variables may be good predictors of psychologically relevant benefits being sought within a functional framework of volunteerism.

In addition to the work on functions of volunteering in psychology, there has been a body of work in the public-administration and volunteer-sector literature (e.g. Sharp, 1980; Whitaker, 1980; Rosentraub and Sharp, 1981; Brudney and England, 1983; Kiser, 1984; Levine, 1984; Warren *et al.*, 1984; Brudney, 1990) that also suggests certain types of programmes will attract volunteers who are motivated by the more recently examined functions of coproduction. There are three distinct volunteer coproduction motives, which have been characterized as: a perception volunteers possess that the programme will not be offered without their help; volunteers have a desire to become more knowledgeable about and be more involved in the governmental infrastructure of their community; volunteers perceive that their volunteering will have a direct benefit on a person they know (usually a family member). While there may be some overlap between these three coproduction functions and those proposed in the VFI, it is generally believed that the coproduction motives address the 'important potential for citizens to improve urban service delivery' (Percy, 1987, p. 83) where 'producers of these services are also among the consumers of the services' (Sundeen, 1985, p. 387). In addition, more recent research has revealed a definite distinction between these three functions, specific to parks and recreation volunteers (Silverberg, 1999; Silverberg *et al.*, 1999a).

In fact, recent research with parks and recreation volunteers has suggested that the set of functions proposed by the functionalist theorists (the VFI, developed by Clary *et al.*, 1998) and the coproduction motives studied in the public-administration and volunteer-sector literature are all relevant to understanding the motivational make-up of this group of volunteers (Backman *et al.*, 1997; Silverberg, 1999; Silverberg *et al.*, 1999a). The more recent of these studies has proposed a typology of public parks and recreation volunteer functions based on reliability and factor analysis procedures (Silverberg, 1999; Silverberg *et al.*, 1999a). The proposed typology currently consists of the six original functions described by Clary *et al.*

(1998), values, understanding, social, career, protective and enhancement, as well as the three coproduction functions, designated by the parks and recreation researchers (Silverberg *et al.*, 1999a) as The Department Needs Me, Knowledge of Governmental Operations and Benefits to People I Know.

The Functionalist Approach: a Greater Understanding of the Volunteer Experience

The next step in utilizing the functionalist approach in research specific to the entire volunteer experience of parks and recreation volunteers was an examination of the nine previously described functions of volunteering as they were correlated to: the volunteer job setting; the level of volunteer job satisfaction; and specific sociodemographic characteristics of volunteers defined as objects with shared meanings, as outlined by functionalist theory (Clary *et al.*, 1998). Functionalist theory (Snyder, 1993) suggests that volunteers seeking particular psychological functions will be most satisfied with their volunteer experience when the job settings in which they are placed tend to facilitate attainment of those functions. Also, functionalist theory suggests that specific sociodemographic characteristics may be predictive of specific psychological functions that volunteers are seeking.

Testing the functionalist propositions with parks and recreation volunteers

A specific study designed to test the three propositions of functionalist theory as they relate to the experience of a sample of public parks and recreation volunteers was conducted in 1998 and 1999 (Silverberg, 1999; Silverberg *et al.*, 2001). The study was conducted with volunteers in the city of Phoenix, Arizona, Parks, Recreation and Library Department (PRLD). The mailed questionnaire included the VFI (Clary *et al.*, 1998) and 12 items to measure the three coproduction motives. The questionnaire also included measures of volunteer job setting, volunteer job satisfaction and specific sociodemographic characteristics used in analyses within this study. A description of each of these measures follows.

The VFI in conjunction with the added coproduction items was the substantial portion of the questionnaire. The VFI measured psychological functions associated with volunteering. The VFI included statements that respondents were asked to identify in terms of how important they were related to their own volunteer experience with the PRLD. An example of some of those statements included: 'Volunteering is a good escape from my own troubles'; 'My volunteer experience will look good on my resume'; and 'Volunteering increases my self-esteem'. Additional statements were added to the VFI for this study to measure coproduction. Examples of the coproduction statements included: 'If I don't volunteer I believe the program will not continue'; 'My volunteering is essential for the success of the program and the inner-workings of my community government'; and 'I volunteer because a family member is a participant in the program'.

In addition to the measures of volunteer functions, other questions were included to assess the additional variables related to the functionalist propositions. Respondents were asked to indicate the type of task (job) that they currently performed as a volunteer with the PRLD (an indication of job setting). To measure volunteer job satisfaction, a job satisfaction scale (Spector, 1997) was utilized. This scale was a commonly used measure of job satisfaction. The scale was chosen with the intent of tapping into the general overall level of job satisfaction associated with volunteering. The following statements are examples of items included in the volunteer job satisfaction scale: 'When I do a good job, I receive the recognition for it that I should receive'; 'I sometimes feel my volunteer work is meaningless'; and 'My super‑ visor shows too little interest in the feelings of the volunteers' (Silverberg *et al.*, 2001). Finally, specific sociodemographic variables were examined. While there were a number of sociodemographic items included, this study specifically examined three characteristics: sex, employment status and ethnicity, strictly from an intuitive standpoint and in an exploratory manner only.

Results of the study

Three (of the nine) volunteer functions, Enhancement, Knowledge of Governmental Operations and Benefits to People I Know, were discovered to be of most importance in relation to volunteer job setting. The two coproduction functions mentioned above (Knowledge of Governmental Operations and Benefits to People I Know) were found to have the largest correlations with volunteer job setting. Based on the results of the analysis it was determined that volunteers in this sample could be characterized by an intention to gain benefits for people they know and not for gaining knowledge of government operations.

Specifically, volunteer coaches (for youth sports leagues) were more likely to volunteer when people they knew were benefiting from their volunteer service (such as their own child being a member of the team they were coaching). On the other hand, volunteer coaches were unlikely to volunteer for knowledge of government operations. Conversely, those individuals who volunteered for the libraries were more likely to do so for knowledge of governmental operations and not for the benefit of people they knew.

The analysis also revealed that volunteers who worked in other operations (such as maintenance and administrative support positions) were more likely to do so for knowledge of the 'inner-workings' of the PRLD and/or government operations within their community. Lastly, the analysis also revealed that there was a high negative correlation between the Enhancement function and individuals who volunteered for the libraries. The library volunteers were less likely to volunteer for growth and personal development reasons (Enhancement).

The following analysis was to determine if the interaction between volunteer function and job setting was significant in terms of volunteer job satisfaction. Functionalist theory would predict that individuals in a particular job setting who are high on the salient function would have higher levels of volunteer job satisfaction (Clary et al., 1998). Once again, the same two coproduction functions that were significant in the first analysis showed significant interactions with job setting in this analysis: Knowledge of Governmental Operations and Benefits to People I Know. The significant correlations were for volunteers who worked as coaches, volunteers who worked in other operations and volunteers who served in recreation programmes. The only positive correlation was for volunteer coaches. Both of the other correlations were negative (volunteers who worked in other operations and recreation programmes). The positive correlation for volunteer coaches was interpreted as these volunteers would have their highest level of volunteer job satisfaction when they were providing their volunteer time in a way that would benefit people they knew. In opposition, volunteers who worked in other operations and recreation programmes would have higher levels of volunteer job satisfaction when they were volunteering and also increasing their knowledge of the 'inner-workings' of the PRLD and other governmental operations within their community.

The final analysis was performed to assess the relationship between sex, employment status and ethnicity with the nine volunteer functions. Five volunteer functions were significant in this analysis: Career, Knowledge of Governmental Operations, Protective, Benefits to People I Know and Understanding. In terms of an individual's sex, only two of the nine volunteer functions had significant relationships with this item. They were the same two coproduction functions that had been significant in the previous analyses (Knowledge of Governmental Operations and Benefits to People I Know). The results in terms of a volunteer's sex indicated that males were more likely to volunteer in order to provide benefits to people they know while females were more likely to volunteer for knowledge of government operations.

The results for volunteers' employment status revealed five significant volunteer functions related to this item. The two volunteer functions were the Career volunteer function and the Understanding volunteer function. The analysis uncovered that students and individuals who were unemployed were more likely to volunteer for career and other learning opportunities (the Career and Understanding functions). In addition, students were also more likely to volunteer for experiences related to knowledge of governmental operations, and based on a feeling of being more fortunate than others (the Protective function). That same group tended to not volunteer in order to provide benefits to people they know. The other group of individuals that showed a significant negative relationship with the Career and Understanding volunteer functions were retired individuals. As one might expect, retired individuals were unlikely to volunteer for career or other learning experiences.

The final relationship examined was ethnicity by volunteer function. Only one volunteer function had a significant relationship in this analysis, the Career volunteer function. The results indicated that this volunteer function had a very strong positive relationship with two ethnic groups, African Americans and Hispanics. These two ethnic groups were most likely to volunteer for experiences that might help them in their career endeavours (the Career function). These findings indicate that volunteer opportunities for these two minority groups should be highly focused on functionally relevant benefits specific to the Career function. It may be that these inner-city volunteers are using their volunteer experience as a way to acquire a job with the PRLD. In fact, many of the minority employees within the PRLD started out just that way (Silverberg, 1999).

Implications of the results of this study

Collectively, the results support a functionalist perspective on volunteerism and lend empirical support for a functional analysis of volunteerism within this particular volunteer sample. The findings are compatible with the tenets of functional theorizing, which describes the phenomenon of volunteerism as a coalescence of people, situations and objects (Lewin, 1946; Snyder and Ickes, 1985; Snyder, 1993; Cantor, 1994; Clary et al., 1998). The findings indicate that psychological functions of volunteers vary across volunteer job settings and by specific (exploratory) sociodemographic variables that would be expected to give rise to shared meanings (as defined in the third proposition). This also suggests that volunteer job satisfaction is, at least in part, a result of the interaction of job setting and the psychological volunteer function being served by the volunteer's job setting.

Results for the analysis on the relationship between volunteer function and volunteer job setting supported previous findings of volunteer functions differing across volunteer experiences (job settings) (Snyder, 1993; Clary et al., 1998). In addition, these findings make a case for the predictive capability of object domains in terms of individual differences in volunteer functions (Shavitt, 1989). In this study, it was found that the individual volunteer functions differed in terms of the three specific sociodemographic variables (object domains) that were examined, similar to the contention by Shavitt (1989, p. 333) that 'differences in individuals' occupations may be associated with differences in the functions of their attitudes toward work relevant objects'. A greater understanding of these concepts and the relationships between them can help in the revision and refinement of the theoretical foundations used to understand the complexities of volunteerism.

As was expected, the results of the analysis of the relationship between the volunteer functions and volunteer job setting are consistent with the notion that many coaches volunteer because their children participate in the programme. This anticipated finding is one that should be helpful to managers of sports programmes in public parks and recreation settings. It is important that these managers understand not only the importance of using volunteers in the success of their programmes, but also that the parents who volunteer as coaches do so for specific coproduction reasons. If coproduction increases as a viable alternative in the delivery of public services, volunteer managers will need to foster volunteer experiences where the perception is that the functionally relevant benefits being derived (both directly and indirectly) are greater than the costs of giving of one's time. Managers who supervise these volunteer coaches would do well to consider reward systems where both coaches and players are recognized for their contribution to the overall success of the programmes.

Other results are consistent with functionalist theory and the coproduction literature as well. In particular, it is logical that volunteers in operation and administrative positions may be doing so to develop a better understanding of how their local government operates. Once again, volunteer managers in these settings need to design experiences that allow volunteers to enjoy this coproduction function. For instance, volunteer managers in administration, when training volunteers, may want to consider providing rotating opportunities for people where they could work in different settings and at different administrative levels. In addition, a possible reward for these volunteers could involve seminars and tours centred on the inner workings of the department and the city government.

Based on prior research in the development of the VFI, the relationship between volunteer function, volunteer job setting and volunteer job satisfaction was also examined. The analysis was designed to detect whether volunteer job satisfaction was a result of the interaction between volunteer function and volunteer job setting. The results are important from the standpoint of understanding the relationship between these three variables. If volunteer managers can offer volunteer jobs tailored to meet the functionally relevant benefits that their volunteers are seeking, those volunteers are going to have higher levels of satisfaction with their experience. In turn, the volunteers may be more likely to continue to volunteer, which should lead to higher levels of productivity in the tasks they complete as volunteers. Because retention of volunteers is crucial to the stability of programmes, volunteer managers must continue to foster experiences that increase the level of volunteer job satisfaction. One possible way for this to occur is through regular discussion with volunteers to be used as an evaluation of those needs being met and those that are not. Because high levels of satisfaction are an important reward for volunteers, it is imperative that volunteer managers do everything possible to keep those levels up.

Additionally, the findings related to volunteer job satisfaction both substantiated previous findings within the functional analysis of volunteerism and contributed to a greater understanding of this phenomenon. These results are important in the continuing study of what motivates volunteers, why they volunteer and what volunteers are seeking from their volunteer experiences. A greater understanding of volunteer experience satisfaction should increase our knowledge concerning the relationship between level of satisfaction and productivity of volunteers, as has occurred in the study of levels of employee satisfaction (Spector, 1997). As with the previous studies that utilized the VFI, the results of this study confirmed that 'volunteers who received benefits congruent with personally important functions had greater satisfaction with their volunteer activity' (Clary *et al.*, 1998, p. 1528). Moreover, level of satisfaction can be related at least in part to the interaction between volunteer function, volunteer job setting and level of volunteer job satisfaction. This relationship appears to play itself out even more within specific volunteer functions of coproduction.

The final analysis within the study was carried out to test the relationship between volunteer function and specific sociodemographic characteristics of the sample. Based on functionalist literature (Shavitt, 1989; Snyder, 1993), the sociodemographic variables chosen were used to test the predictive ability of these objects with socially constructed meanings, within a functional framework of volunteerism. The relationships between volunteer function, sex, employment status and ethnicity yielded some interesting results and opportunity for further contemplation and research. The findings have an intuitive appeal to ask some further questions: Does sex bias play a role in whether males and females are more likely to volunteer for specific types of jobs? Do students volunteer more out of necessity related to academic requirements than as an act of benevolence? Why do so many retired individuals volunteer in public parks and recreation settings? What cultural norms shape the motivations of volunteers from different ethnic groups?

Future directions: still many questions

While the results of this particular study have important management and marketing implications for volunteer managers, giving managers a basis for decision-making processes, the previous questions can become the foundation for a line of research designed to examine the deeper complexities and intricacies of volunteerism and helping behaviour. In particular, the researchers had an interest in considering further investigation of the structure of the 'job satisfaction' concept among volunteer workers (Silverberg *et al.*, 1999b, 2001).

The Next Step: a Greater Understanding of Volunteer Job Satisfaction

Based on the interest generated by the analysis of volunteer job satisfaction within the previous study, attempts were made to examine an enhanced perspective of the complexities of volunteer job satisfaction. Previous research in the employee-management literature had shown that job satisfaction is directly related to employee productivity, customer satisfaction, absenteeism, turnover rates and, ultimately, an organization's bottom-line (Mobley, 1977; Parasuraman, 1982; Schneider and Bowen, 1985; Tompkins, 1992). While volunteer job satisfaction is a key concern for managers of agencies relying on volunteer workers, other than the previous study conducted with public parks and recreation volunteers, little research had focused on the measurement of job satisfaction of volunteers. One study was performed that accomplished certain preliminary research on the measurement of volunteer job satisfaction in parks and recreation settings (Silverberg et al., 2001). Evidence from that study suggested that it might be appropriate to treat volunteer satisfaction as a unidimensional construct. However, in contrast, literature on employed workers suggests that job satisfaction is multidimensional or a rather complex interaction between different conditions and agents (e.g. Herzberg et al., 1959; Smith et al., 1969; Locke, 1976; Spector, 1997).

Furthermore, existing approaches to the measurement of worker satisfaction have been concerned with a 'cause-indicators' perspective. With that perspective, researchers have assumed that job satisfaction must be present if conditions that are thought to 'cause' satisfaction are present in the work environment (e.g. recognition, opportunity for achievement, relations with co-workers, etc.). In contrast, an 'effects-indicator' approach might focus on workers' actual experiences and commitments as part of the workforce. With that approach, investigators might be able to incorporate such factors as workplace happiness and organizational commitment into a measure of job satisfaction. Relationships between such a measure and corresponding 'cause-indicators' as well as job outcomes (e.g. performance, organizational citizenship behaviour and absenteeism) could be examined. Assuming that the previous reasoning could help explain more about the complexities of employee job satisfaction, parks and recreation researchers were determined to produce a causal model of volunteer job satisfaction, and to test the extent to which that model was tenable for volunteers.

Development and Evaluation of an 'Effects-indicator' Model of Volunteer Job Satisfaction

The model that was developed incorporated a set of 'cause-indicators', which have traditionally been used to study employee job satisfaction (e.g. Locke, 1976; Spector, 1997), indicators derived from functionalist theory (Clary et al., 1998), a set of 'effects-indicators' derived from studies of happiness (Waterman, 1993) and organizational commitment (Mowday et al., 1979), and two job-related behavioural outcomes (organizational citizenship behaviours and retention/turnover) (e.g. O'Reilly and Chatman, 1986; Organ and

Konovsky, 1989; Williams and Anderson, 1991; Schaubroeck *et al.*, 1994; Van Dyne *et al.*, 1994; Podsakoff *et al.*, 1997).

'Cause-indicator': job satisfaction measurement: state of the art?

While the proposed model still incorporated a 'cause-indicator' component (Spector, 1997), it was held that it would not be the basis of this new conceptual model of volunteer job satisfaction. Silverberg *et al.* (2001) decided to extend Spector's (1997) model to the challenge of measuring satisfaction of volunteer workers in park and recreation settings. Another approach considered emphasized that an interaction has its roots in functionalist theory (Clary and Snyder, 1991; Snyder, 1993; Cantor, 1994; Clary *et al.*, 1998). As mentioned in the previous study related to the propositions of functionalist theory as it relates to volunteerism, it had been suggested that volunteer job satisfaction depended on the extent to which the conditions of the volunteer work satisfied particular psychological functions that those volunteers bring to their volunteer job settings.

Common to each of these approaches is a 'cause-indicator' perspective. Each model assumes that if particular conditions and agents are present, then it is reasonable to assume that workers will be satisfied. No previous research had conceptualized job satisfaction using an 'effects-indicator' approach that focused on workers' (or volunteers') actual experiences and commitments to the work environment. The causal model that was proposed adopted this unique 'effects-indicator' perspective.

Other components of the 'effects-indicator' model of volunteer job satisfaction

'Effects-indicator': eudaimonic happiness
Central to the 'effects-indicator' approach was the concept of happiness. Happiness points to the experiential, phenomenological character of volunteers' work. This approach was based on Waterman's (1993) discussion of Aristotelian 'eudaimonism'. In contrast to hedonic perspectives on happiness (Tatarkiewicz, 1976; Kraut, 1979), this approach focused on personal expressiveness of the 'true self'. As such, the approach focused on the 'potentialities of each person, the realization of which represents the greatest fulfillment in living, of which each is capable' (Waterman, 1993, p. 678). Application of this orientation to the volunteer job satisfaction measurement challenge implied that satisfied workers expressed and experienced elements of their true selves and their potentialities in their volunteer job setting. In addition, Aristotelian philosophy continues to have an impact on the conceptual understanding of leisure (e.g. Ruddell, 2001; Sylvester, 2001). Because volunteerism may be thought of as a form of 'serious leisure' (Stebbins,

1992), it seemed reasonable to define the experiential quality of volunteer work experiences (and volunteer job satisfaction) in a manner that was consistent with Aristotelian philosophy.

'Effects-indicator': organizational commitment

Organizational commitment refers to long-term relationships between an individual and organization, and the individual's perceptions of future actions by the organization (Brockner and Weisenfeld, 1996). Organizational commitment involves a belief in the organization's goals and values, willingness to exert effort on behalf of the organization, and a desire to remain affiliated with the organization due to an affective response to beliefs about the organization (Porter et al., 1974; Mowday et al., 1979). Commitment has been defined as the strength of individuals' identification with, and involvement in, an organization (Porter et al., 1974).

Higher levels of commitment are associated with several desirable outcomes. Included among these outcomes are greater satisfaction with authorities, increased compliance, greater trust between parties, more pro-social and cooperative exchanges, reduced turnover, greater investments and enhanced willingness to exert behaviours to further the organization's goals beyond those required by the relationship (Porter et al., 1974; Becker, 1992; Lawler and Yoon, 1996; Brockner et al., 1999). In contrast, stakeholders with lower levels of commitment are less trustful of authorities, less supportive of the organization's goals, and may repudiate affiliation, separate and work to discredit or destroy the organization (Scott and Lane, 2000). Further, organizational commitment has been shown to have a significant relationship with organizational citizenship behaviours (Schappe, 1998).

Behavioural outcome: organizational citizenship behaviours

Organizational citizenship behaviour (OCB) has had the most limited exposure in the park and recreation literature. OCB refers to characteristics such as helping behaviours, civic virtue, and providing input and actions on behalf of or to improve the organization and work group performance (e.g. Organ, 1988; Niehoff and Moorman, 1993; Van Dyne et al., 1994; Organ and Lingl, 1995; Podsakoff et al., 1997). In contrast to productivity, which concentrates on specific quantifiable outcomes, OCB addresses the extent to which workers are effective citizens in the workplace. Some highly productive workers may also be very poor organizational citizens, and thereby fail to contribute to teamwork, esprit de corps, loyalty to the organization and support for the organizational mission.

OCBs and positive cooperative relationships are a function of reciprocation (Smith et al., 1983). OCBs extend to contributions that are not part of formal role obligations and expand resources available to the organization through pro-social behaviours that may be managed in response to participants' opinions of organizational fairness through modifications of policies or communications of policies (Organ and Konovsky, 1989). Positive relationships with an organization and organizational effectiveness have been associated with OCBs (Podsakoff *et al.*, 1997).

The proposed causal model extended the concept of OCBs and related behavioural outcomes beyond the formal work environment of paid employees to recreation settings and the efforts of volunteers. Organ (1988) initiated a line of research, based on social exchange theory, that suggested that when employees are satisfied they reciprocate through attachment to the organization and organizational citizenship behaviours that benefit the organization. Organ and Lingl (1995) also pointed out that at least 15 independent studies had found reliable relationships between job satisfaction and organizational citizenship behaviours.

Behavioural outcome: retention/turnover
The majority of theories of employee turnover have viewed this phenomenon as a result of employee dissatisfaction (e.g. Mobley *et al.*, 1979; Bluedorn, 1982). Most studies had shown a causal relationship between job satisfaction and turnover (e.g. Hulin *et al.*, 1985; Crampton and Wagner, 1994). Those studies had shown that negative employee job satisfaction led to higher levels of employee turnover (Spector, 1997). Spector (1997) also noted that there was a high degree of certainty regarding this causal relationship among researchers who were studying employee job satisfaction. This was based on the longitudinally designed nature of most of the past studies of employee job satisfaction. In other words, researchers had measured job satisfaction among samples of employees at one point in time and then, at a later point in time, they had determined which employees had resigned. The researchers then compared the levels of job satisfaction of those employees who had resigned with those employees who had not resigned. It was clear that the causality ran from job satisfaction to turnover because 'the behaviour did not occur until months or in some cases years after the job satisfaction assessment' (Spector, 1997, p. 62). Although it seemed reasonable to assume that similar results would be found among volunteer workers, it is important to note that no similar research on retention of volunteers had been conducted.

Description of the Original Proposed Model

The model that was originally proposed included three sets of concepts. The first set included six traditional 'cause-indicators' from existing research on volunteer satisfaction in park and recreation settings (Spector, 1997; Silverberg *et al.*, 2001). Included were: (i) nature of the work; (ii) communication; (iii) operating conditions; (iv) supervision; (v) contingent rewards; and (vi) relationships with co-workers. In addition, the set of cause-indicators included a concept derived from functionalist theory that represented the extent to which volunteer experiences were consistent with the volunteer's desired psychological functions (Clary *et al.*, 1998).

Concepts in this 'cause-indicators' set were assumed to impact volunteer worker happiness and organizational commitment, which were the second set of concepts in the model. Volunteer worker happiness reflected the 'personal expressiveness' and 'potentiality' of the volunteer worker. A happy volunteer would indicate that she or he: (i) felt intensely involved in her or his work, (ii) felt very alive in the work place, and (iii) maintained a strong sense of enjoyment while in the volunteer workplace (Waterman, 1993). Individuals with high degrees of organizational commitment would 'talk up the organization', contribute to work that transcended their formal work role requirements (e.g. job descriptions), and feel a sense of co-ownership of the organization's goals and initiatives (Mowday *et al.*, 1979). The third set of concepts were behavioural outcomes: organizational citizenship behaviours and retention/turnover. As a whole, those two variables reflected concern for the immediate as well as the long-term health of the organization.

The original proposed causal model is presented in Fig. 5.1. As can be seen from a review of the figure, causal linkages are specified among those sets of concepts. The 'cause-indicators' were assumed to affect the 'effects-indicators'. The model also specified that all the 'cause-indicators' would affect volunteer happiness, and volunteer happiness, in turn, would affect

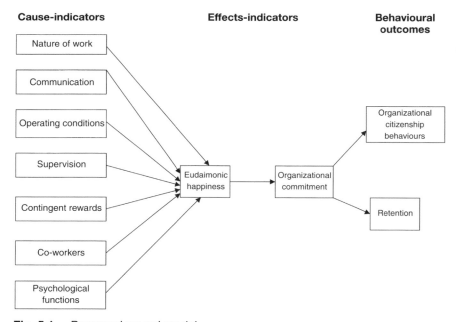

Fig. 5.1. Proposed causal model.

organizational commitment. Organizational commitment, in turn, was assumed to affect the two concepts in the behavioural outcomes set, organizational citizenship behaviours and retention/turnover. There were no feedback loops implied by the model.

Evaluation of the Proposed Model

The sample consisted of agency-maintained lists of volunteers from two park and recreation organizations. One of these agencies was a state park system and the other was a municipal park and recreation department. Eleven components were included in the model. Seven of these were considered to be measures of 'cause-indicators' of volunteer satisfaction. Of these seven, six were subscales from Spector's (1997) job satisfaction scale, as adapted to the context of volunteers by Silverberg *et al.* (2001). In addition, a measure of the extent to which volunteering was serving its intended function was included as a cause-indicator.

The second set of measures included two effects-indicators: eudaimonic happiness and organizational commitment. Finally, measures of organizational citizenship behaviour and retention/turnover were included, representing behavioural outcomes of job satisfaction. A brief description of the scales used to measure these variables follows.

'Cause-indicator': attainment of psychological functions
A single item measured the perceived psychological benefits provided by volunteering. Psychological functions were defined as 'benefits (i.e. needs, motivations, purposes, etc.) that a person gets from their volunteer experience'. Examples of functions were provided, such as 'socializing', 'benefiting people I know' and 'the department needs me'. Respondents were then asked: 'Based on the above definitions, reflect on the function(s) that you want to get from your volunteer experience'.

'Effect-indicator': eudaimonic happiness
The measure of eudaimonic happiness was based on Waterman's (1990, 1993) 12-item scale. Sample items included 'when I engage in this activity I feel more intensely involved than I do in most other activities' and 'I feel a special fit or meshing when engaging in this activity'.

'Effect-indicator': organizational commitment
Organizational commitment was measured with four items adapted from Mowday *et al.* (1979). Items included were as follows: 'my values and the values of [the agency's] managers at my worksite(s) are very similar', 'I am proud to tell people that I am part of [this agency]', 'I care very much about the future of [the agency] services that are provided at my worksite(s)' and 'for me, this is the best of all possible organizations to volunteer for'.

Behavioural outcome: organizational citizenship behaviours
Organizational citizenship behaviours were measured with 20 items derived
from Organ and Konovsky (1989) and Williams and Anderson (1991). These
items were adapted for use in the context of volunteer workers. Examples of
items were 'of all the volunteers I know, I am among the very best at helping
others who have heavy work loads' and 'of all the volunteers I know, I am
among the very best at going out of my way to help new workers'.

Behavioural outcome: retention/turnover
Retention/turnover was measured with two items. These included, 'I intend
to increase the amount of time that I volunteer for my current job with [the
agency]' and 'I plan to continue to volunteer for my current job with [the
agency]'.

Results of the study

Unfortunately, through extensive, exploratory analysis, the original proposed model did not work as well as expected. So, the original model was
revised based on the evidence of poor fit. Revisions included the deletion of
the three non-significant components (communication, operating conditions, contingent rewards) and the addition of paths representing direct
effects of three cause-indicators on commitment. This revised model (Fig.
5.2) showed substantially improved results. The four significant predictors of
eudaimonic happiness in the model were nature of work, quality of supervision, relationships with co-workers and psychological function. Eudaimonic
happiness and three of the cause-indicators (nature of work, quality of supervision and psychological function) were most significant in predicting organizational commitment. Finally, organizational commitment did a moderate
job of predicting the two behavioural outcomes, organizational citizenship
behaviour and retention/turnover.

Implications of the results of this study

As mentioned previously, most existing approaches to the measurement of
employee and volunteer satisfaction have centred on a 'cause-indicators'
perspective. Using that perspective, researchers had assumed that satisfaction was present only if conditions that were thought to 'cause' satisfaction
were present in the work environment. This study took an 'effects-indicator' approach to develop a focus on the 'experiential' nature of the work
performed by volunteers, as well as the commitment those volunteers
felt as part of the workforce of the particular agency. After an exploratory
analysis and a modification of the originally proposed model, the results
demonstrated a strong relationship between the 'cause-indicators', the

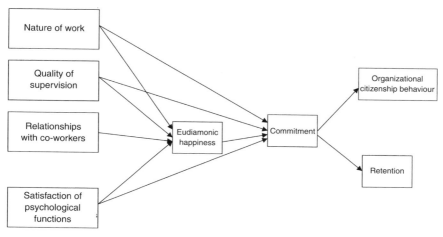

Fig. 5.2. Revised causal model.

corresponding 'effects-indicators' and specific job-related behavioural outcomes.

Another important step that was taken using this new approach to the examination of volunteer satisfaction was the integration of the concepts of organizational commitment and organizational citizenship behaviours into the literature on volunteer job satisfaction (Silverberg *et al.*, 2001). While these concepts had been studied extensively in organizational psychology literature in relation to employee job satisfaction, this was the first time they had been applied to the phenomenon of volunteer satisfaction. Based on the results of this study it was apparent that these concepts would play a significant role in helping both researchers and practitioners develop a greater understanding of the complexity of volunteerism and volunteer worker satisfaction.

Future directions: the questions continue

The conceptual model can provide a foundation for a new research programme on volunteer satisfaction. Further investigations might address measurement concerns. No evidence exists of a previous attempt to measure volunteer happiness or to equate that concept with satisfaction in the workplace. Continued investigation of the 'cause-indicators' drawn from previous research may also be warranted. Silverberg *et al.* (2001) were able to produce a reliable unitary measure of volunteer satisfaction, but did not find support for reliability of the separate, component causes. Additional cause-indicators might also be explored.

Potential additions to the model may include the concepts of procedural justice, trust and perceived organizational support. Conceptual and empirical models suggest relationships between procedural justice, trust and perceived organizational support (Alexander and Ruderman, 1987), perceived satisfaction (Tyler and Caine, 1981), and organizational commitment (Folger and Konovsky, 1989). Similarly, leader fairness, subordinate participation and leader support are correlated with satisfaction and organizational citizenship behaviours (e.g. discretionary efforts taken on behalf of the organization) (Moorman, 1991). Evidence indicates that input for decision making promotes perceptions of organizational support, which leads to reciprocation through OCBs (VanYperen et al., 1999).

It has also been suggested that research should address the relationship between job satisfaction and perceived organizational support (Eisenberger et al., 1986). Perceived organizational support is the degree of generalized belief by an employee or stakeholder that the organization values the individual's contributions and cares about and promotes their well-being (Eisenberger et al., 1986). Perceived organizational support is influenced by the frequency and sincerity of praise and approval, enrichment, and permitted influence over organizational policies, including material aspects such as pay.

References

Alexander, S. and Ruderman, M. (1987) The role of procedural and distributive justice in organizational behavior. Social Justice Research 1, 177–198.

Alter, J. (1997) Powell's new war. Newsweek, 28 April, 28–34.

Backman, K.F., Wicks, B. and Silverberg, K.E. (1997) Coproduction of recreation services. Journal of Park and Recreation Administration 15(3), 58–75.

Becker, T.E. (1992) Foci and bases of commitment: are they distinctions worth making? Academy of Management Journal 35, 232–244.

Bluedorn, A.C. (1982) A unified model of turnover from organizations. Human Relations 35, 135–153.

Brockner, J. and Wiesenfeld, B.M. (1996) An integrative framework for explaining reactions to decisions: interactive effects of outcomes and procedures. Psychological Bulletin 120, 189–208.

Brockner, J., Siegel, P.A., Daly, J.P., Tyler, T. and Martin, C. (1999) When trust matters: the moderating effect of outcome favorability. Administrative Science Quarterly 42, 558–583.

Brudney, J.L. (1990) Fostering Volunteer Programs in the Public Sector. Jossey-Bass, San Francisco.

Brudney, J.L. and England, R.E. (1983) Toward a definition of the coproduction concept. Public Administration Review 43, 59–65.

Cantor, N. (1994) Life task problem solving: situational affordances and personal needs. Personality and Social Psychology Bulletin 20, 235–243.

Cigler, B.A. (1987) Setting Smalltown Research Priorities the Service Delivery Dimension. Economic Research Service Report. Department of Agriculture, Washington, DC.

Clary, E.G. and Snyder, M. (1991) A functional analysis of altruism and prosocial behavior: the case of volunteerism. In: Clark, M. (ed.) *Review of Personality and Social Psychology*, Vol 12. Sage, Newbury Park, California.

Clary, E.G., Snyder, M., Ridge, R.D., Copeland, J., Stukas, A.A., Haugen, J. and Miene, P. (1998) Understanding and assessing the motivations of volunteers: a functional approach. *Journal of Personality and Social Psychology* 74, 1516–1530.

Cnaan, R.A. and Goldberg-Glen, R.S. (1991) Measuring motivation to volunteer in human services. *Journal of Applied Behavioral Science* 27, 269–284.

Crampton, S.M. and Wagner, J.A., III (1994) Percept–percept inflation in microorganizational research: an investigation of prevalence and effect. *Journal of Applied Psychology* 79, 67–76.

Crompton, J.L. (1999) *Financing and Acquiring Park and Recreation Resources*. Human Kinetics, Champaign, Illinois.

Crosby, P. (1979) *Quality is Free*. New American Library, New York.

Deming, W.E. (1986) *Out of Crisis*. MIT Center for Advanced Engineering Study, Cambridge, Massachusetts.

Eisenberger, R., Huntington, R., Huthcison, S. and Sowa, D. (1986) Perceived organizational support. *Journal of Applied Psychology* 71, 500–507.

Ferris, J.M. (1988) The use of volunteers in public service production: some demand and supply considerations. *Social Science Quarterly* 69(1), 3–23.

Folger, R. and Konovsky, M.A. (1989) Effects of procedural and distributive justice on reactions to pay raise decisions. *Academy of Management Journal* 32, 115–130.

Herzberg, F. (1968) One more time: how do you motivate employees? *Harvard Business Review* 46, 53–62.

Herzberg, F. (1971) *Work and the Nature of Man*. World Publishing, Cleveland, Ohio.

Herzberg, F., Mausner, B. and Snyderman, B. (1959) *Motivation to Work*. John Wiley & Sons, New York.

Holderman, K. (1996) Public–private partnership is a success story of the government reinvention movement. *Business America*, October, 5–7.

Hulin, C.L., Rozonowski, M. and Hachiya, D. (1985) Alternative opportunities and withdrawal decisions: empirical and theoretical discrepancies and an integration. *Psychological Bulletin* 97, 233–250.

Juran, J. (1988) *Juran on Planning for Quality*. The Free Press, New York.

Kiser, L.L. (1984) Toward an institutional theory of citizen coproduction. *Urban Affairs Quarterly* 19, 485–510.

Kraut, R. (1979) Two conceptions of happiness. *Philosophical Review* 87, 167–196.

Lawler, E.J. and Yoon, J. (1996) Commitment in exchange relations: test of a theory of relational cohesion. *American Sociological Review* 61, 89–108.

Levine, C.H. (1984) Citizenship and service delivery: the promise of coproduction. *Public Administration Review* 44 (special issue), 178–189.

Lewin, K. (1946) Action research and minority problems. *Journal of Social Issues* 2, 34–46.

Locke, E.A. (1976) The nature and causes of job satisfaction. In: Dunnette, M.D. (ed.) *Handbook of Industrial and Organizational Psychology*. Rand-McNally, Chicago, pp. 1297–1349.

McClelland, D.C. (1953) *The Achievement Motive*. Appleton-Century-Crofts, New York.

Mobley, W.H. (1977) Intermediate linkages in the relationship between job satisfaction and employee turnover. *Journal of Applied Psychology* 62, 237–240.

Mobley, W.H., Griffeth, R.W., Hand, H.H. and Meglino, B.M. (1979) Review and conceptual analysis of the employee turnover process. *Psychological Bulletin* 86, 493–522.

Moorman, R.H. (1991) Relationship between organizational justice and citizenship behaviors: do fairness perceptions influence employee citizenship? *Journal of Applied Psychology* 76, 845–855.

Mowday, R.T., Steers, R. and Porter, L. (1979) The measurement of organizational commitment. *Journal of Vocational Behavior* 14, 224–247.

Nanetti, R.Y. (1980) From the top down: government promoted citizen participation. *Journal of Voluntary Action Research* 9(1), 149–162.

Niehoff, B.P. and Moorman, R.H. (1993) Justice as a mediator of the relationship between methods of monitoring and organizational citizenship behavior. *Academy of Management Journal* 36, 527–556.

O'Reilly, C. and Chatman, J. (1986) Organizational commitment and psychological attachment: the effects of compliance, identification, and internalization on prosocial behavior. *Journal of Applied Psychology* 71, 492–499.

Organ, D.W. (1988) *Organizational Citizenship Behavior.* Lexington Books, Lexington, Massachusetts.

Organ, D.W. and Konovsky, M. (1989) Cognitive versus affective determinants of organizational citizenship behavior. *Journal of Applied Psychology* 74, 157–164.

Organ, D.W. and Lingl, A. (1995) Personality, satisfaction, and organizational citizenship behavior. *The Journal of Social Psychology* 135, 339–350.

Osborne, D. and Gaebler, T. (1993) *Reinventing Government*. Plume, New York.

Parasuraman, S. (1982) Predicting turnover intentions and turnover behavior: a multivariate analysis. *Journal of Vocational Behavior* 21, 111–121.

Percy, S.L. (1987) Citizen involvement in coproducing safety and security in the community. *Public Productivity Review* 42, 83–93.

Podsakoff, P.M., Ahearne, M. and MacKenzie, S.B. (1997) Organizational citizenship behavior and the quantity and quality of work group performance. *Journal of Applied Psychology* 82, 262–270.

Porter, L.W., Steers, R.M., Mowday, R.T. and Boulian, P.V. (1974) Organizational commitment, job satisfaction, and turnover among psychiatric technicians. *Journal of Applied Psychology* 59, 603–609.

Rosentraub, M.S. and Sharp, E.B. (1981) Consumers as producers of social services: coproduction and the level of social services. *Southern Review of Public Administration*, 4, 509–539.

Ruddell, E. (2001) The relationship between Schole and Eudaimonia: an Alderian interpretation of Schole in the Nicomachean Ethics. Paper presented at 2001 Leisure Research Symposium, Denver, Colorado, October.

Schappe, S.P. (1998) The influence of job satisfaction, organizational commitment, and fairness perceptions on organizational citizenship behavior. *The Journal of Psychology* 132, 277–291.

Schaubroeck, J., May, D.R. and Brown, F.W. (1994) Procedural justice explanations and employee reactions to economic hardship: a field experiment. *Journal of Applied Psychology* 79, 455–460.

Schneider, B. and Bowen, D. (1985) Employee and customer perceptions of service in banks: replication and extension. *Journal of Applied Psychology* 70, 423–433.

Scott, S.G. and Lane, V.R. (2000) A stakeholder approach to organizational identity. *The Academy of Management Review* 25(1), 43–62.

Sharp, E.B. (1980) Toward a new understanding of urban services and citizen participation: the coproduction concept. *Midwest Review of Public Administration* 14(2), 105–118.

Shavitt, S. (1989) Operationalizing functional theories of attitude. In: Pratkanis, A.R., Breckler, S.J. and Greenwald, A.G. (eds) *Attitude Structure and Function*. Lawrence Erlbaum, Hillsdale, New Jersey.

Silverberg, K.E. (1999) An identification and explication of a typology of public parks and recreation volunteers. Doctoral dissertation, Clemson University, Clemson, South Carolina.

Silverberg, K.E., Ellis, G.D., Backman, S.J. and Backman, K.F. (1999a) An identification and explication of a typology of public parks and recreation volunteers. *World Leisure & Recreation* 41(2), 30–34.

Silverberg, K.E., Ellis, G.D. and Marshall, E. (1999b) Development and evaluation of a volunteer job satisfaction scale. Abstracts from the Symposium on Leisure Research, Nashville, Tennessee.

Silverberg, K.E., Ellis, G.D. and Marshall, E. (2001) Development and evaluation of a volunteer job satisfaction scale. *Journal of Park and Recreation Administration* 19(1), 79–92.

Silverstein, M. (1996) The public entrepreneurship revolution. *Business and Society Review* 15–18.

Smith, C.A., Organ, D.W. and Near, J.P. (1983) Organizational citizenship behavior: its nature and antecedents. *Journal of Applied Psychology* 68, 653–663.

Smith, P.C., Kendall, L.M. and Hulin, C.L. (1969) *The Measure of Satisfaction in Work and Retirement*. Rand-McNally, Chicago.

Snyder, M. (1993) Basic research and practical problems: the promise of a 'functional' personality and social psychology. *Personality and Social Psychology Bulletin* 19, 251–264.

Snyder, M. and Ickes, W. (1985) Personality and social behavior. In: Lindzey, G. and Aronson, E. (eds) *The Handbook for Social Psychology*, Vol. 2, 3rd edn. McGraw Hill, New York, pp. 883–948.

Spector, P.E. (1997) *Job Satisfaction*. Sage, Thousand Oaks, California.

Stebbins, R.A. (1992) *Amateurs, Professionals, and Serious Leisure*. McGill-Queen's University Press, Montreal.

Sundeen, R.A. (1985) Coproduction and communities. *Administration and Society* 16, 387–402.

Sylvester, C. (2001). Slavery and leisure in Aristotle's ethical theory. Paper presented at 2001 Leisure Research Symposium, Denver, Colorado, October.

Tatarkiewicz, W. (1976) *Analysis of Happiness*. Martinus Nijhoff, The Hague.

Tompkins, N.C. (1992) Employee satisfaction leads to customer service. *HR Magazine* 37, 93–95.

Tyler, T.R. and Caine, A. (1981) The influence of outcomes and procedures on satisfaction with formal leaders. *Journal of Personality and Social Psychology* 41, 642–655.

US Census (1990) *1990 Census Lookup*. venus.census.gov/cdrom/lookup.

Van Dyne, L., Graham, J.W. and Dienesch, R.M. (1994) Organizational citizenship behavior: construct redefinition, measurement, and validation. *Academy of Management Journal* 37, 765–802.

VanYperen, N.W., van den Berg, A.E. and Willering, M.C. (1999) Towards a better understanding of the link between participation in decision-making and organizational citizenship behavior: a multilevel analysis. *Journal of Occupational and Organizational Psychology* 72, 377–392.

Walter, V. (1987) Volunteers and bureaucrats: clarifying roles and creating meaning. *Journal of Voluntary Action Research* 16(3), 22–32.

Walton, M. (1990) *Deming Management at Work*. G.P. Putnam's Sons, New York.

Warren, R., Rosentraub, M.S. and Harlow, K.S. (1984) Coproduction, equity and the distribution of safety. *Urban Affairs Quarterly* 19, 447–464.

Waterman, A.S. (1990) Relevance of Aristotle's conception of eudaimonia for the psychological study of happiness. *Theoretical and Philosophical Psychology* 10, 39–44.

Waterman, A.S. (1993) Two conceptions of happiness: contrasts of personal expressiveness (eudaimonia) and hedonic enjoyment. *Journal of Personality and Social Psychology* 64, 678–691.

Whitaker, G.P. (1980) Coproduction: citizen participation in service delivery. *Public Administration Review* 40, 240–246.

Williams, L.J. and Anderson, S.E. (1991) Job satisfaction and organizational commitment as predictors of organizational citizenship behaviors. *Journal of Management* 17, 601–617.

A Logistic Regression Model of the Decision of Volunteers to Enter a Sports Coach Education Programme

6

Brian E. Wilson

Background

Since at least the 19th century, the voluntary sector of the UK economy has been a significant provider of social and community services. The voluntary sector provides the majority of the population with much of its sport and leisure activities. This is despite the growth of public- and private-sector involvement during the latter half of the 20th century (Holt, 1989; Cox, 1994; Brailsford, 1997; Polley, 1998).

In 1996 there were 150,000 sports clubs in the UK, with 6.5 million members, including 200,000 voluntary coaches. This compares to 75,600 people employed by local authorities and 120,000 employed in the commercial sector. In 2000, it was estimated that the financial contribution of the voluntary sector to the UK economy was £12.8 billion a year, or nearly 2% of the Gross National Product (Longley, 2000).

During the 1960s in the UK, there was a decline in the time devoted to sport in schools. This resulted in sharp increases in junior memberships of the local voluntary sports clubs. These created a need for expansion of voluntary coaching. The national governing bodies of sport (NGBs) responded by establishing coach education courses.

Government strategies have resulted in increasing sums of public money being put into volunteers in sport, including coaching. Yet there has been very little research conducted into how and why individuals choose to become voluntary coaches. There is a lack of conceptual models, hampering the testing of theories. There is a need for better understanding by policy makers of the processes of becoming a coach, especially as some research indicates that volunteering may be declining (Deckers and Gratton, 1995; Smith, 1998).

The research set out to develop a conceptual model suitable for decisions on volunteering in sport and to test such a model with quantitative and qualitative data. It was anticipated that the research would confirm the multivariable nature of the phenomenon, the need for further research into the nature of the underlying variables and the need for better metrics for some variables.

Conceptual Model

Much of the research on the reasons why people became involved in an organization has been based upon the concept of expectancy theory. The concept implies that an individual engages in an activity in order to obtain a reward. Research on volunteer involvement indicates that the act of volunteering is highly multivariate. The motivations can change during entry to and throughout a career in an organization (Kessler, 1975). A development of expectancy theory, social exchange theory, makes the concept more relevant to sports clubs as it incorporates a dynamic element into the choice process. In social exchange theory, incentives are based upon exchange of costs and rewards within a continual process of evaluation of expected and actual costs and benefits.

These theories can be put into the specific context of coaching voluntary sport by considering an adult club member or a parent of a junior (child) club member.

- The person has an idea about a sport with expectations of health and social gain.
- A decision is taken for the person to become associated with a club.
- Perceptions of benefits and costs are formed and continuously reviewed.
- Means of improving these benefits are considered.
- Coaching is perceived as a means of added benefit.
- A decision is taken by the individual to become a coach or to not do so.
- The perceived benefits and costs are continuously reviewed.

The decision process is dynamic, being continuously affected by the environment. As changes are recognized, some or all of the above steps are re-iterated.

Such a conceptual model lacks a specific mechanism for determining whether or not a decision is taken or deferred. Brandenberg et al. (1982) developed the model to cover how people adopt recreational activities. They set out to determine how the preoccupations and interests of an individual become linked to a specific activity. Their definitions of 'preoccupations', 'interests' and 'activities' followed those in the earlier concept of family life cycles (Rapoport and Rapoport, 1975). Brandenberg and his co-workers hypothesized that the decision to take up an activity was triggered by the occurrence of what they termed a 'key event'. 'Key events' included many of the events identified by Rapoport and Rapoport in their study of family life cycles, namely change of job, move of residence, marriage, birth, retirement, as well as being personally asked to participate.

Mintern (1994) refined the generalized Brandenberg model to a single decision. In this case, deciding to join and use a new leisure centre, the opening being the 'key event'. His theory was that there was a 'threshold' value for the net sum of the expected costs and rewards, above which an individual decided to join and below which the individual decided not to join.

This research developed these concepts to a Sports Decision model. It is illustrated in Fig. 6.1 with respect to the decisions to become associated with a club and to become a coach. 'Associate' encompasses either joining or being the parent of a child who joins. The example is deliberately simplistic in order to illustrate a complex and multivariate process. It shows the net

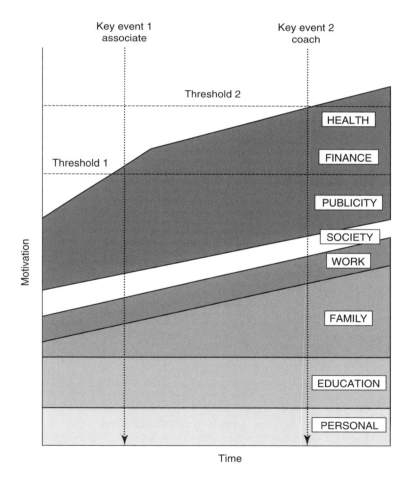

Fig. 6.1. Sports Decision model.

sum of perceived costs and rewards for a number of groups of variables, each set changing with time. The sums are measured in terms of motivation. The values are personal and may be perceptual or actual, feelings or monetary costs.

Mathematical Model

A specific decision, to register to train as an athletics coach, was chosen. The Sports Decision model was transformed into a mathematical model which could be tested against field data related to a specific point in time. For an individual at a point in time, the result of the decision is binary with two mutually exclusive categories 'yes', enter, or 'no', not enter. This is the response variable of the mathematical model.

The explanatory variables of the mathematical model are the motivational factors, measured in terms of the net benefit from each factor, as perceived by the individual. Each variable will have a different weighting. The conceptual model suggests that these weighted benefits are additive in their overall effect. The mathematical model can be represented as a classic regression:

$$Y_i = X_0 + \beta_1 X_{i1} + \beta_2 X_{i2} + \beta_3 X_{i3} + \beta_4 X_{i4} + \ldots \beta_j X_{ii}$$

where Y_i represents the decision of individual 'i', the binary result of the decision, the response variable; X_0 is a constant; $\beta_1, \beta_2, \beta_3, \ldots \beta_j$ are the weighting factors for each of the 'j' explanatory variables; and $X_{i1}, X_{i2}, X_{i3}, \ldots X_{ij}$ are the perceived values of each of the 'i' individuals, the explanatory variables.

A mechanism is also needed to represent the 'threshold' in the conceptual model. When the threshold is exceeded, the decision of the individual will change from 'no' to 'yes'. This ensures that the value of the response variable is always binary.

The model can be tested by collecting values of potential explanatory variables for a number of individuals and the actual state of the response variable for each variable. At a given point in time, the latter state will always be one of the two binary states, 'yes' (entered) or 'no'. These can be numerically represented as '1' or '0', respectively.

This model cannot be solved using the classic least squares linear regression method because it will violate some of the conditions required by least squares:

- The response variable is binary and not continuous.
- Explanatory variables may be binary (e.g. gender), categorical (e.g. number of children) or continuous (e.g. travel distance).
- Variables may not be normally distributed (e.g. education).
- A 'threshold' mechanism is required.

A solution can be found using the statistical technique of logistic regression (Hosmer and Lemeshow, 1989; Collett, 1991; Rice, 1994; Hutcheson and Sofroniou, 1999; SPSS Inc., 1999). It has been used in studies of volunteering (Schanning, 1999) and of education (Willis, 1998). Logistic regression treats the problem in probability terms. The weighted explanatory variables give a probability value which lies between zero and one. This continuous value for the response variable is then set at '0' or '1' by a threshold value. Generally, this threshold is set at 0.5.

Logistic regression has another advantage over linear regression. The S statistic, degree of dispersion, can be calculated. A value greater than 1 may indicate that one or more significant explanatory variables are missing. There is no comparable measurement with linear regression. Indication of missing explanatory variables can be a catalyst to new research to find them. High or low dispersion also indicates other potential peculiarities of the data, including inadequate scales of measurement (Collett, 1991; Hutcheson and Sofroniou, 1999).

Logistic regression does have some disadvantages. One is that the results are difficult to interpret. The coefficients relate to odds, not to absolutes as in linear regression, and are relative. Odds are related to, but not the same as, probabilities or likelihoods. A logistic regression coefficient of 2.0 indicates 2:1 odds that the response variable will change to '1' if that explanatory variable increases by one unit, everything else being equal.

This leads to a further problem. Explanatory variables are often measured on different scales. For example, the explanatory variable 'number of children in the household' is likely to range from 0 to 6 or more. The variable 'travel distance' can take an infinite number of values from 0. The value of a one-unit change in a variable will depend upon the unit of measurement, as well as the magnitude of the effect. This means that model coefficients cannot be used directly to compare the relative impacts of explanatory variables. To overcome this, the model coefficients can be transformed into standardized coefficients (Menard, 1995). The standardized coefficients indicate the relative influence of each explanatory variable in relation to the others.

Unlike linear regression, logistic regression may not have a unique solution. This is because there is no one statistic corresponding to the linear regression coefficient, R^2. The mechanism of computing a solution is iterative and analogous to mountain climbing without a map and in cloudy conditions. Having reached a peak, it is not possible to be certain that a higher peak does not exist. The solution arrived at is also dependent upon the starting point, upon whether explanatory variables are added or removed during model building and upon the criteria used to add or remove variables during building.

As a result, solutions to logistic regression models are found by striking a balance from a number of objective measures of fit. In the case of this research, four measures considered were:

1. The reduction in a statistic referred to in the literature as $-2LL$ (log-likelihood) between a model using no explanatory variables (the Initial Model) and a model with selected explanatory variables (the Final Model). The significance of this reduction can be measured by the chi-squared test, the degrees of freedom being calculated from the number of variables included.
2. The Nagelkerke coefficient, referred to as Nagelkerke R^2. It varies between 0.0, no association, and 1.0, perfect association, but has no sign. It gives some indication of the proportion of the overall variability which is accounted for by the independent variables in the model.
3. The proportional change in error, ϕ_p. This is a measure of the predictive ability of a logistic regression model. It compares the proportion of observed cases where the predictions from the model agree and disagree with the observed value (coach or not coach). It is calculated from the four values in the 2×2 frequency table of these comparisons. It can take a value between 0.0, no predictive ability, and 1.0, perfect predictive ability. It has a weakness in that it can have high values even with a model which has a manifestly poor fit.
4. The C statistic is a measure of the extent to which the model correctly assigns a high probability to those cases where the individual is a coach and assigns a low probability to those individuals who are not coaches. It takes into account the extent to which correct assignments might have occurred by chance. It can take a value between 0.5, could have occurred by chance, and 1.0, all assignments correct. This measure emphasizes predictive ability. It has the advantage of taking into account the threshold.

Explanatory Variables

Published literature suggests a large number of potential variables (Schindler-Rainmann and Lippett, 1971; Johnson, 1973; Anderson and Moore, 1978; Dowling *et al.*, 1997). The sample size required to test all these potential variables is impractical. As the objective of the research was to test the model, not to calculate relative significance of individual variables, the research was restricted to one sport, athletics, and the sampling restricted to two similar clubs both located in south-east England. The following variables were used.

Gender

The hypothesis of many researchers is that males are more likely to become coaches than females (Anderson and Moore, 1978; Humble, 1981; Jackson, 1985; Williams and Ortega, 1986; Willis, 1998). The data collected showed high correlations between gender and other variables. This indicates that the set of variables influencing the decision of males may be significantly different to the set influencing the decision of females and that the weighting associated with common variables may differ between the genders. To overcome this, separate models were built for men and for women.

Dependants

Studies of sports volunteers (Brandenberg *et al.*, 1982; Butt, 1987; Deckers and Gratton, 1995) indicate that involvement of children and partners can be a major reason to volunteer, especially as coaches. This was reinforced during negotiations with athletic clubs at the commencement of this research. What was not clear was whether it was the number or proportion or gender or age which was important. In this study, each member of each household was placed into one of eight categories:

1. Males under 18, neither parent a member of an athletic club.
2. Females under 18, neither parent a member of an athletic club.
3. Males under 18, members of athletic clubs.
4. Females under 18, members of athletic clubs.
5. Males 18 and over, not members of athletic clubs but with one or more children members of athletic clubs.
6. Females 18 and over, not members of athletic clubs but with one or more children members of athletic clubs.
7. Males 18 and over, members of athletic clubs.
8. Females 18 and over, members of athletic clubs.

The age of 18 was used to differentiate a child from an adult as this was then the minimum age for entry into the coach education programme. Combinations of categories were used to form other variables (e.g. adults in household).

Distance

Research on volunteering often contains references to 'lack of time'. In this study, respondents were asked to say how long it took them to reach their athletics club. At the same time, the physical distance was measured between their residence and the club. These provided a perceptual and a real measure of accessibility of a facility.

Transport

Accessibility is also related to transport. The decline of public transport, especially in the evening, and the perceived risks to children from abuse, now make personal use of a car almost a necessity. Competition for transport in a multi-person household could be a problem. Respondents were asked how many cars were available for their use in their free time. This variable was used in combination with the dependent variables to further variables (e.g. number of cars available per adult in household).

Education

A Scottish survey found that coaches in athletics had significantly fewer years of formal education than coaches in other sports (Lyle *et al.*, 1997). Other research (e.g. Smith, 1998; Schanning, 1999) has indicated that the age at which full-time education ceased and the highest level of educational attainment were important in volunteering in general. This study measured the number of years of school attendance after the age of 15 and the number of years of further or higher education since leaving school. A broad definition of the latter was taken to accommodate both part-time and full-time courses.

Free time

Whilst logic might indicate that lack of free time may deter people from volunteering, especially as athletic coaches give an average of 12 hours a week (Lyle *et al.*, 1997, p. 26, table 10), anecdotally people with the least spare time are said to 'make time'. It is known that the time given by sports volunteers is highly variable (Sports Council, 1996). There is also the question of work irregularity and ability to commit oneself to regular volunteering.

Respondents were asked to say the earliest time on a Tuesday or Thursday evening at which they were normally home and free from work or household duties or study. These are the main training days in the UK for most amateur sports. Each respondent was also asked if their work involved them in regular overtime or shift work or being away from home. This gave a second binary variable of 'irregular hours'.

Association with sport

Volunteering was long considered to have a high degree of altruism: serving others without regard for personal benefit. As volunteering became a subject for serious research, it was realized that voluntary organizations could be seen as two groups, each with differing motivations:

- Motivated by organizational and or individual objectives, primarily related to the provision of financial help and services to others. Volunteering is without expectation of tangible reward for the volunteer.

- Motivated by desires for mutual self-help amongst their members. Volunteering takes place to benefit oneself and others from a collective interest and is to help them to attain shared aims.

Most amateur sports clubs fall into the latter category, the aims being to share expensive facilities and to organize competitions. More recently, the growth of professional sport and of the health and leisure industries may have motivated some people to participate in sport and gain coaching qualifications not only for their own satisfaction, but also to gain entry to a leisure-based course or to advance a career. To measure work-based motivation, respondents were asked to estimate how much of their work time was related to sport or leisure.

Research indicates that the more a respondent has personal experience of sport, the more they are likely to take up voluntary posts. But it may be that volunteering in sport is a means to retain a relationship with a club beyond normal competitive years. This could explain the anecdotal evidence that those active in road running or in veterans (masters) are less likely to volunteer, especially to coach. Veterans or masters are male athletes over the age of 40 and female athletes over the age of 35.

In the data collection for this research, each respondent was asked to estimate the number of years since leaving school that they had competed in any sport. They were also asked to estimate how frequently over the past 12 months they had helped with or competed in any formal organized sport or exercise. They were further asked if other members of their household were involved in any sports other than athletics. This was to cover conflicts of interest in the household. They were also asked if their main interest was in road running (as opposed to track and field) and if they competed in, or intended to compete in, veteran athletics.

Literacy

Unpublished research by the author indicated that the number of voluntary coaches in an area showed statistical association with the overall literacy level of the area. This reinforced anecdotal evidence that some volunteers were deterred from becoming coaches because of fears of science and of examinations.

This study followed other research (Nicoll and Harrison, 1984) in measuring normal reading capabilities from the periodical most frequently read. Readability used the well-established Flesch Ease of Reading Score (Flesch, 1948; Lunzer and Gardner, 1979). It is one of the few measures of readability developed for adults. Preliminary studies showed that account must be taken not only of the preferred periodical, but also the preferred type of article in terms of whether or not the writing was predominantly in a personal style or a factual style. The Flesch Ease of Reading Score requires measurement of the average word length and the average sentence length. Each respondent was also asked if they read or did not read scientific or technological articles.

Attitudes

A study by Sundeen (1992) found that the attitude of respondents to whether or not other people should volunteer was significant. This study also used logistic regression. Measurement was on a five-point Likert scale answering the statement 'People should volunteer some of their time to people elsewhere'. The same question and response scale was used in this study. The same technique was used to discover attitudes to the payment of coaches. The statement posed was 'coaches at *local* sports clubs, generally, should be paid'.

Age

Research indicates that the probability of volunteering increases with age to a certain point and then decreases, especially around the retirement age of 60. Research indicates that the peak age is approximately 40 years old for athletic coaches (Sports Council, 1996; Lyle *et al.*, 1997). This confirms the work of Rapoport and Rapoport (1975) in which they hypothesized that there were events in the family life cycle that tended to be associated with individuals making decisions on volunteering. Two such events frequently occur at about the age of 40:

- Children reaching the age of about 10, the age at which many start sport in clubs outside school.
- Reaching stability and peak earnings in career.

However, the data collected for this research found that age was highly correlated with other variables: dependants, transport and attitudes. It could not be used in its own right. But the conceptual model used in this research hypothesizes both a threshold and, after the threshold has been reached, a life event to trigger a decision to volunteer.

Club association

Research has shown that the probability of any individual choosing to volunteer may be associated with the 'culture' of the organization. It has also shown that 'being asked' was one of the key reasons for volunteering. Both reasons are likely to be related to the socioeconomic, demographic composition and history of the club. A binary variable was used in this study to indicate the two clubs sampled. If this variable was found to be significant, then 'culture' is likely to be important as the two clubs were selected to be very similar.

Data Collection and Analysis

Data collection

The data were collected from the membership and from the parents of junior members of two athletics clubs in the south-east of England using the membership lists supplied by the clubs. Quota samples were taken from 12 sub-populations:

- Male and female qualified coaches from both clubs.
- Male and female members (not coaches), 18 and over, from both clubs.
- Male and female parents (not members) of junior members under 18 from both clubs.

The data obtained from each sub-population were weighted by the ratio of the sample obtained to the total sub-population. The overall sample contained data from 112 respondents from a total population of 1055 (10.6%). The quota sample for coaches was deliberately set high due to their relatively small numbers; 67% of coaches, 7% of members and 11% of parents were sampled. This was fairly consistent between the two clubs and the genders. Data were obtained from face-to-face interviews, mainly at the respondent's home. Each interview was planned to last 30 minutes and was recorded.

The first part of the interview collected quantitative data for each of the explanatory variables mentioned previously. Questions on topics such as age, number of children, years at school and years at college required whole-number answers, whilst other questions were phrased to elicit a 'yes' or 'no' answer, e.g. if any dependants were involved with sports other than athletics. Some questions involved estimations. These included how long to travel from home to the athletics club, what percentage of work hours were related to sport or exercise and how many years competed in any sport after leaving school. Whilst such answers are subjective, they are justified on the basis that they measure the perception of the respondent to the topic, and that perception may be more influential in decisions than actuality. Other questions required answers on five-point Likert scales, particularly questions related to attitudes towards volunteering. A few questions required the ticking of alternative answers presented to the respondent on a show card. All quantitative questions were put to each respondent in the same wording and in the same order.

The second part of the interview sought personal experiences and views on coaching in athletics. This was conducted using a series of open-ended questions delivered in an order dictated by the flow of the conversation. The two objectives of the qualitative section were to allow respondents an opportunity to feed back, in confidence, to the sport and to collect information to triangulate and fill out the results of the logistic regression and the possible trigger events put forward in the conceptual model.

Interviews were initially requested by mail shot with a reply paid card. These were reinforced by telephone calls. The overall conversion rate of requests to interviews obtained was 55%, this being highest for coaches (79%) and lowest for members (42%); 51% of the requests not converted proved to be either because the respondent or child was no longer a member or because they had moved away. This resulted in a participating sample size of 112.

The data for members and for parents who were not coaches were collected as at the date of the interview. At that date, either they had decided not to be a coach or they had not made a decision, in some cases because they had not been made aware of the opportunity. The data for coaches were collected as at the date that they entered the coach education programme. This did create a danger of imperfect recall. But the indications are that the errors were small. Dates could be cross-checked and there were no obvious time trends in replies. The quantitative data collected are summarized in Table 6.1. Results are given in averages which are not weighted.

Data analysis

The quantitative data were subjected to data vetting to ensure that they complied with two essential requirements of logistic regression: independence and linearity.

All the explanatory variables used in a model must be independent of each other. That is to say that the effect on the response variable of one explanatory variable is independent of the effect of any other explanatory variable. Lack of independence was measured by the tolerance statistic and by inspection of the correlation matrix and variance decomposition proportions in its calculation. A tolerance statistic of less than 0.20 was taken as indicating unacceptable collinearity. In such cases, the presence of this explanatory variable with the other explanatory variables was rejected. The same reasoning was used when the variance decomposition proportions in the correlation matrix exceeded 0.50 (Menard, 1995; Hutcheson and Sofroniou, 1999). Methods for calculating these tests are found in many statistical programs, including SPSS, which was used in this research.

Three potential explanatory variables were found to have tolerance statistics below 0.20: Age, School Leaving Age and Years of Further or Higher Education. A further five potential explanatory variables were found to have low tolerance statistics and high correlations: Word Complexity, Sentence Length, Flesch Score, Time to Club and Distance to Club. As a result, 'Age' was omitted from all model building. When 'Flesch Score' was used in model building, the 'Word Complexity' and 'Sentence Length' were omitted and *vice versa*. When 'Minutes to Club' was included, then 'Distance to Club' was excluded and *vice versa*.

The second important criterion for logistic regression is that the effect of an explanatory variable on the response variable is linear throughout its entire range. A test for non-linearity was used: the Box-Tidwell test (Hosmer and Lemeshow, 1989; Menard, 1995). Whilst this can indicate non-linearity, it gives no information on the actual shape of the relationship. One means of overcoming this problem is to plot the averages of groups of data (Demaris, 1992, pp. 49–51). Such plots indicate the positions and directions of possible non-linear effects. For example, the explanatory variable 'Time to Club' appears to initially decrease the probability of becoming a coach and then flatten out and remain constant. Interpreted, distance appears to be an increasing deterrent, but reaches a value beyond which any further increase exerts no greater an effect.

Two transformation methods are available to rectify non-linear data. One is to apply a mathematical transformation, e.g. the square root of the data. The second is to treat the data series as a set of steps. The series method represents a continuous curve as a set of straight lines, each spanning a specified range of the data. The step method transforms the data to a categorical form. The latter may also be used with intrinsically categorical data, such as the number of dependants.

Categorical variables can substantially increase the number of variables. The simplest categorical data is a binary variable. The two states can be represented by one variable which can take the values of '0' or '1' to represent the two states. A categorical variable which can have three states (e.g. none, one, and two or more children) can be represented by a set of two variables, each capable of having a value of '0' or '1'. In the example, no children can be represented by the set of '0' '0'; one child as '1' '0' and two or more children as '0' '1'. In general, a categorical variable with 'm' categories requires a set of '$m - 1$' variables.

Binary and categorical variables add to the difficulties of interpreting results of logistic regression. The logistic coefficient calculated for a binary explanatory variable represents the change in the response variable, decision to coach, that occurs when the explanatory variable changes from '0' to '1'. For a three-state categorical variable, there will be two logistic coefficients. In the example given, the first could represent the change in the response variable when the explanatory variable changes from 'no children' to 'two or more children'. The second could represent the change between 'one child' to 'two or more children'. Other coding schemes are possible. In this research the coding scheme used compares each category to the last category, usually the one measuring the largest numbers or amounts of the variable. In the example given, the reference category is 'two or more children'.

In this research, testing for non-linearity proved to be essential. The majority of potential explanatory variables exhibited non-linear effects. The

Table 6.1. Summary of descriptive and potential explanatory variables.

		Male		Female	
		Coach	Not	Coach	Not
Sample	Number interviewed	23	41	11	37
Club association	Count club A	9	19	7	18
	% club A	39%	46%	64%	49%
Year of birth	Average year	1946	1954	1949	1956
Year of coach registration	Average year	1986		1991	
Age at coach registration	Average age	40		42	
Boys NOT in athletics	Average number in household	0.26	0.22	0.09	0.43
Boys IN athletics	Average number in household	0.39	0.20	0.36	0.22
Girls NOT in athletics	Average number in household	0.26	0.44	0.36	0.30
Girls IN athletics	Average number in household	0.70	0.27	0.73	0.43
Men NOT in athletics	Average number in household	0.09	0.15	0.73	0.62
Men IN athletics	Average number in household	0.04	0.02	0.27	0.22
Women NOT in athletics	Average number in household	0.61	0.73	0.09	0.19
Women IN athletics	Average number in household	0.30	0.12	0.00	0.08
Distance to track	Average units	42	79	83	66
Minutes to track	Average minutes	13	21	14	15
Cars available	Average number	1.4	1.7	1.3	1.7
School leaving age	Average years old	16.7	17.0	17.0	17.1

Post-school education	Average number of years	2.3	2.4	1.5	2.4
Hour home	Average hour, p.m.	5.81	5.21	5.25	4.64
Irregular working hours	Number with irregular work hours	10	23	1	12
	% irregular working hours	43%	56%	9%	32%
Other sport, respondent	Number of respondents	14	22	8	26
	% respondents with other sports	61%	54%	73%	70%
Other sport, dependants	Number of households	11	13	5	19
	% households with other sports	48%	32%	45%	51%
Post-school competition	Average % of years	66%	50%	54%	28%
Interest in veteran athletics	Number interested	12	27	6	16
	% interested in veterans	52%	66%	55%	43%
Main interest road running	Number main interest	6	18	1	4
	% main interest in road running	26%	44%	9%	11%
Participation in sport	1 = at least 1 per week, 5 = none	1.5	2.0	1.8	2.2
Sport in work	Average % of work time	16%	12%	3%	15%
Flesch Reading Score	Higher = easier	51.5	51.5	54.7	52.8
Word complexity	Average syllables per word	1.55	1.57	1.51	1.54
Sentence length	Average words per sentence	23.0	22.6	20.8	22.0
Read science (and technology)	Number who read science and technology	15	32	4	13
	% read science and technology	65%	78%	36%	35%
Attitude to volunteering	1 = strongly disagree, 5 = strongly agree	3.7	3.8	3.7	3.9
Attitude to paying coaches	1 = strongly agree, 5 = strongly disagree	3.6	2.7	3.8	2.6

most suitable transform for the majority was conversion into a categorical variable with a limited number of categories. In other cases, a square root transform was satisfactory.

Model Building

Twenty-six potential variables were identified. The ideal method of building a model would be to enter all 26 variables and allow the computer program to decide automatically which variables were significant at a given level of probability. This is not feasible for two reasons.

1. Programs do not test for collinearity and will allow combinations of variables to be entered that are not independent of each other.
2. The number of variables and the data density of each variable may produce matrices that are either too dense or too sparse for the program to proceed.

As a consequence, it was decided to build a first model by introducing one variable at a time, starting from the variable that appears to be most significant. Within a logistic regression program, a number of alternative methods are usually available to introduce explanatory variables into the model. In this research the method chosen was stepwise forward selection using likelihood ratio criterion (Forward:LR). The method starts with only a constant (cut off) in the model and adds one variable at a time. Each time, variables in the model are examined again and eliminated if not significant. The default minimum probability value of 0.05 was chosen to allow variables to enter the model and the default probability value of 0.10 was chosen to eliminate variables.

Steps in the building were rejected if they gave no improvement in the number of correctly predicted cases. Steps resulting in perfect fits were rejected as they indicate mathematical failures in the model-building algorithm. Additions of variables giving no further improvements in fit were rejected on the grounds of parsimony.

At the conclusion of the initial building, collinearity tests were again conducted. Any alternative explanatory variables were tested, for example 'Time to Club' or 'Distance to Club'. The alternative giving the best fit was selected. Tests were then conducted to ensure that the removal or the addition of every potential explanatory variable did not give a better result. The constant was always found to be not significant. This accords with logic in that if there were no explanatory variables, the probability of an individual not becoming a coach would be zero.

Because of the collinearity which exists between the explanatory variable 'Gender' and many other explanatory variables, two models were constructed. It was found that the set of explanatory variables differed between the two genders.

Having built two models giving good fits, each model was then subjected to two further tests. One was designed to look at the sensitivity to the threshold value (0.5). This was achieved by plotting the frequencies of the calculated values of response variable, probability of being a coach, and distinguishing the plots for those who were actually coaches from those who were not. In this research, the result was an elongated 'S' plot with almost all the 'coaches' along one limb and almost all the 'non-coaches' along the other limb. Very few plots lay in the middle, indicating low sensitivity to the threshold value. A further test of fit was made by plotting the deviance values of the residuals (SPSS Inc., 1999). These should be normally distributed. The plots indicate reasonable fits for a sociological model, although there are substantial deviations associated with the extreme ends.

The male model

The nine significant explanatory variables are shown in the Table 6.2. The first two columns describe the variable. Where a variable is binary or categorical,

Table 6.2 Male model.

Explanatory variable		Standardized coefficient	Model coefficient	−2LL lost
Cars available	None or 1 cf. 3 or more	1.47	26.40	108.7
	2 compared to 3 or more	0.88	15.72	
Girls in athletics	None cf. 2 or more	−0.52	−11.40	90.6
	1 cf. 2 or more	−0.12	−2.89	
% of sport in work	Less than 50% cf. 50% or more	0.48	12.69	50.6
Time to club	20 minutes or less cf. more than 20 minutes	0.47	8.89	47.5
Participation rate	Once a month or more cf. less than once a month	0.38	7.75	55.1
Boys NOT in athletics	None cf. 2 or more	0.35	−8.35	21.3
	1 cf. 2 or more	0.24	−2.22	
Time home	By 4 p.m. cf. after 6 p.m.	−0.33	−6.55	36.5
	After 4 p.m., by 6 p.m. cf. after 6 p.m.	−0.32	−5.68	
Boys in athletics	None cf. 2 or more	−0.32	−8.35	34.9
	1 cf. 2 or more	−0.07	−2.22	
Word complexity	Sq. root of average word length	−0.01	−24.45	37.4

the second column shows the category and the category to which it is being compared. For example, the most significant variable is the number of cars available. This is categorical. The first category is where there is no or one car available. This category is compared to where there are three or more cars available.

The third column gives the standardized coefficient. It indicates the relative influence of that variable (and category) compared with other variables. The variables are ranked in Table 6.2 by the standardized coefficients. The fourth column gives the unstandardized, model coefficient. This is for record purposes only. These coefficients demonstrate the difficulties of interpretation where there are wide ranges in the measurement scales of the variables. The fourth column, $-2LL$, indicates the amount of fit contributed by that variable. In the case of categorical variables, only one value is shown, as such variables can only exist in the model as a complete set of categories.

The number of cars available has the strongest influence. This influence is the opposite to what might have been expected in that the fewer the cars available, the more the respondent is likely to be a coach. The effect is not linear, decreasing with the number of cars. The explanation may be that the number of cars available is a proxy for socioeconomic category. Anecdotal evidence indicates that voluntary coaching in athletics tends to be the domain of lower-income persons rather than high-income earners. It also corresponds to work by Lyle et al. (1997) which found that coaches in athletics had significantly fewer years of formal education than coaches in other sports. The omission of a variable specifically measuring socioeconomic condition is indicated by the fact that a measure of the degree of dispersion of the model, the S statistic, is 5.26, considerably greater than the perfect value of 1.00. One reason for over-dispersion is the absence, or partial absence, of a significant explanatory variable.

The number of girls in the household who are members of an athletics club has an effect almost as strong as that of car availability. It is not a linear effect. Compared to having two or more girls involved, having no girls has a strongly negative influence. Having one girl markedly reduces this negative influence. Interestingly, the influence of having boys involved with athletics is less strong. The influence of having boys in the household who are not involved in athletics has the reverse influence. The overall influence of these variables indicates that being a coach is probably associated with altruistic motivations related to perceived benefits to the family.

Three variables have similar influences on the model. The probability of being a coach is significantly associated with work situations involving 50% or more of work time being related to sport or leisure. This includes many teachers and staff employed in leisure and health centres. In these cases, a strict definition of 'voluntary' coach may not apply, in the sense that monetary payment may be related to the activity of being a coach or of possessing a coach award.

The perceived time to reach the club is influential. If more than 20 minutes are required, the probability of being a coach decreases. This is an expected result reflecting the influence of perceived accessibility or availability of time.

As might be expected, the frequency of participation in sport has a positive influence on the likelihood of being a coach, as measured by whether or not the respondent has participated more than once a month in the last 12 months.

The least significant variable is the square root transformation of the average word length of the periodical normally read. This has a negative effect, perhaps contrary to what might have been expected. The reason may be that the variable may be associated with the probable socioeconomic effect mentioned previously.

The 'fit' of the model to the data can be judged from the following statistics. The inclusion of the nine explanatory variables reduces the log-likelihood ($-2LL$) of the initial model from 776.6 to 73.9. This reduction has 14 degrees of freedom and is significant at a probability of less than 0.001. The Nagelkerke R^2 coefficient (0.95) indicates that about 95% of the variance has been accounted for by these nine variables. All 521 (weighted) cases of 'Not Coach' were correctly assigned and 82% of the 39 cases 'Coach' were correctly assigned. This assignment rate has a ϕ_p value of 0.83, which is significant at the probability level of 0.010. The C statistic has a value of 0.93, indicating that this assignment rate is better than chance.

The female model

The seven significant variables are shown in Table 6.3 with the statistics as described previously. The explanatory variable 'cars available' in the male model is still in the female model, but with a reduced influence. The most influential explanatory variable is the attitude of the respondent to the statement 'coaches at *local* sports clubs, generally, should be paid'. Agreement with this statement significantly reduced the probability of being a coach, compared to disagreeing with the statement. A neutral stance also reduced the probability, but to a lesser extent.

The next three explanatory variables were not significant in the male model. As might be expected, having regular work hours, as compared to irregular hours, increased the probability of being a coach. Conversely, having an interest in either veteran athletics or road running, compared with not having such interests, reduced the probability of being a coach. These confirm the anecdotal evidence concerning both these activities.

Another result which might have been expected is that, for women, the more adults that there are in the household, the less likely the respondent is to become a coach.

Finally, the number of girls in the household involved in athletics has the same type of influence as it did in the male model. However, in contrast with

Table 6.3. Female model.

Explanatory variable		Standardized coefficient	Model coefficient	−2LL lost
Pay coaches	Agree cf. disagree	−1.07	−184.33	104.9
	Neutral cf. disagree	−0.19	−38.36	
Cars available	None or 1 cf. 3 or more	0.37	63.59	59.6
	2 cf. 3 or more	0.07	12.76	
Irregular hours	Work hours regular cf. irregular	0.24	43.62	41.3
Veteran interest	Not interested cf. interested or active	−0.23	−40.25	28.6
Road running interest	Not interested cf. interested or active	−0.22	−61.24	32.6
Adults in household	Number in household, other than respondent	0.17	19.30	13.3
Girls in athletics	None cf. 2 or more	−0.089	−16.29	27.7
	1 cf. 2 or more	−0.13	−24.69	

the male model, the numbers of boys involved or not involved was not significant.

The 'fit' of the model is similar to that for the male model. The inclusion of the seven explanatory variables reduces the log-likelihood (−2LL) of the initial model from 681.5 to 25.5. This reduction has 10 degrees of freedom and is significant at a probability of less than 0.001. The Nagelkerke R^2 coefficient (0.98) indicates that about 98% of the variance has been accounted for by these seven variables. All 480 (weighted) cases of 'Not Coach' were correctly assigned and 74% of the 16 cases 'Coach' were correctly assigned. This assignment rate has a ϕ_p value of 0.82, which is significant at the probability level of 0.010. The C statistic has a value of 0.99, indicating that this assignment rate is better than chance.

Qualitative Evidence

The qualitative data were analysed for evidence related to the variables found to be significant in the logistic regression models and for indications of 'key events'. The following evidence was found.

Over 30% of the respondents said that they would not become an athletics coach because they had other leisure activities. There was a statistical association between the number of cars available and household interests outside athletics. These may partially correspond to the strong negative association for men and for women between car availability and becoming a coach.

Women expressed strong views about paying coaches. The majority were strongly against the concept. Their main reason was that payment could lead to coaches pressuring children to compete. This conflicted with their views that the greatest benefits of sport to their child were social. It was the men who saw the main benefit of sport as learning to compete. They expressed less concern about paying coaches.

Of the respondents, 22%, including some single parents, stated that they would not coach because they had no spare time after work or because of family commitments. This corresponds to the negative associations in both models between time to the club and irregular work hours. A further 9% felt that they could not commit their leisure time on a regular basis.

Of the coaches, 25% said they started coaching to help their own child. A further 30% said they started coaching either to fill their time waiting for their child at the club or because they had observed a shortage of coaches. Women tended to want to coach their son, less so their daughter. Men tended to want to coach their daughter. These correspond to the sibling variables in the two models.

Of the respondents, 22% said that their personal priority was to compete in sport for as long as they could, leaving them no time to coach. They saw veteran competition and road running as being a means of extending their competitive careers. These were reflected in the female model, but not in the male model. In addition, many women stated that they did not want to spend leisure time with children, especially if they were teachers. This may partially explain why there are fewer female coaches. It relates to statements such as 'I want my leisure to be different to my everyday life'.

Men perceived coaches as successful sports people. Consequently, the more a man participated in sport, the greater the likelihood that a man saw himself as a coach. Similarly, as women participated significantly less in sport and many had no interest in sport at all, women were less likely to see themselves as coach potential.

Of the coaches, 32% had not or were not actively coaching. Half of these were under the age of 35. This corresponded with 20% of coaches stating that their prime reason for qualifying was to enhance their career or study prospects. The start to a career constitutes a 'key event' triggering a threshold for a decision.

Of the coaches, 35% took the decision to train following being invited to do so by somebody in the club. This reinforces the findings of other research that being asked is a common 'key event' to volunteering.

The younger the respondent, the more likely it was that they intended to continue to compete as a veteran and that this would take priority over them actively coaching. The evidence from this study indicates that whilst young people may continue to enter the coach education programme, few of them may actively coach, if ever. Their careers and their desires to personally compete are greater priorities.

Summary and Conclusions

Summary

Amateur sport in the UK is based upon a network of clubs run by unpaid volunteers. The voluntary coaches devote much of their leisure time to developing the sporting abilities of young people. They ensure that the public and private investments in sports facilities are used effectively and that athletes experience a healthy and safe life in the community. From this network come the international sporting stars. Despite the number of people involved, the financial investment made and the responsibility for youth development, very little is known about the decision making of these volunteers.

Starting from social exchange theory and incorporating Brandenberg's work on the recreational activity adoption process, a conceptual model was developed for decision processes in voluntary sport. This conceptual model can be mathematically represented by a logistic regression (LR) model. Unlike other regression methods, LR can handle the binary nature of an individual's decision: to volunteer or not. It can also handle binary, categorical and non-normally distributed variables, e.g. gender, number of children and distance travelled.

Information was collected by personal interview from 112 individuals associated with athletics in the UK. They were qualified athletics coaches, adult athletes and parents of junior athletes, all of them unpaid volunteers. The objective of the research was to test a substantive model of the decision to become a voluntary coach. This objective did not include identification of all significant variables or the accurate measurement of their effects. Qualitative information from the interviews was analysed to supplement and to triangulate the quantitative results.

The conceptual model was verified and LR modelling gave a satisfactory fit to the data. The effects of some of the variables in published literature were found to be at variance with previous hypotheses. The set of significant variables for men differed from the set for women. Several of the variables suggested in published literature were found to be significantly correlated with each other and could not be used together. The models indicate that one or more significant variables have not yet been identified or do not have adequate measuring systems.

Conclusions

Logistic regression offers a quantitative means of testing theories in decision situations which can be conceptualized by the Sports Model developed in this research. The specific situation studied for this research shows the multivariate nature of such decisions; the non-linear effects of variables; the existence of motivational thresholds; the importance of 'key events'; and the effects of gender. More research is needed to identify and to adequately measure basic underlying variables, especially those related to socioeconomics.

References

Anderson, J.C. and Moore, L.F. (1978) The motivation to volunteer. *Journal of Voluntary Action Research* 7, 120–125.

Brailsford, D. (1997) *British Sport: a Social History*. Lutterworth, Cambridge.

Brandenberg, J., Grenier, W., Hamilton-Smith, E., Scholten, H., Senior, R. and Webb, J. (1982) A conceptual model of how people adopt recreational activities. *Leisure Studies* 1, 273–277.

Butt, D.S. (1987) *Psychology of Sport*, 2nd edn. Van Nostrand Reinhold, New York.

Collett, D. (1991) *Modelling Binary Data*. Chapman & Hall, London.

Cox, R.W. (1994) *History of Sport: a Guide to the Literature and Sources of Information*. British Society of Sports History, Frosham.

Deckers, P. and Gratton, C. (1995) Participation in sport and membership of traditional sports clubs: a case study. *Leisure Studies* 14, 117–131.

Demaris, A. (1992) *Logit Modeling Practical Applications*. Sage, London.

Dowling, D., Potrac, R.P. and Jones, R. (1997) *Women & Leisure: a Qualitative Analysis of Constraints & Opportunities*. Brunel University, London.

Flesch, R.F. (1948) A new readability yardstick. *Journal of Applied Psychology* 32, 221–233.

Holt, R. (1989) *Sport & the British: a Modern History*. Clarendon Press, Oxford.

Hosmer, D.W. and Lemeshow, S. (1989) *Applied Logistic Regression*. John Wiley & Sons, New York.

Humble, S. (1981) *Voluntary Action in the 1980's: a Summary of the Findings of a National Survey*. Volunteer Centre, London.

Hutcheson, G. and Sofroniou, N. (1999) *The Multivariate Social Scientist*. Sage, London.

Jackson, H. (1985) *Recruiting Volunteers*. Home Office, London.

Johnson, R.H. (1973) Motivating the volunteer worker. *Volunteer Administration* 7, 44–48.

Kessler, R.C. (1975) A descriptive model of emergency on-call blood donation. *Journal of Voluntary Action Research* 4, 159–171.

Longley, C. (2000) Charities must resist government's embrace. *The Daily Telegraph*, 25 August, 31.

Lunzer, E. and Gardner, K. (eds) (1979) *The Effective Use of Reading*. Heinemann, London.

Lyle, J., Allison, M. and Taylor, J. (1997) *Factors Influencing the Motivation of Sports Coaches*. Scottish Sports Council, Edinburgh.

Menard, S. (1995) *Applied Logistic Regression*. Sage, London.

Mintern, J.H. (1994) Effect of new provisions on non-elite sports careers. DPhil thesis, Liverpool University, Liverpool, UK.

Nicoll, A. and Harrison, C. (1984) The readability of health-care literature. *Developmental Medicine and Child Neurology* 26, 596–600.

Polley, M. (1998) *Moving the Goalposts: a History of Sport*. Routledge, London.

Rapoport, R. and Rapoport, R.N. (1975) *Leisure and the Family Life Cycle.* Routledge & Kegan Paul, London.

Rice, J.C. (1994) Logistic regression: an introduction. In: Thomson, B. (ed.) *Advances in Social Science Methodology*, Vol. 3. JAI, Greenwich, Connecticut, pp. 191–247.

Schanning, K.F. (1999) Doing good deeds: a multi-dimensional model of volunteerism. PhD thesis, University of Virginia, USA. [*Dissertation Abstracts International* 70(10), 3807A.]

Schindler-Rainmann, E. and Lippett, R. (1971) *The Volunteer Community.* The Volunteer Community Centre for a Voluntary Society, Washington, DC.

Smith, J.D. (1998) *The 1997 National Survey of Volunteering.* National Centre for Volunteering, London.

Sports Council (1996) *Valuing Volunteers in UK Sport.* Sports Council, London.

SPSS Inc. (1999) *SPSS Regression Models 9.0.* SPSS Inc., Chicago.

Sundeen, R.A. (1992) Differences in personal goals and attitudes among volunteers. *Nonprofit and Voluntary Sector Quarterly* 21, 271–291.

Williams, J.A., Jr and Ortega, T. (1986) The multidimensionality of joining. *Journal of Voluntary Action Research* 15(4), 35–44.

Willis, P.L. (1998) The effect of career and family transitions and selected variables on the decision to enrol in a graduate program in developmental education. EdD dissertation, Grambling State University, Louisiana. [*Dissertation Abstracts International* 70(2), 375A.]

Politics of Volunteering and Active Citizenship: Policy Issues

The chapters in this section report on the volunteer scene in Canada, Australia and The Netherlands. Edwards's chapter is based on a survey of volunteer participation, in contrast with the chapters of Arai and Meijs, which are more purely theoretical. The focus here is on active citizenship and the policy issues that emerge when volunteers, serious or casual, become central to the functioning of a local or national service or organization.

Deborah Edwards observes in Chapter 7 that, despite various external pressures and a changing environment, little research has been undertaken to explore the context in which general museums and art museums in Australia attempt to organize their volunteers. Her chapter addresses this issue from a distinct perspective. It draws on institutional analysis to explain the organizational context in which volunteers participate. Edwards examines this context in three parts. The first part provides a definition of volunteering in Australia. In the second she presents an overview of volunteer participation in general museums and art museums in that country. In the third part she defines the organizational field of these two types of museum and identifies for Australia the characteristics that shape this field.

Susan M. Arai's chapter describes the nature of volunteering in Canada. She explores the ever-changing character of volunteering and its spaces in that country. As we look back over the history of voluntary associations in Canada, we can see the richness and diversity that has developed there. From this background Arai discusses some of the current issues that have tended to undermine the experience of volunteering and the existence of voluntary associations in Canada. She then works up a set of vignettes to highlight the impact of changes in political philosophy and in demographic trends, among them an ageing population and new challenges of the economy in the postmodern world. These current issues and challenges are best understood in the context of civic participation, historical development of the volunteer sector and workings of democracy. In short, this chapter provides a succinct overview of the role that volunteers have played in Canada in developing its human services and its welfare state.

In Chapter 9 Lucas Meijs concludes, after examining the writing of Christer Leopold, that no generic model exists that applies equally well to all volunteering and volunteer management contexts. Volunteering, volunteers, and the ways they are organized and managed differ from context to context. This chapter looks further into the growing understanding of diversity in volunteering and volunteer management. It concentrates on the different settings in which volunteering takes place. These settings are linked to two distinct managerial approaches: membership management and programme management. In the first part of the chapter, Meijs examines the differences between these two approaches to managing volunteers. In the second part he links the two to a variety of organizational and emotional settings in which people volunteer. In the final part Meijs presents his conclusions on the relation between organizational context and the ways volunteers should be managed.

Defining Field Characteristics of Museums and Art Museums: an Australian Perspective

7

Deborah Edwards

University of Western Sydney, Locked Bag 1797, Penrith South, NSW 1797, Australia

Introduction

There is a developing discourse on volunteer participation in tourism centred on management, the economic value of volunteer services, motivation, recruitment, participation rates and roles, retention and leadership (Caldwell and Andereck, 1994; Stebbins, 1996; Tyzack, 1996; Farrell *et al.*, 1998; Green and Chalip, 1998; Farmer and Fedor, 1999; Holmes, 1999; Rochester, 1999). In Australia, thousands of volunteers are involved in museums and art museums (Australian Bureau of Statistics, 2000), offering their services and skills in a variety of roles including visitor information, guiding, conservation management and administration. Holmes (1999), in a long-term study of heritage museums, found that the heritage sector is becoming increasingly more specialized in its management of volunteers in response to increasing numbers of both volunteers and museums and heritage organizations. Additionally, museums and art museums are increasingly required to diversify their products and services in order to increase their cash flow. Volunteer participation is not financially remunerated but it greatly contributes to the market activity of the entity. Indeed, the productive performance of the volunteer contributes to the organization's overall market success. Despite these external pressures and changing environment, little research has been undertaken in establishing the context in which museums and art museums must organize their volunteers.

This chapter addresses this issue from a distinct perspective. It draws on institutional analysis in order to explain the organizational context in which volunteers participate. Organizational context is examined in three parts. Firstly, it provides a definition of volunteering in Australia. Secondly, it provides an overview of volunteer participation in museums and art museums.

Thirdly, it defines the organizational field of museums and art museums and identifies the characteristics that shape the field within Australia.

An Australian Definition of Volunteering

Lyons *et al.* (1998) maintain that different people will draw the line between what is volunteering and what is not at different points, and that this will vary across different societies. It has been suggested that the terminology (volunteer work, voluntary activity, volunteer) have different connotations for different people. Definitions of volunteering (Australian Bureau of Statistics, 1996; Boulay, 1996; Stebbins, 1996; Ellis, 1997; Fisher and Ackerman, 1998; Cordingly, 2000; Warburton and Oppenheimer, 2000) vary in their focus from broad to narrow, formal and informal, and with significant variations of emphasis. However, they agree that volunteering is an activity in which people participate for no financial gain. From an Australian perspective the peak body for the volunteering sector in Australia defines volunteering as 'an activity that takes place in not-for-profit organizations or projects and is of benefit to the community and undertaken of the volunteer's own free will, without coercion; for no financial payment; and in designated volunteer positions only' (Volunteering Australia, 2001, p. 4). Although lengthy, the definition is simple in its message and incorporates five characteristics of volunteering:

1. Unpaid work that benefits the community;
2. Is undertaken by choice;
3. For no payment;
4. In non-profit organizations; and
5. Volunteers participate in designated volunteer positions only.

Cordingly (2000) clarifies these characteristics. She argues that the type of organization in which volunteering is undertaken is relevant to any definition of volunteering for the following reasons. Firstly, not-for-profits exist for a social purpose and any financial surplus is reinvested back into the organization. This is in contrast to a commercial organization that, as a result of its access to a pool of volunteers, would have the opportunity to increase its profits by either decreasing or not increasing their paid staff, leaving volunteers open to exploitation. The second characteristic is important as it highlights the benefits that volunteers and communities gain from their involvement as distinct from other unpaid work such as in the home or work for unemployment benefits. The third characteristic is fundamental to volunteering and that is that individuals enter into the activity of their own free will, they are not imposed upon nor are they obligated to be involved. The fourth characteristic distinguishes volunteers from paid staff because once volunteers receive payment it must be declared as income and they then become paid workers. The fifth characteristic focuses on the role of the volunteer. Where organizations do not have clearly defined volunteer positions then the lines of employment between paid staff and volunteers become blurred, which may confuse both groups of people and lead to disharmony in the workplace. These criteria are important, as they set out the parameters for volunteer involvement in Australian organizations, including museums, and are legitimated by the national volunteering association. The following section highlights the significance of volunteer involvement in Australian museums.

The Participation of Volunteers in Museums and Art Museums

The Australian Bureau of Statistics (1996, 1997, 2001) has conducted three studies of museums and art museums, 1994–1995, 1996–1997 and 1999–2000, and defines a museum establishment as 'an enclosed area which stored artefacts, artworks and museum objects and which was open to the general public' (Australian Bureau of Statistics, 1996, p. 1). For the year 2000 Australian museums attracted over 27.5 million visitors, employed close to 7000 people and used approximately 30,000 volunteers in the provision of their services (Australian Bureau of Statistics, 2001). The largest of these museums attract over a million visitors each. Museums and art museums received 68% of their total income from federal, state and local government funding (Australian Bureau of Statistics, 2001). However, this is somewhat higher for large museums (75%). Large museums are those museums with more than 100 paid employees and they account for 34% of all admissions. Further funding is derived from fund-raising (7.5%), admissions (7.2%) and sales (7.2%) (Australian Bureau of Statistics, 2001).

Of all staff employed by large museums, 44% are volunteers and 56% are paid staff (Australian Bureau of Statistics, 2001). The economic contribution of volunteers to museums is documented formally in financial reports by only a few large organizations. Table 7.1 represents work groupings of those people employed in large museums.

Table 7.1. Work groupings of volunteers and paid staff in museums of 100 or more persons (Australian Bureau of Statistics, 2001).

	Volunteers (%)	Paid staff (%)
Security, front of house and guides	23.5	13.9
Research, conservation and collection management	3.0	14.4
Managerial and administrative	1.4	13.6
Exhibition design and display	NA	6.6

NA, not applicable.

Large museums with high proportions of volunteers are presented with significant challenges when dealing with different types of personnel that undertake similar activities. These challenges include recruiting and retaining volunteers (Getz and Frisby, 1988), filling important roles with people who may be motivated by a search for enjoyment (Stebbins, 1996), dealing with unrealistic volunteer expectations and dissatisfaction (Green and Chalip, 1998) and the volunteer service encounter (Oakes et al., 1998). The organization of volunteers in large museums and art museums varies from self-autonomous groups to management by a paid volunteer coordinator. In a number of museums and art museums new volunteer intakes are conducted biannually or triennially whilst at others it is on an as-needed basis. With respect to volunteer guides, both experienced guides and paid staff shape the recruitment committees. Guide training is extensive and senior guides are predominantly responsible for training new volunteers. Length of training varies and in many institutions guides are not permitted to take tours until they have completed a minimum of 1 year's training. Where volunteers are organized autonomously, the link between them and other museum functions is tenuous and volunteers feel that the role they play is not always appreciated or taken seriously by all staff members (D. Edwards, 2002, unpublished field notes, University of Western Sydney, Australia).

Organizational and managerial challenges are also exacerbated when organizations interact with their external environments such as competitors, suppliers, consumers, regulatory agencies, trade associations and other organizations. Thus, the internal activities of organizations may be connected to and affected by larger systems of relations (Scott and Meyer, 1991). The following section explores this connectedness by defining the organizational field of museums and art museums and identifying the characteristics that shape the field within Australia.

Method

The delineation of a field is to some extent subjective and is complicated by the multiplicity of levels within a society (Greenwood et al., 2002). However, it is possible to make the task more manageable by focusing on one level. Here that level of interest is large Australian museums and art museums that employ more than 100 paid staff members and utilize more than 100 volunteers. This study is informed by research notes for a medium-term project that is studying the management of volunteers at three major museums and art museums in New South Wales and the Australian Capital Territory. These research notes are drawn from three areas, semi-structured interviews which were conducted with paid and unpaid volunteer coordinators, volunteer focus groups which were held at each venue, and observational notes from the Australian Association of Gallery Guides Organisation (AAGGO, a solely volunteer group) 2003 conference and AAGGO representative and general meeting.

Organizational Field

Institutional theory affirms that organizations do not operate in isolation from each other, they exist in connection with other similar organizations and as a group tend to become increasingly homogenous over time (Benson, 1975; DiMaggio and Powell, 1983; Hinings and Greenwood, 1988; Hannan and Freeman, 1989; Hall, 1991; Meyer and Scott, 1992). Organizations are strongly embedded in environments, and environmental influences penetrate organizations in many ways (Aldrich, 1999). 'A common theme running through all faces of institutional theory is environmental influence over organizations' and it can be seen as a shaping force, one in which 'organizations change their structures to conform to an institutionalized pattern supported by powerful legitimating forces outside their boundaries' (Aldrich, 1999, p. 50). The external environment's influence and effect on and relationship to organizations has been identified as important to understanding the context in which organizations operate (Ranson *et al.*, 1980; Hall, 1991; Powell and DiMaggio, 1991; Meyer and Scott, 1992; Scott, 1995; Anand and Peterson, 2000; R. Suddaby, 2000, unpublished manuscript, University of Alberta, Canada). Greenwood and Hinings (1996), in particular, argue that 'developments in the market context can have an impact on the level of capacity for action in the organisation, increasing the possibility for radical change' (p. 1034). The 'environment' is problematic, as it is not a uniform or single entity, but made up of multiple characteristics where some aspects are of little concern to an organization while others are so dominant that they can affect an entire organization. However, it is important to explain the patterns of inter-organizational competition, influence, coordination, and flows of communication and innovation because they define the boundaries within which these processes operate (Powell and DiMaggio, 1991). Institutional theory's use of organizational field reflects the 'totality of relevant actions' (Scott, in Meyer and Scott, 1992, p. 162) that occur within and between organizations and their external environments.

According to Scott (1995), 'the notion of field connotes the existence of a community of organizations that partakes of a common meaning system and whose participants interact more frequently and fatefully with one another than with actors outside the field' (pp. 207–208). He argues that this interaction critically influences individual organizational activities and tends to cause units within the field to resemble each other. Organizational fields can be distinguished by unique characteristics and rules that, in turn, define and distinguish the operations of organizations within that field. Prominent work on defining field characteristics has been undertaken by:

- Hinings *et al.* (2003), who state that repeated patterns of organizational interaction lead to a consensus of beliefs and values in a field which then enforces particular ways of behaving.

- Scott (2001), who delimits fields using four areas: boundaries, logics, governance and structuration.
- Anand and Peterson (2000), who believe that 'the market serves as a magnet around which groups of organizations begin to cohere' (p. 270). This, they argue, results in the consolidation of organizational fields, and organizations will seek to reduce uncertainty and ambiguity about their markets by processing the collection, delivery and interpretation of market information.
- Powell and DiMaggio (1991), who identified the influence, coalitions and competing values which lead to the structuration of the field of US art museums.
- Greenwood and Hinings (1996), who emphasize archetypes/templates (models) around which organizations converge.

The following framework brings together the various elements discussed by these authors to delimit the field of museums and art museums in Australia and include:

- Standard industrial classification codes.
- Microprocesses.
- Common information-gathering systems.
- Existence and level of inter-organizational interaction and patterns of coalition.
- Common structure of relations/governance within which these organizations may function.
- The linkages that bind both similar and dissimilar organizations.
- Predominant belief systems and related practices.
- Technical and institutional aspects of organizations and their environments.

These characteristics are discussed in turn.

Standard industrial classification codes identify groupings of businesses which carry out similar economic activities. In the Australia New Zealand Standard Industrial Classification (ANZSIC, 2001), classes are created if certain conditions are met.

> The most important of these are that they represent recognisable segments of Australian and New Zealand industry, meet user requirements for statistics, are homogeneous in terms of industrial activity, are economically significant, and align as closely as practicable with the international standard.
>
> (ANZSIC, 2001).

The subdivisions and groups listed under division 'P' are units that engage in providing cultural and recreational facilities and services (ANZSIC, 2001). Grouping 92 is libraries, museums and the arts. From this perspective, museums and art museums in Australia have their own institutional order distinct from that of other organizational fields such as theme parks or accommodation. Additionally, Australian museums are aligned with international associations such as the International Council of Museums (ICOM) through a national committee that represents the interests of Australian museums within ICOM.

Standard industrial codes will alert organizations to their competitive set but managers will also categorize other firms as being within or outside their competitive set. They identify those firms that are relevant to their strategic choices and will continually scan the environment, evaluating what business they are in, identifying their competitors and identifying organizations from whom they can learn (Scott, 2001). This is referred to as *microprocesses*. Key actors of larger museums and art museums in Australia over the past 8 years have become more active in competitively competing for coveted tourism awards against other attractions such as theme parks or entertainment activities. But even though they compete with organizations outside their field, museum managers consider their product and services to be clearly differentiated from those other attractions. A major differentiating feature is their use of volunteers. This differentiation is important, as it influences managers' conceptions of their field while enforcing beliefs about the appropriateness of particular organizational practices and forms across the field (Scott, 2001). Volunteer coordinators from museums and art museums in Canberra come together quarterly as an informal group to share information, discuss issues and compare strategies related to managing volunteers. Thus, managers in categorizing other firms with whom they have organizational and operational commonalities are performing boundary-setting processes. The outcome is a divergence in the perceptions and beliefs of managers that leads to acceptable rules of organizational behaviour, both in procedures related to the organization's tasks and in terms of the organizational structures they have adopted from those inside their competitive set (McDonald and Mutch, 2000).

Anand and Peterson (2000) found, in a study of the commercial music industry, that the market 'serves as a magnet around which groups of organizations begin to cohere' (p. 270). Thus, within a field a *common information-gathering system* develops to collect, deliver and interpret market activity information that organizations can use to reduce uncertainty and ambiguity about their common markets. Museums and art museums derive common market data from a wide variety of sources including museum and art museum associations (Australian Museums On-Line (AMOL); ICOM), volunteer associations (Australian Volunteering, AAGGO), the Australian Bureau of Statistics, national and state tourist offices, and their own specific information-gathering systems (ticket sales, visitor counts, etc.). These sources provide objective information about field activities to all museums, which can be analysed and used to guide strategic plans and organizational action. Specifically, the analysis of visitor needs has influenced museums to look for more innovative ways to present and deliver their displays. This has had an impact on 'old guard' volunteers who are critical of 'production for the masses' and who find it difficult dealing with increasing numbers of children.

The *existence and level of inter-organizational interaction and patterns of coalition* is considered to be a defining field characteristic because 'the structure of a field not only influences managers' cognitions but is also shaped by them' (Scott, 2001, p. 138). Organizations exhibit a particular mode of organizing or way of operating within a framework of the 'rules of the game' or widely held and articulated characteristics. The structure by which museums and art museums operate requires them similarly to deal with Commonwealth, State and Local Government agencies, as well as embassies, universities, galleries, other museums, art schools, and other professional associations within Australia and internationally. Key occupational groups within museums and art museums interact and share their beliefs, opinions and conceptions through the many opportunities available to them such as AMOL, e-mail discussion groups, AAGGO, Australian Museum Forum, Australia Council for the Arts, Australia's Cultural Network and Council of Australian Museum Associations. These organizations and associations allow members to interact, collectively representing themselves and 'it is from these interactions that understandings of reasonable conduct and the behavioural dues of membership emerge' (Greenwood *et al.*, 2002, p. 61). Large museums and art museums dominate the field and are influential through their links with regional museums and galleries across Australia. They provide collaborative and ongoing dialogue, strategic alliance, and relationships with other cultural institutions (National Museum of Australia, 2002). Repeated interaction and coalition strengthens the rules of the game, enforces organizing routines and standardizes organizational practices within the field. It is exemplified by the following comment: 'My director gave me this the other day. It is a system for recruiting volunteers. They said it was a good way of doing it. They got it from a meeting they attended. So we will adapt this for our own program' (D. Edwards, 2002, unpublished field notes, University of Western Sydney, Australia).

'What is perhaps less obvious is the great variety of mechanisms and arrangements employed to govern different sectors or fields in the same society' (Scott, 2001, p. 140). *Governance structures* are imposed by rule and sanction from higher authorities, by actions of members in the field or by a combination of both. In Australia, large museums and art museums are subjected to similar enforced hierarchies and regulatory structures. They are responsible to their relevant minister, and to financial accountability under the Commonwealth Authorities and Companies Act. They are administered through a Council or Board of Trustees and are managed by a Director or General Manager. Thus their institutional processes are linked by governance structures to the wider environment and the rules and conceptions that arise from these agencies. Theoretically, organizations that confront a highly regulated environment will develop more formal internal administrative structures (Aldrich, 1999). This is evidenced in some large museums, as they have formalized their volunteer management systems in a similar way to bureaucratic human resource practices found in other fields, in order to conform to federal and state regulatory guidelines. Volunteers have met these changes with resistance, as in the past they enjoyed a certain freedom and self-rule, which they are reluctant to give up, 'they wouldn't try that here there would be a revolt' (D. Edwards, 2002, unpublished field notes, University of Western Sydney, Australia). 'The establishment of a professional association is a specific way in which an occupation can formalise its identity, make claims about its occupational status, and participate in the governance of a field' (Lounsbury, 2002, p. 256). The AAGGO was formed in 1976 as volunteer guides sought to cope with changes in their institutions, a lack of information and a lack of general organizational guidance (Wharton and Harper, 2003). Today the aim of AAGGO is to advance the professionalism of gallery guides through their biennial conferences, which are held at a different gallery each time, and the circulation of newsletters twice a year.

Organizations are involved in both horizontal and vertical connections with *similar and dissimilar organizations* (Scott and Meyer, 1991). The State Library, the Art Gallery of New South Wales and Taronga Park Zoo are organizations within the respective fields of libraries, art museums and zoos. These organizations can be vertically and horizontally linked, as they are also a part of and operate in the broader *sector* of 'visitor attractions', of which there are many players (Oakes *et al.*, 1998). For example, the Powerhouse Museum, a contemporary museum in New South Wales, adopted (and subsequently adapted) a volunteer programme that was developed by the New South Wales National Parks and Wildlife Service. Aldrich (1999, p. 300) notes that a field 'may well encompass an entire regional, national, or global economic system, depending on the core chosen'. The field of museums and art museums transgresses state borders, through associations and events such as AMOL, AAGGO and the Museums Australia Conference. These connections can provide opportunities for organizations to stay abreast of volunteer management practices, and to discuss and adopt new ways of organizing. At the same time, other players such as theme parks and leisure precincts inadvertently place pressure on museums to compete, forcing them to focus on the delivery of services that are more market-oriented, to run a prominent museum 'shop' and 'café' (Chong, 2000), to mount spectacular displays or host events that are both related and unrelated to core activities. To meet the new demands the role of the volunteer is diversifying while at the same time they must achieve best practice in customer service in order to realize positive customer experiences. In one museum, volunteers are recruited on the basis that they will commit for 4 years, of which their first 18 months are devoted solely to training in order to achieve high levels of knowledge and appropriate customer-related skills (D. Edwards, 2002, unpublished field notes, University of Western Sydney, Australia).

Belief systems and related practices provide guidelines to field participants as to how they are to carry out work (Scott, 2001). Key actors are viewed as knowledgeable and reflexive, capable of understanding and taking account of everyday situations and of routinely monitoring the results of their

own and others' actions (Scott, 2001, p. 76). According to McDonald and
Mutch (2000), ways of organizing and behaving are 'created, enacted, replicated or revised, and turned into routines' (p. 131). Thus, their actions can
lead to creating and transferring new ways of organizing. But the strength and
unity of field participants such as trade associations will affect belief systems
and practices, the stronger these associations are the more influential they are.
Museum guides are networked through AAGGO, which provides an opportunity for guides to hone their skills, increase their knowledge and become tech-
nically efficient. AAGGO is open only to volunteers and membership and
participation is taken very seriously. It has become an arena in which membership and formal interaction enables volunteers to play a notable role in cen-
tralizing beliefs within the field. Powell and DiMaggio (1991), in a study of
American art museums, demonstrate how the fragmentation of organizations
enabled a professionalizing occupation (museum workers) to dominate reform
and influence the emergence of fieldwide structures. For the first time, at the
2003 AAGGO conference, accreditation of guides was raised as an important
consideration, the implementation of which would lead to the professionalizing occupation of volunteer guides. Some fields can be characterized by a
single set of beliefs while others are characterized by multiple belief systems
(Scott, 2001). Furthermore, the articulation of shared values and beliefs leads
to the formalizing of principles and charters. Australian museums and art
museums are characterized by a coherent set of beliefs, which are enforced by
strong national and international associations, these include:

- Conserving and promoting cultural identity.
- Professional cooperation, collaboration and exchange.
- Access to multiple stakeholders.
- Dissemination of knowledge and raising public awareness of museums.
- Training of personnel.
- Advancement of professional standards.
- Elaboration and promotion of professional ethics.

In turn they are reinforced by museum staff at museum association meetings,
in museum journals and by members positioned within the field.

Lastly, *technical* characteristics are those in which a product or service
is produced and exchanged in a market such that organizations are rewarded
for effective and efficient control of their production systems (Scott and
Meyer, 1991, p. 123). '*Institutional* characteristics are the elaboration of
rules and requirements to which individual organisations must conform if
they are to receive support and legitimacy' (Scott and Meyer, 1991, p. 123).
Museums have become more accessible to a broader range of classes, and
the sovereignty of the consumer and trends in popular taste are colluding to
transform the role of the museum (Chong, 2000), forcing them to rethink
the presentation and interpretation of displays and package their corporate
identity. This affects museums in two ways. Firstly, they must view 'visitors
as knowledgable consumers of attraction experiences with opinions and

expectations' (Graham and Lennon, 2002, p. 218) and creatively interpret their exhibitions to meet changing visitor demands. Secondly, they will have to re-evaluate their dominant field belief systems and related practices in order to deal with new efficiency and effectiveness challenges that arise from the first outcome. Technology and the internet are providing museums with a rich opportunity for dealing with some of these issues. Larger museums are expanding and developing their electronic access in order to provide greater opportunities for people to access their products and services. In another example, multimedia is being used to redevelop displays in order to enhance presentations, which will provide more variety in interpretation, deeper layers of information, and increased opportunities for visitor interaction and participation in the museum experience. Simultaneously, museums are pressured to review their training, management and organization of volunteers in front-of-house and guiding activities, to meet these new challenges. But, autonomous volunteer groups are often left to cope with these challenges with little management assistance or guidance.

The characteristics discussed here are not independent; they are complex and interrelated and at times difficult to disentangle from each other. Greenwood *et al.* (2002) caution that field boundaries are constantly under review and subject to redefinition of interpretation and emphasis that may be temporarily resolved by socially negotiated consensus.

According to Greenwood and Hinings (1996), fields will vary in their insulation from other fields, and how open or closed they are to ideas from other fields will depend on their level of coupling. Coupling refers to the adoption of clearly endorsed organizational templates (ways of organizing) and the transmission of those templates to organizations within the field by highly articulated agents, such as the state, professional associations, regulatory agencies and leading organizations (Greenwood and Hinings, 1996). Tight coupling limits the amount of influence that other fields may have while loose coupling permits greater influence. The mechanisms in the museum field (federal government, state government, professional associations, regulatory agencies and leading organizations) act to communicate a consistent set of expectations and to monitor compliance of field members. When taken with other field characteristics, the outcome is strong mimetic, normative and coercive processes (Greenwood and Hinings, 1996) that influence organizational conformity within the museum field. Thus, it can be argued that the field of museums and art museums is tightly coupled. However, museums and art museums are simultaneously flexible in that environmental changes are leading them to seek organizational solutions from other fields. For example, changing market needs have forced the museum field to be more novel in the delivery of its products and services and to look to the fields of events and hospitality for innovative ideas and new ways of doing things.

In this framework, organizational field-level analysis has been used to outline the complex environments in which volunteers at museums and art museums in Australia operate. Organizational field characteristics facilitate an understanding of the external environment by taking account of the inter-relationship between organizations within the field and the effect they may have on the internal environment of the organization. It appears that although the field of museums and art museums is well institutionalized, it is evolving in response to external environmental changes. The solutions, it seems, come from lead organizations and associations such as the Art Gallery of New South Wales, the Australian War Memorial, AMOL, ICOM and AAGGO, and the volunteers themselves.

Conclusion

Organizations do not operate in isolation, they exist in connection with other similar organizations and their exogenous environment – the organizational field. This interaction critically influences individual organizational activities. The use of fields enables a more comprehensive view of understanding the complex connections and interactions between organizations and their environments. The purpose of this chapter was to present a concept, 'the organizational field', to reveal the contextual dynamics in which museums and art museums operate and how those dynamics may affect the organization of volunteers. Field-level analysis provides a multidimensional focus to analysing this interaction – the field, the organization and the individual. Such an analysis enables actors within organizations to better understand how their environment affects their organizational structures, internal processes and managerial decision making. Although the framework provides a useful tool for analyses, it is illustrative only and more empirical work is required to extend the analyses such that more can be learnt about how volunteer management is affected by fieldwide activity.

References

Aldrich, H.E. (1999) *Organizations Evolving*. Sage Publications, London.
Anand, N. and Peterson, R.A. (2000) When market information constitutes fields: sensemaking of markets in the commercial music industry. *Organization Science* 11, 270–284.
Australia New Zealand Standard Industrial Classification (ANZSIC) (2001) Chapter 1: About the Classification: Industrial Classification. Australian Bureau of Statistics, Canberra. http://www.abs.gov.au/ausstats/ABS (accessed 10 July, 2001).
Australian Bureau of Statistics (1996) *Voluntary Work – Australia*, Australian Bureau of Statistics, Canberra.
Australian Bureau of Statistics (1997) *Service Industries: Libraries, Museums and Commercial Art Galleries*. Australian Bureau of Statistics, Canberra. http://www.abs.gov.au/ausstats (accessed 15 October, 2002).
Australian Bureau of Statistics (2000) *Culture and Recreation: Museums and Art*

Museums. Australian Bureau of Statistics, Canberra. http://www.abs.gov.au/ausstats/ABS% (accessed 15 October 2002).

Australian Bureau of Statistics (2001) *Museums* (Catalogue No. 8560.0, Vol. 2001). Australian Bureau of Statistics, Canberra.

Benson, K. (1975) The interorganizational network as a political economy. *Administrative Science Quarterly* 20, 229–249.

Boulay, C. d. (1996) What does it take to manage volunteers? *Australian Journal on Volunteering* August, 4–15.

Caldwell, L.L. and Andereck, K.L. (1994) Motives for initiating and continuing membership in a recreation-related voluntary association. *Leisure Sciences* 16, 33–44.

Chong, D. (2000) Institutional identities and national museums in the United Kingdom. *The Journal of Arts Management Law and Society* 29, 271–289.

Cordingly, S. (2000) The definition and principles of volunteering: a framework for public policy. In: Warburton, J. and Oppenheimer, M. (eds) *Volunteers and Volunteering*. The Federation Press, Sydney, pp. 73–82.

DiMaggio, P.J. and Powell, W.E. (1983) The iron cage revisited: institutional isomorphism and collective rationality in organizational fields. *American Sociological Review* 48, 147–150.

Ellis, S.J. (1997) Trends and issues in volunteerism in the U.S.A. *Australian Journal on Volunteering* 2(2), 29–33.

Farmer, S.M. and Fedor, D.B. (1999) Volunteer participation and withdrawal: a psychological contract perspective on the role of expectations and organisational support. *Non-profit Management and Leadership* 9, 349–367.

Farrell, J.M., Johnston, M.E. and Twynam, D.G. (1998) Volunteer motivation, satisfaction, and management at an elite sporting competition. *Journal of Sport Management* 12, 288–300.

Fisher, R.J. and Ackerman, D. (1998) The effects of recognition and group need on volunteerism: a social norm perspective. *Journal of Consumer Research* 25, 262–275.

Getz, D. and Frisby, W. (1988) Evaluating management effectiveness in community run festivals. *Journal of Travel Research* 26, 22–27.

Graham, M. and Lennon, J. (2002) The dilemma of operating a strategic approach to human resource management in the Scottish visitor attraction sector. *International Journal of Contemporary Hospitality* 14, 213–220.

Green, C.B. and Chalip, L. (1998) Sport volunteers: research agenda and application. *Sport Marketing Quarterly* 7(2), 14–23.

Greenwood, R. and Hinings, C.R. (1996) Understanding radical organizational change: bringing together the old and the new institutionalism. *Academy of Management Journal* 21, 1022–1054.

Greenwood, R., Suddaby, R. and Hinings, C.R. (2002) Theorizing change: the role of professional associations in the transformation of institutionalized fields. *Academy of Management Journal* 45, 58–90.

Hall, R.H. (1991) *Organizations: Structures, Processes and Outcomes*, 5th edn. Prentice Hall, Englewood Cliffs, New Jersey.

Hannan, M.T. and Freeman, J. (1989) *Organizational Ecology*. Harvard University Press, Cambridge, Massachusetts.

Hinings, C.R. and Greenwood, R. (1988). *The Dynamics of Strategic Change*. Blackwell, Oxford.

Hinings, C.R., Greenwood, R., Reay, T. and Suddaby, R. (2003) Dynamics of change in organizational fields. In: Poole, M.S. and Van de Ven, A.H. (eds) *Handbook of Organizational Change and Innovation*. Oxford University Press, New York.

Holmes, K. (1999) Changing times: volunteering in the heritage sector 1984–1998. *Voluntary Action* 1(2), 21–35.

Lounsbury, M. (2002) Institutional transformation and status mobility: the professionalization of the field of finance. *Academy of Management Journal* 45, 255–266.

Lyons, M., Wijkstrom, P. and Clary, G. (1998) Comparative studies of volunteering: what is being studied. *Voluntary Action* 1(1), 45–54.

McDonald, C. and Mutch, A. (2000) The future of volunteering as institutionalising practice. In: Warburton, J. and Oppenheimer, M. (eds) *Volunteers and Volunteering*. The Federation Press, Sydney, pp. 125–139.

Meyer, J.W. and Scott, W.R. (eds) (1992) *Organizational Environments: Ritual and Rationality*. Sage Publications, Newbury Park, California.

National Museum of Australia (2002) *Online Action Plan*. National Museum of Australia. http://www.nma.gov.au/actionplan/onlineactionplan.pdf (accessed 8 April 2002).

Oakes, L., Townley, B. and Cooper, D. (1998) Business planning as pedagogy: language and control in a changing institutional field. *Administrative Science Quarterly* 43(2), 257–292.

Powell, W.W. and DiMaggio, P.J. (eds) (1991) *The New Institutionalism in Organizational Analysis*. The University of Chicago Press, Chicago.

Ranson, S., Hinings, B. and Greenwood, R. (1980) The structuring of organizational structures. *Administrative Science Quarterly* 25 (March), 1–17.

Rochester, C. (1999) One size does not fit all: four models of involving volunteers in small voluntary organisations. *Voluntary Action* 1(2), 7–20.

Scott, W.R. (1995) *Institutions and Organizations*. Sage Publications, Thousand Oaks, California.

Scott, W.R. (2001) *Institutions and Organizations*, 2nd edn. Sage Publications, Thousand Oaks, California.

Scott, W.R. and Meyer, J. (1991) The organisation of societal sectors: propositions and early evidence. In: Powell, W.W. and DiMaggio, P. (eds) *The New Institutionalism in Organizational Analysis*. The University of Chicago Press, Chicago, pp. 108–140.

Stebbins, R.A. (1996) Volunteering: a serious leisure perspective. *Nonprofit and Voluntary Sector Quarterly*, 25, 211–224.

Tyzack, H. (1996) Volunteering: laissez faire or managed? *Australian Journal on Volunteering* 1(1), 23–27.

Volunteering Australia (2001) *A National Agenda on Volunteering: Beyond the International Year of Volunteers*. Volunteering Australia. www.iyv2001.net (accessed 16 October 2002).

Warburton, J. and Oppenheimer, M. (2000) *Volunteers and Volunteering*. The Federation Press, Sydney.

Wharton, L. and Harper, J. (2003) *A Seed that Flourished: a Commemorative Publication*. Australian Association of Gallery Guiding Organisations, Melbourne, Victoria.

Volunteering in the Canadian Context: Identity, Civic Participation and the Politics of Participation in Serious Leisure

8

Susan M. Arai

Department of Community Health Sciences, Brock University, 500 Glenridge Avenue, St Catharines, Ontario, Canada, L2S 3A1

Introduction

Volunteering as leisure is a complex pursuit of individuals that takes place during leisure time and enables people to find personal meaning and identity, and to express through action their needs, interests, and social and political values. It is important to note that volunteering as leisure is a dynamic pursuit that brings the individual into a diverse network of networks and in direct engagement with the structures of society. As such, volunteering as leisure is affected by the changing social and political context, which at various times may emphasize acts of benevolence, community governance, political action and social change, or social control. Building from this position, the purpose of this chapter is to paint a picture of the current nature of volunteering in Canada, and to explore the ways that volunteers and the spaces for volunteering are ever changing on the Canadian landscape.

When we look back over the history of voluntary associations in Canada we can see the richness and diversity that developed. Our challenge today is to conduct research and to develop theory that reflects that richness, for the way that we define the volunteer and the sector, and the questions that we choose to ask (or not ask), have a large bearing on our understanding of their role and contribution to society. We know that in 1987, approximately 5.3 million Canadians (27% of the population) donated over 1 billion hours of time to formal volunteering activities in voluntary associations and non-profit organizations (Duchesne, 1989). In the decade that followed, there was a 40% increase in the total number of volunteers, such that in 1997 some 7.5

million, or 31.4% of the population aged 15 years and over, indicated that they volunteered for a charitable or non-profit organization (Hall *et al.*, 1998). By the year 2000, the rate of volunteer participation had decreased to the previous rate of 27% (Hall *et al.*, 2001). This 'determinants' approach, although an important starting point in understanding who volunteers, obscures some important underlying issues, including questions such as:

- Why do people volunteer?
- What larger purpose does volunteering serve in Canadian society?
- What is the current social and political context for volunteers and the voluntary sector?
- What is the future of the voluntary sector and volunteering in Canada?

While we often think of volunteering as a fairly neutral and static activity, volunteering is *socially constructed and is affected by the changing social and political context* and therefore theories and research on volunteering as leisure must continue to be dynamic. The current issues that challenge the experience of volunteering and the existence of voluntary associations in Canada will be discussed. A series of vignettes is used to highlight the impact of changes in political philosophy, demographic trends such as an ageing population and the challenges of the economy in the (post)modern world. These current issues and challenges are best understood in the context of civic participation, the historical development of the voluntary sector and notions of democracy. Thus, this chapter provides a brief overview of the history of volunteering in Canada and the role that volunteers played in the development of human services and the welfare state. From this we may learn from our rich heritage and address the current issues of globalization with an appropriate degree of complexity.

The Canadian landscape echoes themes experienced elsewhere in Western nations. This chapter highlights current economic and social policies in Canada that affect the voluntary sector and our volunteers. As in Britain and the USA, the Federal and some of the Provincial governments in Canada are attempting to solve economic problems via neo-conservative shifts in social and economic policies (e.g. deficit reduction), leading to questions about the roles played by the public, private and voluntary sectors within the social welfare system. Research indicates that these shifts emphasize the role of volunteers in direct service delivery and preparing people for the workforce; and in doing so, may be reinforcing the notion of volunteering as an act of benevolence or social control and may undermine the ability of voluntary associations to play a role in social change and democracy in Canada. This chapter concludes by reflecting on the current themes in leisure research on volunteers and raises questions to address as we – scholars, managers and supporters of volunteers – proceed into the future.

Volunteering in Canada: a Century of Proliferation, Expansion and Increasing Complexity

From pre-Confederation (1867) onward, the nature of volunteering in Canada has changed significantly. As the nature of the public-sector provision of services has increased, voluntary associations have added to their range of activities not only the delivery of human services but also community development and social action.

Pre-Confederation: volunteering as benevolence

The pre-Confederation period in Canada is characterized by the dominance of social structures such as class and religion within the voluntary sector, and a *laissez-faire* philosophy in government, which restricted its role to that of preserving law and protecting the rights of property (Guest, 1985). In 1840, municipalities were delegated responsibilities for social welfare; however, programmes and services were minimal (Splane, 1965). The provinces were generally only involved in the development of facilities for corrections and some asylums.

This period is best described as an era dominated by charities and institutions, in which large institutions were established for persons who were sick, mentally ill, developmentally disabled and punished for some crime (including poverty) (Splane, 1965; Strong, 1969; Carter, 1975; Guest, 1985). During this period the church provided a dominant collectivist element and voluntary associations arose, both religious and lay, to make provisions in the areas of health and welfare (Splane, 1965). Hospitals were established in larger communities under voluntary associations to serve the poor (Hastings and Mosley, 1966), and asylums for the insane and houses of industry for the indigent and poor developed (Splane, 1965; Strong, 1969; Guest, 1985). Volunteering was often an act of upper-class women, often leaders in their churches. The motivations of volunteers within these early associations were 'not always a simple response to the obvious needs which presented themselves; the programmes they established usually expressed a strong moral and evangelical emphasis' (Splane, 1965, p. 18). It was during this time that ideas such as benevolence – good will, an act of kindness – and charity – an act of pity, help given to the deserving poor, kindness in judging the faults of other people – prevailed. Fraternal organizations also emerged during this period, beginning with the establishment of the first Masonic Lodge in 1817 (Donnison, 1958). These organizations were collectives for men based on religious denomination or employment in a trade.

Post-Confederation to the 1950s: expansion of service volunteering and the rise of protest organizations

In the 100 years following Confederation, Canada underwent many changes as a nation, including: industrialization, the expansion of the West, the promotion of large-scale immigration and the beginning of a long trend in rural to urban migration (Splane, 1965; Guest, 1985). The Depression brought with it unemployment and poverty. The World Wars continued the processes of industrialization and urbanization, and the shift in the population to larger centres (Guest, 1985). In addition, the needs of people with physical disabilities and mental health problems were brought to the forefront as veterans returned from abroad.

As a whole, these rapid social changes led to the rise of new social problems, and to new ways of thinking about old ones. At the end of the 1800s there began a shift in ideologies. Problems such as unemployment, poverty and delinquency began to be viewed as risks associated with life in an urban–industrial society, rather than problems associated with personal inadequacy. In addition, as an outcome of industrialization, increases in affluence, social mobility and immigration, the cohesion of traditional elements in society such as the family and church began to decline (Triandis, 1995) and new collectives took root. While volunteer activity under the direction of religious organizations continued to develop, there was an expansion in the number and type of voluntary associations including:

- Voluntary health organizations, e.g. Victorian Order of Nurses (1897) originating in the National Council of Women, the Canadian National Institute for the Blind (1917), the Canadian Paraplegic Association (1945).
- Voluntary mental health organizations, e.g. Committee on Mental Health (1918) now the Canadian Mental Health Association.
- Health organizations developed by the medical profession for the purposes of fund-raising and research, e.g. beginning with the development of the Canadian Cancer Society (1938).
- Welfare associations, e.g. as part of the urban reform movement, voluntary associations arose to combat a wide variety of social ills including the establishment of parks and playgrounds and the first voluntary children's aid society (1891); churches set up departments of social service to run and coordinate their expanding social welfare and social reform activities.
- Civic organizations and service clubs (1920s) to fulfil the dual role of social club and service to community, e.g. Rotary, Lions Club, Kiwanis (Donnison, 1958; Govan, 1966; Guest, 1985).

As a result of the needs that developed, and in response to lobbying and advocacy on behalf of various groups (and sometimes in spite of it), government has shifted from a *laissez-faire* approach toward an institutional response. During this period, many of the services performed by voluntary associations have been taken over by the public sector (e.g. Childre.. public health, town planning and utilities, education, health care and libra. ies) (Splane, 1965; Hastings and Mosley, 1966; Guest, 1985).

Associated with rural–urban migration and industrialization, and as an outcome of the First World War, this period also gave rise to voluntary associations whose primary function was to serve the interests of its members, including: fraternal organizations, farmer's groups (e.g. Cooperative Commonwealth Federation (CCF), which later became the foundation of the New Democratic Party in Canada), organized labour, and women's organizations (e.g. Women's Institutes) whose principal aims were in the lobbying and advocacy of government or the private sector (Guest, 1985; Carbert, 1995). The focus of these social movements was often on the fact that the sacrifices and ill effects of society were, in reality, falling on some segments of society while others reaped huge profit and advantage.

1960s to the late 1970s: volunteering as political action and social change

The period of the 1960s to early 1970s represents a period of expansion of the welfare state in Canada as government services arose to fill gaps and extend inherited approaches (Heclo, 1981; Guest, 1985). During this period voluntary health and welfare associations continued to spread and flourish and the concepts of democratic involvement and citizen participation became dominant (Hastings and Mosley, 1966; Guest, 1985) as volunteers engaged in political and social action in various social movements around disability, mental health and other human services. This period represents the proliferation of political activity and social action to acquire a wider array of social rights for marginalized groups. As a result, there was increased activity in the area of welfare rights, consumer rights and tenant associations (Govan, 1966; Guest, 1985). As Strong stated in 1969:

> (the) new ideals of public welfare involve concepts of protection, preservation, and the development through preventative methods and to an increasing degree, the intelligence, social consciousness, and standards of democracy of a community are being judged by the extent to which it has recognized these principles in providing for those members who belong to disadvantaged groups and accordingly have little influence themselves on the operations of government.
>
> (Strong, 1969, p. 105)

1980s and beyond: the downturn in support for volunteering

By the end of the 1970s, Canada had a complex array of voluntary associations at local, provincial and national levels with roles and functions in a variety of areas (e.g. recreation, health, welfare, religion, culture). With the historical emergence of voluntary associations came an expansion in the spaces for, and nature of, the participation of volunteers. However, at the end of the 1970s, cutbacks to the universal system of family allowances indicated that the expansion period was at an end (Guest, 1985). During this period, government involvement in social programmes began to be seriously questioned. In Canada, from the 1980s to the current day there has been a decline in the political consensus that was present in the previous stages (Guest, 1985). Beginning in the 1980s, there was a crisis of faith in the welfare state and the notion arises that the welfare state has 'accelerated dramatically, resulting in what is variously termed as "bloated", "excessive", or "runaway" public sector' (Heclo, 1981, p. 399). Government action in previous stages was based on the assumption of continuous economic growth. However, when economic surplus was no longer assured, critics turned on the democratic state, citing it as a primary drain on the forces of economic progress, and therefore the quality of society (Heclo, 1981). Consequently, many advocated the return to the residual tradition of restricting government help only to those in greatest need (Guest, 1985). As a result, voluntary associations are now being described as able to meet the continuing needs of individuals and communities. However, the emphasis that society has come to place on individual rights and competition, and the decreased involvement of government in the provision of public services and in supporting the voluntary sector, calls into question the potential of voluntary associations to promote citizenship, democracy and community, and to deliver enabling services to those in need of aid (Billis and Harris, 1992; Nowland-Foreman, 1998; Arai, 1999, 2000).

Volunteering in Canada: a Current View

At the present time, volunteering in Canada reflects an array of activities from the delivery of direct services (e.g. food banks, childcare, day programmes for older adults), self-help initiatives, community planning activities and social action (e.g. healthcare policy reform, environmental protest). Spaces for these activities to occur are provided by voluntary associations that reflect the diversity that arose during the history of the sector described in the previous section. On a national level, significant developments have been made over the past decades toward a comprehensive look at the contributions of Canadians to volunteering. In 1987, the Voluntary Activity Survey (VAS) was conducted (Duchesne, 1989). In 1997 and 2000 the National Survey of Giving, Volunteering and Participating (NSGVP) was conducted in Canada with plans to administer the survey again in 2003. The NSGVP results from a partnership between federal government and voluntary-sector organizations including: the Canadian Centre for Philanthropy, Canadian Heritage, Health Canada, Human Resources Development Canada, Statistics Canada and Volunteer Canada (Hall *et al.*, 2001). The information provided by this research is supplemented by a number of qualitative and quantitative studies that provide depth and insight into the experiences of voluntary associations and their volunteers (cf. Carbert, 1995; Arai, 1999, 2000; Plummer, 2002).

Between 1997 and 2000 there was little change in the types of organizations for which Canadians volunteered in the proportion of either events or hours (Hall *et al.*, 2001). Continuing earlier trends, in 2000 the greatest percentage of participation took place in arts, culture and recreation (including sports) organizations (23% of all volunteers), accounting for more than a quarter of the total number of volunteer hours that occurred during that same year. Volunteering in social service organizations comprised 20% of all volunteer events and involved 20% of the total volunteer hours. Together, religious organizations (14% of events and 16% of hours), education and research organizations (13% of events and 11% of hours), and health organizations (13% of events and 9% of hours) accounted for less than half of the total number of events and hours. Other types of organization (e.g. environmental, housing, law, advocacy and political, international and business, and professional organizations) accounted for the remaining 17% of both volunteer events and volunteer hours (Hall *et al.*, 2001).

Within these organizations, volunteers fill a number of roles and are engaged in an array of activities. The NSGVP asked Canadians about their participation in 15 general types of volunteer activities. The top three activities that volunteers are involved in continue to be: organizing and supervising events (57% in 2000); sitting as a Board member (41% in 2000); and canvassing, campaigning and fund-raising (40% in 2000). Other activities of volunteers include: office work, providing information, teaching/coaching, providing care or support, collecting/serving/delivering food, and driving. Each of these activities is engaged in by 20–30% of volunteers. Maintenance/repair activities are engaged in by less than 20% of volunteers. Comparisons of the results from 1997 to 2000 indicate that the types of activities undertaken by volunteers appear to be changing. Compared with 1997, results from the NSGVP 2000 indicate the largest increase has been in the percentage of volunteers who organized or supervised events. In contrast, there has been a decline in the percentage that took part in canvassing, campaigning or fund-raising (44% in 1997 to 40% in 2000) (Hall *et al.*, 2001).

People's motivations for volunteering are complex and diverse; however, the NSGVP provides some insight into people's reasons. The top three reasons that volunteers indicated are: believing in the cause of the organization (95%), putting their skills and experience to use (81%) and because they had been personally affected by the cause the organization supports (69%). In addition, 57% of all volunteers saw it as an opportunity to explore their strengths, while 23% volunteered because they wanted to improve their job opportunities. Compared with results from 1997, there has been little change in the percentage of volunteers reporting these reasons for volunteering. The desire to fulfil religious obligations or beliefs by performing volunteer activities declined from 29% to 26%, while volunteering because one's friends volunteered showed the largest increase, from 25% to 30%.

Other research on volunteers focuses on the motivations of volunteers, or why people choose to volunteer (Henderson, 1981; Caldwell and Andereck, 1994; Silverberg *et al.*, 2003), and the benefits experienced by volunteers (Stebbins, 1992, 1996; Arai and Pedlar, 1997). In addition, the meaning and centrality of volunteering as a leisure experience is also examined in the context of the whole individual and in the context of community. For example, Stebbins (1992, 1996) discusses the differences between casual and serious leisure; Cuskelly and Harrington (1997) discuss the differences among volunteers on the work–leisure continuum; Thompson (1997) questions whether employment-based volunteering can be considered leisure; Wearing and Neil (2000) write on the creation of self and identity through volunteering; and Arai (2000) looks at the contributions of volunteering to civil society and democracy. These studies raise the question of what sorts of contexts are required for individuals to experience serious leisure, to create identity, and for civil society and democracy to flourish. However, if we keep looking inside the system at the individuals we miss seeing the path that the voluntary sector as a whole is being led down. There is the need to look up at policy decisions and the nature of voluntary associations to see the political nature of volunteering and its role in civil society. In the following section, our attention turns toward four case studies that highlight the spaces in which volunteering occurs, and some of the challenges to the experience of volunteering as leisure.

Changing spaces for volunteering at the local level: vignettes of four voluntary associations

Local-level voluntary associations provide important spaces for voluntary activity. The following vignettes provide an insight into the diversity of spaces where volunteers donate their time. They also shed light on the various purposes or functions of these organizations and the ways in which they are structured, and highlight the current issues and challenges that volunteers grapple with as they attempt to function within the changing social and political climate. Vignette 1 – the cultural centre (CC) – represents a mid- to large-size cultural centre in Canada (see Box 8.1). This vignette has been developed as an amalgam of several cultural centres across a number of diverse ethnic groups. The CC today provides a social space and support for members sharing a similar culture or country of origin. One of its continuing functions is the maintenance of language and cultural traditions for members, the development of an ethnic identity and community. The vignette also highlights the contributions that the CC makes to the broader community, and the challenges that are unique to organizations of this type, including the loss of volunteer support among successive generations.

Box 8.1. Vignette 1: the cultural centre (CC).

In most communities in Canada, cultural centres (CC) have been developed by members of the community sharing an ethnic background. While these organizations are often diverse in their structure, level of bureaucracy and specific set of programmes and services, those that are larger share some common characteristics. Many cultural organizations have developed in larger communities over the last 50–100 years, their history of development varying with waves of immigration from their country of origin. For many of the cultural organizations, immigration was predominant in the 1950s through to the 1970s and these organizations formed to support the settlement of new members, to provide a social space and support for members of the cultural group, and to share the culture and traditions of the group with the broader community. In general, these organizations provide social and leisure opportunities for the members of the organization, such as: creating business connections and networks for its members; and direct services to members of the organization including youth groups, sport and recreational opportunities (e.g. dance classes), and language classes. Cultural organizations also play a significant role in the broader community, including: education about the language and culture of the country of origin; participation in multicultural events and open houses; and in the case of the larger cultural organizations, the operation of halls and restaurants for community use; and fund-raising and donations to other community organizations (e.g. hospital, United Way). These organizations generally operate with few, if any, paid staff and the majority of the roles and tasks are taken on by volunteers. Volunteers in cultural organizations sit on boards and committees, cook for cultural events and festivals, conduct building maintenance and repair, supervise and instruct in cultural programmes and perform a myriad of other tasks. At the present time a number of challenges and concerns are described by the volunteers within the organization and highlight significant challenges around the longevity of the organization, including:

- The reliance of the organization on a core group of volunteers (often first- or second-generation Canadians) who are active members on boards and committees, and provide the majority of the labour for open houses and other community events. The majority of these core and active members are ageing and are now in their 70s or 80s.
- The lack of adult volunteers to support the demands of the organization. As some of the volunteers describe, the young adults are working, raising their families and taking their children to dance classes and piano lessons, leaving them little time to volunteer. Further concerns are raised about the lack of youth involvement, including the loss of cultural traditions and language and the preference of their youth for spending time with friends.
- Financial challenges are another significant influence on the longevity

(continued)

(Box 8.1 continued)

of the organization, specifically the lack of government dollars available to assist with the ongoing maintenance and improvement and property taxes. To cope with this challenge many organizations have turned to a business approach, which includes renting out their halls to the broader community and operating restaurants or catering businesses to ensure revenue.

Source: S.M. Arai, Department of Community Health Sciences, Brock University, St Catherines, Ontario, Canada, unpublished data.

Vignette 2 – the Social Planning Organization of Newtonville (SPON) – highlights a voluntary association that focuses on community planning, information, research on human services and increasing the participation of citizens in these decisions (see Box 8.2). This vignette highlights the impact of Provincial and Federal policy decisions about income and welfare at the local level and on the experience of the volunteers.

Box 8.2.   Vignette 2: Social Planning Organization of Newtonville (SPON). The Social Planning Organization of Newtonville (SPON) serves a large northern community. SPON has been in existence for several decades and, in keeping with the nature of a social planning organization, its mission emphasizes a response to current social issues and improvements in the delivery of human services in a way that values the inherent worth and dignity of all individuals, the strength of individuals, organizations and community, citizen participation, collaborative partnerships, equal opportunity and diversity. The goals of the organization are to promote social and economic justice, to bring people together to develop programmes and services for the community, link individuals and organizations through information, and to conduct research into social issues. Some of the recent initiatives of SPON include: providing community information and referral services for the community, coordinating and developing networks in multicultural services, conducting research and policy analysis, public education, creating networks and advocating on issues of poverty. SPON is involved in many joint committees, partnerships, task forces with other planning bodies (e.g. local government, district health council, other social planning organizations) and local organizations (e.g. churches, the library, universities and colleges, local business, and the municipal parks and recreation department).

Like many social planning organizations, SPON is committed to the facilitation of citizen participation in the development and critique of social policy and improvements in human service delivery, and in decentralizing

(continued)

(*Box 8.2 continued*)

decision making so that local communities have a voice in the issues that affect them. SPON is a non-profit organization with charitable status. The Board is comprised of individual community members (volunteers) and works on a consensus model of decision making around policy, management and the operations of the organization; the organization is fuelled by four staff members (full- and part-time), and a large pool of volunteers involved in the programmes and projects of the organization, administration within the organization and fund-raising. Recent challenges and concerns of the organization include:

- The loss of funding received from municipal and provincial governments, leading to the loss of paid staff and increased demand for local dollars from the United Way, has placed a financial strain on the organization. There is a lack of funds for initiatives to keep up with community needs and demands.
- There is increased demand for SPON to assist the community in addressing increases in community need as government funding for the public provision of human services (e.g. health and welfare) has been decreased and geographic isolation limits people's access to core services (e.g. health care).
- Decreases in funding led to the increased need for SPON's volunteers to be involved in fund-raising. While this led to an increase in the number of individuals in contact with the organization as volunteers, there has been a shift in the nature of the volunteer's role in the organization, with many being asked to fund-raise for the organization. For many long-term volunteers involved in the policy and planning of the organization this has been a source of frustration.
- Overall there is a lack of available and committed volunteers, or loss of volunteers through moves, burnout and personal circumstances.
- Changes in government reporting and project administration requires more staff time spent on administration, which in turn decreases time that can be spent on the programmes, services and initiatives of the organization.
- Many volunteers expressed concerns about the shift toward a business model and the emphasis on fund-raising, efficiency and outcomes rather than the core concerns of their mission statement.

Source: Arai (1999).

Vignette 3 – the Valleytown Minor Softball League (VTMSL) – has been chosen as it reflects an aspect of sport at the community level that is often overlooked (see Box 8.3). Like many voluntary associations it operates without paid staff, and a particularly unique feature is that it operates in partnership with the local Legion to provide opportunities for children to play softball.

Box 8.3. Vignette 3: Valley Town Minor Softball League (VTMSL).

Valley Town Minor Softball League (VTMSL) is a volunteer-driven, summer softball league for children aged 5–15. All games are held at the same three diamonds in the Valley Town neighbourhood. This past summer there were approximately 225 children registered in the league and organized into three age divisions: Squirts (ages 5–7), Juniors (ages 8–11) and Bantam (ages 12–15). The league has been operating in this community in southern Ontario for over 50 years. A unique feature of this league is the involvement of the Valley Town Legion. The league was developed as a community service arm of the Valley Town Legion, which has 'positively serving youth' as part of its organizational mandate. The league operates under the mission of 'promoting fun and fair play for all'. Parents describe the league as a 'house league' with an emphasis on learning and fun rather than competition. A significant number of families have been involved in the league for between 5 and 10 years. Because all games are held at the same diamonds, spectators and players tend to see each other frequently and develop a familiarity with one another.

The VTMSL is organized and operated solely by volunteers, including a small Executive Committee of five (Head Commissioner, Assistant Commissioner, Umpire-in-Chief, Secretary, Treasurer). Presently, the Executive oversees league promotion, registration and finances, scheduling, assigning players and coaches, and the maintenance of equipment/supplies. Each of the softball teams are organized by volunteer coaches, who are often the parents of players. The coaches plan practices (the equipment is provided by the league), act as a liaison between the Executive and parents, and provide on-field supervision and instruction. Presently, the need for new coaches is high. As a result, while some coaches are highly skilled and committed, others have less baseball experience and/or are less committed to the team and the league. In addition to registration income and fund-raising, the league recruits one sponsor for each team, who, in exchange for $300, has a team named after them and their name silk screen printed on to the team jersey. The Valley Town Legion also supplies nominal financial support to the league (approximately $500 and free building rental). Recent challenges and concerns of the organization include:

- The number of registered players has dropped significantly from past years, raising a concern about the detrimental effect of low participation rates on the experience. In past seasons over 500 children were registered, and approximately 400 children are required for the league to thrive. Low numbers in the Squirts girls division, for example, meant that the division had only two teams in it. Further decreases in enrolment may develop as parents have indicated that they may register their children in other leagues or sports that are thriving.
- The VTMSL is a small league run by volunteers with extremely limited funds available for marketing and promotions. The volunteers themselves have little business-related training, and, further, their time is

(continued)

> (*Box 8.3 continued*)
>
> constrained by their paying jobs and families. Opportunities for fund-raising have been limited by external constraints. In past years, the league raised some funds for the league through food sales from bar-becues held at the fields, one Saturday a month. However, due to a recent tightening of the city regulations surrounding operating propane and uncooked food, this fund-raiser no longer occurs. As a result, the league has only engaged in limited fund-raising efforts with minimal success.
>
> • There are a number of organizational efficiency issues that have arisen over the last summer including the late arrival of team jerseys and errors detected in book-keeping records. Many of the participants overlook some of these inefficiencies due to the voluntary nature of the people helping to support the league (coaches and organizers); however, some of these issues affect the longer-term viability of the league.
>
> Source: E.K. Sharpe, Department of Recreation and Leisure Studies, Brock University, St Catherines, Ontario, Canada, unpublished data.

Vignette 4 – Friends of the Canes Watershed (FCW) – represents a newer initiative in the area of environmental planning and management, which formed as a result of budget cuts in the Province of Ontario and the decentralization of decision making with respect to natural resources (see Box 8.4). In this initiative, outdoor enthusiasts, government stakeholders, local landowners and concerned citizens have come together to form an initiative around the Canes Watershed.

Collectively, these vignettes highlight a number of the common issues encountered by voluntary associations in Canada, including:

• The benefits of volunteer-driven organizations and community governance not only to the individual volunteer but also to the development of community. The horizontal and consensus-based nature of decision making that is essential for the establishment of trust within these voluntary associations is often at tensions with a 'business mindset' that emphasizes outcomes and effectiveness in the battle for scarce resources (all vignettes).

• The changing nature of the roles of volunteers created by forces external to the organization (vignette 2-SPON, vignette 4-FCW).

• The lack of volunteers and issues of commitment that threaten the long-term viability of the organization (all vignettes).

• That fund-raising (the act of) cannot be looked at in isolation for: (i) it impacts on the experience of volunteering as leisure (vignette 2-SPON), (ii) it is impacted by the availability of volunteers (vignette 2-SPON), (iii) it changes the activities of the organization (vignette 1-CC), and (iv) the ability of the organization to fund-raise is affected by broader changes and constraints (e.g. city regulations) (vignette 3-VTMSL).

Box 8.4.   Vignette 4: Friends of the Canes Watershed (FCW).
In the mid-1990s, changes in government policy in the Province of Ontario led to acute budgetary reductions and the decentralization of decision making among the government agencies responsible for natural resources. Consequently, an initiative was struck by a number of parties interested in the Canes Watershed in southern Ontario. Initial meetings brought together parties interested in the environmental integrity of the Canes Watershed including: government representatives of resource agencies, local politicians, outdoor recreation participants, landowners and concerned citizens. This diverse group of affiliated government staff and outdoor enthusiasts – including canoers, hikers, mountain bikers and horse riders – created an interesting menagerie.

As a result of initial meetings a group formed and became known as the Friends of the Canes Watershed (FCW) and an innovative management strategy was adopted. Although it comprised diverse interests, the agencies and actors agreed upon a shared mission statement. Effort was directed toward maintaining and enhancing the natural features of the Canes Watershed. Developing and maintaining an inventory of natural features, advocating responsible stewardship and investigating opportunities for resource protection became an initial goal. The organization compiled and distributed information pertaining to natural features of the watershed, hosted community awareness events and formalized a watershed planning process.

The FCW is an example of co-management in a process involving representatives of the public sector as well as the private interests of landowners and outdoor enthusiasts. As an informal network this organization brings together the specific interests of agent and actor and provides a forum to address common interests about the natural environment, facilitating the sharing of information, which leads to collective action. To avoid the perception of being a closed or restricted group, the organization maintains an informal atmosphere. This is of particular importance to maintaining an invitational stance for both the private and the public domains, ensuring that they feel comfortable in each other's company during organizational debates and functions. Organizational responsibilities and duties are shared equally among the participants. Although FCW does not boast financial resources, members volunteer and make various contributions. An excellent example is the compilation of information regarding natural features of the area. A partnership of representatives of government resource agencies found sufficient funds to hire a university student to engage in research; the members of FCW collectively shared information; an agency bound the documents; and citizens volunteered to deliver them to the community. Challenges and issues confront the FCW, though they have effectively undertaken initiatives toward their goal. The following comprises the areas needing attention:

• Learning how to work together in an atmosphere of trust. Working collectively was a notable challenge to representative government re-

(continued)

> (*Box 8.4 continued*)
>
> source agencies, who felt solely responsible for the management of natural resources.
>
> - The shared nature of resources represents a challenge to the organization. The perspective of resources as public property may restrict private interests and access, thus limiting opportunities. Landowners offer a paramount challenge as their interests are specific to themselves.
>
> - Changes in environmental governance result in an increase in expectations toward the FCW to manage natural resources. Absence of any formal legal standing, reliance on the goodwill of volunteers and the minimal availability of resources by government agencies pose significant threats to the organization and, ultimately, environmental integrity.
>
> Source: R. Plummer, Department of Recreation and Leisure Studies, Brock University, St Catherines, Ontario, Canada, unpublished data.

To a certain degree, each vignette reflects the changes associated with the downloading of government responsibility coupled with a lack of resources, support and authority of the voluntary association. At the current time, this is most prevalent in vignette 4-FCW and vignette 2-SPON. The relationship between the voluntary sector and local, Provincial and National governments is complex. However, there is general agreement, and as the vignettes reflect, that the health of the voluntary sector relies on support from and a relationship with government. While the foundation for volunteering and citizenship lies in the voluntary exercise of civil and political rights, the rights of citizenship also invoke duties in others, including government (Brown, 1996; Torjman, 1997). The vignettes reflect a return to themes that existed pre-Confederation and during the early 1900s with an emphasis on the service nature of volunteering, benevolence and the *laissez-faire* notions of government. What this does is pose a challenge to the environment, culture, health and sport in Canadian society, which raises larger questions about the future of the things which Canadians value: multiculturalism, the environment, universal health care, and the health and well-being of our children; in other words, the 'public goods' upon which society rests. Further, as reflected in the vignettes, the following section of this chapter also reveals that the voluntary sector increasingly relies upon a decreasing pool of volunteers.

National data on volunteering in Canada

Who volunteers? In an attempt to respond to this question, there has been much support for structural theories, most prominently in the literature on the 'determinants of volunteering'. For example, in her study of volunteers across Canada, Duchesne (1989) found that volunteer participation is higher for women than men; it rises with education and income, and increases up to age 44 and then declines with advancing age. This reflects a determinants of volunteering approach in which sociodemographic variables (e.g. age, gender, income) are correlated with voluntary affiliation (cf. Duchesne, 1989; Smith, 1994; Day and Devlin, 1996). As Bell and Force state, it is as 'if one knew a person's economic, family and ethnic status, age and sex . . . one should be able to predict closely that person's participation in the various activities of society' (in McPherson and Rotolo, 1996, p. 179).

Building on a determinants of volunteering approach, an examination of the national data enables us to paint a picture of the following: the overall number or *how many* people volunteer, demographic shifts in *who* volunteers their time and the *intensity* or number of hours that they contribute. The results from the national data indicate that there are variations from Duchesne's original observations about the predictability of volunteering at the end of the 1980s.

How many volunteer . . . and how much?
Since 1987 there have been significant fluctuations in the number of Canadians who contribute their time as volunteers. As indicated in Table 8.1, in 1997, 7.5 million Canadians over the age of 15 (31.4% of the population) donated their time to charitable and non-profit organizations (Hall *et al.*, 2001). Since 1987, there had been a 40% increase in the time Canadians formally donated to voluntary associations (5.3 million Canadians or 27% of the population over the age of 15 volunteered in 1987). From 1997 to the year 2000, there was an overall decline in volunteers, with the proportion of volunteers returning to the 27% (6.5 million Canadians) found in 1987. This occurred despite the increase in the population of Canada by 2.5% (see Table 8.1).

Despite the decline in the numbers of Canadians volunteering, between 1997 and 2000 we observe an increase in the intensity of volunteering among those who do volunteer. In 1997, the 7.5 million Canadians who volunteered donated 1.1 billion hours of their time to charitable and non-profit organizations (Hall *et al.*, 2001). In 2000, with fewer Canadians volunteer-

Table 8.1. Rates of volunteering among Canadians aged 15 and older, 1987, 1997 and 2000 (from Hall *et al.*, 2001, p. 34).

	2000 NSGVP	1997 NSGVP	1987 VAS
Total population	24,383,000	23,808,000	19,202,000
Total volunteers	6,513,000	7,472,000	5,337,000
Volunteer participation rate (%)	26.7	31.4	26.8

ing, the total number of hours volunteered declined by an estimated 5% to 1.05 billion hours (Hall *et al.*, 2001). Almost half (42%) of these hours were supplied by 11% of Canadians (Hall and Febbraro as cited in Hall *et al.*, 2001), suggesting variations among volunteers in their level of contribution. In 2000, the top quarter of volunteers, for example, contributed an average of 471 hours of their time throughout the year and accounted for 73% of the overall total hours. This is similar to 1997, when the top quarter of volunteers accounted for 72% of the overall total hours, but contributed, on average, 431 hours of their time. It is also worth noting that in absolute numbers there are fewer volunteers in the top quarter than there were in 1997 – approximately 1.6 million in 2000 versus about 1.9 million in 1997 (Hall *et al.*, 2001).

On average, each individual volunteer in 2000 contributed 162 hours over the year, which is an increase from the 149 hours contributed during 1997. The greatest increases were found among those who were widowed (67 more hours per year, on average), those who were 65 years and older (67 more hours), those with household incomes under $20,000 (59 more hours) and those who were unemployed (54 more hours) (Hall *et al.*, 2001). In addition, the differences between men and women may be decreasing. These results are considered more closely in the following sections.

Who volunteers?

Overall there has been a decline in the proportion of Canadians who volunteer across all characteristics (e.g. age, gender, income level, etc.). However, the results indicated in Table 8.2 reveal which segments of the population make higher contributions of volunteer time.

AGE   In general, the average number of hours that people volunteer increases with age. As indicated in Table 8.2, from 1997 to 2000 the volunteer rate declined across all age groups. However, among the people in each age group who volunteer there have been marginal to significant increases in the average number of hours that they contribute (except among individuals aged 25–34). In 2000, the highest levels of volunteering rates are found among individuals in their mid-adult years. However, this age group also shows the highest rate of decline since 1997 (declining 7%) with small increases in the average number of hours that these individuals volunteer (11 hours among those aged 35–44; 1 hour among those aged 45–54). The age group indicating the second largest proportion of volunteers is the youth group (29% aged 15–24, a decrease of 4% since 1997). Among this group there has been a marginal increase in the number of hours that people volunteer (5% increase since 1997). Individuals aged 55–64 have maintained a fairly steady rate of volunteering, showing a decline of only 2% between 1997 and 2000, and an increase of 21 hours in the average hours volunteered. However, the greatest contribution in volunteer hours (and the greatest increase since 1997) is found among individuals 65 years and older (269

Table 8.2. Percentage volunteering and average hours volunteered during the year, Canadians aged 15 and older, 1997 and 2000 (from Hall *et al.*, 2001, p. 34).

Characteristic	2000 (%)	1997 (%)	2000 (average hours)	1997 (average hours)
Age				
15–24	29	33	130	125
25–34	24	28	131	133
35–44	30	37	153	142
45–54	30	35	158	157
55–64	28	30	181	160
65 and older	18	23	269	202
Sex				
Male	25	29	170	160
Female	28	33	155	140
Marital status				
Married or common-law	28	33	165	151
Single, never married	26	31	136	133
Separated, divorced	25	29	181	157
Widowed	17	20	253	186
Education				
Less than high school	19	21	154	126
High school diploma	23	29	150	159
Some post-secondary	33	36	173	153
Post-secondary certificate or diploma	28	34	165	149
University degree	39	48	166	159
Labour force status				
Employed	28	34	147	138
Full-time	27	32	145	138
Part-time	33	44	155	139
Unemployed	25	29	175	121
Not in the labour force	24	27	193	176
Household income				
Less than $20,000	17	22	207	148
$20,000–39,999	21	29	179	163
$40,000–59,999	26	33	162	150
$60,000–79,999	31	36	156	144
$80,000–99,999	35	42	127	128
$100,000 or more	39	45	150	143

average hours volunteered in 2000) (see Table 8.2). Among this age group there has been an increase of 67 hours in the average number of hours volunteered; however, there has also been a 5% decrease in the number of individuals in this age range who volunteer. Individuals between the ages of 25 and 34 show a decline in both the proportion of individuals who volunteer (decrease of 4% since 1997) and the average number of hours that individuals in this age group volunteer (decline of 2 hours since 1997).

SEX   As shown in Table 8.2, participation rates among men and women have decreased since 1997, and gender differences in the overall rates continue to persist. In 2000, 28% of women and 25% of men volunteered. However, during that same time period there has been a decrease in the differences between men and women in the average number of hours that they contribute. In 1997 men and women differed by an average of 20 hours (140 hours for women, 160 hours for men) but by 2000 this gap had narrowed to a difference of 15 hours (155 hours for women, 170 hours for men) (see Table 8.2).

MARITAL STATUS   When considering people based on marital status there has been a decrease in the proportion of people who volunteer, and an increase in the average number of hours volunteered, across all groups. The highest participation rates continue to be found among individuals who are married (28% in 2000), and the lowest among individuals who are widowed (17% in 2000). However, as Table 8.2 depicts, widows account for the largest increase in the average number of hours volunteered (increase of 67 hours since 1997).

EDUCATION   In general, the pattern continues that volunteering increases with education (see Table 8.2). However, there may be a trend towards a narrowing of the gap. Individuals possessing a university degree are more likely to volunteer (39% in 2000, 48% in 1997), while a lower proportion of individuals whose maximum educational attainment does not consist of a high school diploma volunteer (19% in 2000, 21% in 1997). In 1997 there was a range of 27% in the participation rates across volunteers according to educational attainment, by 2000 this gap had narrowed to 20%. As shown in Table 8.2, a similar pattern was found in the average number of hours that individuals volunteer (a 33-hour range in 1997, 23-hour range in 2000).

LABOUR FORCE STATUS   Overall, higher rates of volunteering are found among individuals who are employed (28% in 2000). As shown in Table 8.2, a greater proportion of individuals who are employed part-time volunteer (33% in 2000). However, this group also shows the greatest decline in participation rates since 1997 (an 11% decrease) and the smallest increase in the average number of volunteer hours. The lowest rates of volunteering are found among individuals who are either not in the labour force (24% in 2000) or unemployed (25% in 2000). However, between 1997 and 2000, individuals in these groups show the greatest increases in the average number of volunteer hours and the smallest decrease in the proportion of people who volunteered (see Table 8.2). Individuals who are unemployed showed an increase of 54 hours since 1997, and those who are not in the labour force show an increase of 17 hours.

For many who volunteer, perceptions are that volunteer activities provide vital linkages to the job market, including: finding work, development of employment skills and increased chance of success in the workplace. According to Hall *et al.* (2001), more than one in every five volunteers (23%) agreed that improving job opportunities was a reason for volunteering, with younger volunteers aged 15–24 being even more likely (55%) to indicate this as a reason. This belief is held even more highly among those who are unemployed or looking for work. Close to two-thirds of unemployed volunteers (62%) held this belief in 2000 compared with 54% in 1997. More than three out of four youths looking for work (78%) thought volunteering would help them get a job. Nevertheless, unemployed youth volunteers devoted a relatively low number of hours to volunteering (132 hours per year, on average).

HOUSEHOLD INCOME   In general, the pattern continues that volunteer participation rates increase as the level of income increases (see Table 8.2). In 2000, 17% of individuals earning less than $20,000 volunteered, compared to 39% of individuals earning $100,000 or more. With the exception of individuals in the $80,000–99,999 group, there has also been an increase in the average number of hours volunteered across all groups. However, the highest increase in the number of hours contributed has been among individuals earning less than $20,000, showing an increase of 59 hours since 1997 (from 148 to 207 hours) and individuals earning $20,000–39,000 show an increase of 16 hours (from 163 to 179 hours). In comparison, between 1997 and 2000 individuals in the top two income brackets show either a decrease in the average number of hours volunteered (from 128 to 127 hours for individuals earning $80,000–99,999) or a slight increase (from 143 to 150 hours for individuals earning $100,000 or more).

Where are Current Forces Pushing Us?

We must look beyond a determinants approach if we are to understand volunteering and the nature of this form of leisure in Canada. Overall, the number of volunteers in Canada has decreased by 4%. One must question whether that decrease is due to a demographic shift (i.e. in the determinants of volunteering), due to a change in the spaces available for volunteers to participate, or some other external force. The vignettes highlighted some of the social and political forces in Canada that have acted to change the nature of the public spaces that are available for volunteers. As in Britain and the USA, Federal and some of the Provincial governments in Canada are attempting to solve economic problems via neo-conservative shifts in social and economic policies (e.g. deficit reduction), leading to questions about the roles played by the public, private and voluntary sectors within the social welfare system. While several authors connect volunteering to citizen participation and the outcomes of democracy (cf. Putnam, 1993a,b, 1995; Arai, 1999,

2000; Reed and Selbee, 2000), research indicates that these shifts may be reinforcing the notion of volunteering as an act of benevolence or social control and may undermine the ability of voluntary associations to play a role in social change and democracy in Canada.

Recent policy decisions connected with the shift toward neo-conservativism promote volunteering for its ability to provide service. The other functions that have historically emerged in the voluntary sector are diminished (e.g. collective social action, the acquisition of social rights for marginalized groups). Nyland (in Nowland-Foreman, 1998) refers to this as the shift of voluntary associations away from their function as 'representatives of the community' to deliverers of service 'to the community'. This may lead to decreases in choice and in the freedom of the volunteer, thereby undermining the basic definition of the volunteer. Furthermore, the nature of volunteering as a leisure experience and its contribution to civil society is called into question by the following policy developments:

*   Mandatory volunteering under the work-for-welfare policy (Social Assistance Reform Act, Province of Ontario) and for high school completion credits in the Province of Ontario.
*   Emphasis on the utility of volunteering for skill development and preparation for the workforce.
*   Volunteering as a resource in the wake of cuts to social programmes.

As neo-conservative shifts such as this have come into force, the work of Parker (1997) and Arai (1999, 2000) are of particular interest. Parker (1997) describes volunteering as one of the three main types of relationship that exist between people in the production of goods and services; the other two being marketing (buying, selling and exchanging goods) and coercion (some of us compel action, others submit). Arai (1999, 2000) has created a typology of volunteers that emphasizes the political nature of volunteering and its contribution to civil society. Citizen, Techno and Labour Volunteers differ in their experiences of benefits and responsibilities and in the way that they view their contributions (Arai, 1999, 2000). For the Citizen Volunteer, the emphasis is on a contribution to the broader community, in developing knowledge about the community, and about the people in the community, including their perceptions and experiences. Citizen Volunteers describe the richness and importance of developing relationships and friendships with other volunteers and staff people within the voluntary association, and the importance of building and experiencing a sense of community. Techno Volunteers tend to place greater emphasis on benefits of a more rational and technical nature. They discuss their ability to make a contribution to the organization and to develop knowledge about fund-raising, and issue and computer networks that will assist with work. While they also describe the importance of relationship formation, this is often discussed in terms of the development of contacts and networking. Labour Volunteers emphasize the benefit of being able to make a resource contribution to the organization and to develop specific skills (e.g. fund-raising skills, marketing and promotional skills). Labour Volunteers are individuals that are involved in frontline service delivery, fund-raising and/or administration within the voluntary association. They demonstrate limited knowledge of the organization and/or the social issues that the organization attempts to address. For Labour Volunteers, relationships are described in terms of developing acquaintances. While presented here as ideal types, volunteers may approach their volunteering in a way that reflects one or more of these types.

Opportunities for volunteering in the array of voluntary associations in Canada (cultural organizations, minor softball leagues, local branches of Rotary International, the Red Cross, environmental organizations, community planning organizations and local aid-giving groups) provide the mesh between private interest and the public realm. In the context of service provision, volunteering is the meshing together of private interest (personal meaningfulness of the environment, an individual desire to give of oneself to others, the enjoyment of camaraderie) and our collective endorsement of a social safety net and the preservation of the environment, a belief in the social rights of citizens of our country with respect to a minimum standard of living (universality), and a healthy public sector. In other words, it is the blending of self-interest and the common good. However, Citizen, Techno and Labour Volunteers differ in their ability to contribute to the formation of social capital (Arai, 2000). Social capital is created when relations among people change in ways that facilitate action (Coleman, 1988, 1990). Thus, at the foundation of social capital is the notion of trust (Putnam, 1993a,b, 1995; Fukuyama, 1995; Newton, 1997), with different contexts giving rise to different types of trust. *Thick trust* is an essential ingredient of mechanical solidarity or *gemeinschaft* societies and occurs in small face-to-face communities generated by intensive daily contact between people. *Abstract trust* is the foundation of imaginary, empathic or reflexive communities, and its formation is linked to the connections created between individuals in national social movement organizations (Minkoff, 1997; Newton, 1997). *Thin trust* is associated with organic solidarity, *gesellschaft*, or looser forms of relationship and produces weak ties that 'constitute a powerful and enduring basis for social integration in modern, large-scale society' (Newton, 1997). Particularly important to the development of thin trust are the overlapping and interlocking networks of voluntary associations. For Citizen Volunteers – volunteers most integrally involved in the decision making and discussion of social issues – the opportunity exists to develop thick trust or abstract trust (Arai, 2000). Through the nature of their involvement (in management and operations), Techno Volunteers tend to be involved in the formation of thick trust or thin trust, and for Labour Volunteers the emphasis is on thin trust (Arai, 2000).

Vignette 2 (the SPON) indicates that neo-conservative shifts (policy shifts, decrease in funding and in-kind supports etc.) decrease the spaces for participation as a Citizen Volunteer, and there is increasing reliance on Techno and Labour Volunteers as organizations tend toward direct service delivery and focus inward on organizational survival (e.g. fund-raising) (Arai, 1999, 2000). As vignette 4 (the FCW) highlights, decentralization in decision making to the local organizations can increase spaces for Citizen Volunteers but an appropriate level of resources and authority is required by the organization. When care is not taken to preserve spaces for the Citizen Volunteer there may be decreases in the nature of participatory democracy (who can participate, and where and how they may participate) and in the emergence of social capital. Further, as spaces for participation narrow, and the freely chosen nature of volunteering is diminished by mandatory approaches, participation in the voluntary sector may in fact be shifting from Parker's (1997) description of 'volunteering' to that of 'coercion' for individuals on social assistance, and 'marketing' – or the buying or acquisition of experience and course credits, and the selling of labour – for high school students. In essence, we may describe this as the commodification of the volunteer.

A significant finding from the NSGVP is that volunteering activity (as well as donating and civic involvement) is extremely unevenly distributed. According to Dreessen (2000), it is possible to define a 'civic core' of volunteers, which consists of 28% of the total population aged 15 and over. This core group of citizens donates 83% of the total volunteer hours, 77% of total dollars donated and 69% of all participation in civic events (Dreessen, 2000). Furthermore, as indicated earlier in this chapter, the greatest increases in the number of volunteers were found among those who were widowed (67 more hours per year, on average), those who were 65 years and older (67 more hours), those with household incomes under $20,000 (59 more hours) and those who were unemployed (54 more hours) or not in the labour force. This raises an interesting tension between the importance of voluntary associations as spaces for creating personal meaning and identity and building community, and questions about who really bears the weight of the voluntary sector in the face of current cuts in the public sector.

The shifting role of government raises additional concern about the health of the voluntary sector. As government policies and spending shift, many organizations rely increasingly on donations and fund-raising initiatives. However, the number of volunteers who indicated that they participate in canvassing, campaigning and fund-raising has decreased by 4% between 1997 and 2000. This at a time when some organizations (e.g. vignette 2, SPON; vignette 4, FCW) indicate increased demand from the community for their support and services. Vignette 2 (SPON) also raised additional questions about the supports required by volunteers involved in government initiatives such as mandatory volunteering programmes (e.g. Work for Welfare, educational initiatives) and the impact that has on the resources of the voluntary sector and the experience of the volunteers.

Driving the Voluntary Sector: Where Do We Really Want to Go?

Each phase in the development of society has the seeds of the next phase embedded within it. What will the seed we are planting in the present proliferate? Who will volunteer? Why will people volunteer? Will volunteering promote greater diversity and social cohesion? These questions raise important issues to be addressed by researchers and managers in the voluntary sector. Are we merely trying to improve the functioning and efficiency of the current 'system' or are we advocates for a larger goal, in this case the flourishing of civil society?

Globalization presents challenges for which there are no simple solutions, requiring both global and local action. We have at once the task of maintaining the integration of individuals in society, and advocating our collective social rights at a global level. Complex problems such as this will not be addressed by simple solutions, it will require both diversity and complexity in our system of human services, and, specifically, in the voluntary sector. Our social and cultural history within the voluntary sector creates the foundation for this complexity. From each period we may take the best aspects that emerged. With techno-rational and economic solutions we risk losing the moral and philosophical ideals and the trust that are at the roots of the voluntary sector, and will provide the capacity for action in the future. As Wuthnow (1995) states, the value of voluntary associations is that they are 'able to reinforce basic human values that cannot be encouraged directly by political or economic institutions. They may, in fact, preserve values that are in danger of being undermined by those other institutions' (p. 210). Wuthnow refers to this as the preservation of the moral dimensions, consisting of virtues such as cooperation, collective identity, altruism, social relationships as ends in themselves, intimacy for its own sake, moral absolutes such as integrity and honesty, or the love of beauty and truth. At the current time the dominant message is the proliferation of volunteering for its contribution to the market (Techno and Labour Volunteers and skill development for participation in the labour force). There is also an emphasis on volunteering as an act of social control, which makes voluntary associations the 'fingers of government' (Nowland-Foreman, 1998), whose primary function is the efficient delivery of direct services that the government no longer provides, and as a means for people to earn their welfare payments. What then will be the primary contributor to civil society and democracy? Is that the path we really want to take?

References

Arai, S.M. (1999) Voluntary associations as spaces for democracy: toward a critical theory on volunteers. Doctoral dissertation, University of Guelph, Guelph, Ontario, Canada.

Arai, S.M. (2000) Typology of volunteers for a changing sociopolitical context: the impact on social capital, citizenship and civil society. *Loisir et Societe/Society and Leisure* 23, 327–352.

Arai, S. and Pedlar, A. (1997) Building communities through leisure: citizen participation in a healthy communities initiative. *Journal of Leisure Research* 29, 167–182.

Billis, D. and Harris, M. (1992) Taking the strain of change: UK local voluntary agencies enter the post-Thatcher period. *Nonprofit and Voluntary Sector Quarterly* 21, 211–225.

Brown, P. (1996) *Love in a Cold World? The Voluntary Sector in an Age of Cuts*. Canadian Centre of Policy Alternatives, Ottawa.

Caldwell, L. and Andereck, K.L. (1994) Motives for initiating and continuing membership in a recreation-related voluntary association. *Leisure Sciences* 16, 33–44.

Carbert, L. (1995) *Agrarian Feminism: the Politics of Ontario Farm Women*. University of Toronto Press, Toronto.

Carter, N. (1975) *Volunteers: the Untapped Potential*. Canadian Council on Social Development, Ottawa.

Coleman, J.S. (1988) Social capital in the creation of human capital. *American Journal of Sociology* 94 (Suppl.), S95–S120.

Coleman, J.S. (1990) *Foundations of Social Theory*. The Belknap Press of Harvard University Press, Cambridge, Massachusetts.

Cuskelly, G. and Harrington, M. (1997) Volunteers and leisure: evidence of marginal and career volunteerism in sport. *World Leisure and Recreation* 39, 11–18.

Day, K.M. and Devlin, R.A. (1996) Volunteerism and crowding out: Canadian econometric evidence. *Canadian Economic Association* 24, 37–53.

Donnison, D.V. (1958) *Welfare Services in a Canadian Community: a Study of Brockville Ontario*. University of Toronto Press, Toronto.

Dreessen, E.A.J. (2000) *What Do We Know About the Voluntary Sector? An Overview 2000*. Statistics Canada, Ottawa.

Duchesne, D. (1989) *Giving Freely: Volunteers in Canada*. Statistics Canada, Ottawa.

Fukuyama, F. (1995) *Trust: the Social Virtues and the Creation of Prosperity*. Penguin Books, Toronto, Ontario.

Govan, E.S. (1966) *Voluntary Health Organizations in Canada*. Royal Commission on Health Services, Ottawa.

Guest, D. (1985) *The Emergence of Social Security in Canada*, rev. edn. University of British Columbia Press, Vancouver.

Hall, M., Knighton, T., Reed, P., Bussiere, P., McRae, D. and Brown, P. (1998) *Caring Canadians, Involved Canadians: Highlights from the 1997 National Survey of Giving, Volunteering and Participating*. Minister of Industry, Ottawa.

Hall, M., McKeown, L. and Roberts, K. (2001) *Caring Canadians, Involved Canadians: Highlights from the 2000 National Survey of Giving, Volunteering and Participating*. Minister of Industry, Ottawa.

Hastings, J.E.F. and Mosley, W. (1966) *Organized Community Health Services*. Royal Commission on Health Services, Ottawa.

Heclo, H. (1981) Toward a new welfare state? In: Flora, P. and Heidenheimer, A.J. (eds) *The Development of Welfare States in Europe and America*. Transaction Books, New Brunswick, New Jersey, pp. 383–406.

Henderson, K. (1981) Motivations and perceptions of volunteerism as a leisure activity. *Journal of Leisure Research* 13, 208–218.

McPherson, J.M. and Rotolo, T. (1996) Testing a dynamic model of social composition: diversity and change in voluntary groups. *American Sociological Review* 61, 179–202.

Minkoff, D. (1997) Producing social capital. *American Behavioral Scientist* 40, 606–619.

Newton, K. (1997) Social capital and democracy. *American Behavioral Scientist* 40, 575–586.

Nowland-Foreman, G. (1998) Purchase-of-service contracting, voluntary organizations, and civil society. *American Behavioural Scientist* 42, 108–123.

Parker, S. (1997) Volunteering – altruism, markets, causes and leisure. *World Leisure and Recreation* 39, 4–5.

Plummer, R. (2002) Managing natural resources together: the role of social capital in the co-management process. Doctoral dissertation, University of Guelph, Guelph, Ontario, Canada.

Putnam, R. (1993a) *Making Democracy Work: Civic Traditions in Modern Italy.* Princeton University Press, Princeton, New Jersey.

Putnam, R. (1993b) The prosperous community – social capital and public life. *The American Prospect* 4(13), 27–40. http://epn.org/prospect/13/13putn.html

Putnam, R. (1995) Tuning in, tuning out: the strange disappearance of social capital in America. *Political Science & Politics* 28(4), 664–683.

Reed, P.B. and Selbee, L.K. (2000) *Patterns of Citizen Participation and the Civic Core in Canada.* Statistics Canada, Ottawa.

Silverberg, K., Ellis, G.D., Whitworth, P. and Kane, M. (2003) An 'effects-indicator' model of volunteer satisfaction: a functionalist theory approach. *Leisure* (special issue on volunteerism).

Smith, D.H. (1994) Determinants of voluntary association participation and volunteering: a literature review. *Nonprofit and Voluntary Sector Quarterly* 23, 243–263.

Splane, R. (1965) *Social Welfare in Ontario 1791–1893: a Study of Public Welfare Administration.* University of Toronto Press, Toronto.

Stebbins, R.A. (1992) *Amateurs, Professionals, and Serious Leisure.* McGill-Queen's University Press, Montreal.

Stebbins, R.A. (1996) Volunteering: a serious leisure perspective. *Nonprofit and Voluntary Sector Quarterly* 25, 211–224.

Strong, M.K. (1969) *Public Welfare Administration in Canada.* Patterson Smith, Montclair, New Jersey.

Thompson, M. (1997) Employment-based volunteering: leisure or not? *World Leisure and Recreation* 39, 30–33.

Torjman, S. (1997) *Civil Society: Reclaiming Our Humanity.* The Caledon Institute on Social Policy, Ottawa.

Triandis, H.C. (1995) *Individualism and Collectivism.* Westview Press, Boulder, Colorado.

Wearing, S. and Neil, J. (2000) Refiguring self and identity through volunteer tourism. *Loisir et Societe/Society and Leisure* 23, 389–420.

Wuthnow, R. (1995) Between the state and market: voluntarism and the difference it makes. In: Etzioni, A. (ed.) *Rights and the Common Good: the Communitarian Perspective.* St. Martin's Press, New York, pp. 209–221.

Managing Volunteers in Different Settings: Membership and Programme Management

9

Lucas C.P.M. Meijs[1] and Linda Bridges Karr[2]

[1]Business Society Management, Rotterdam School of Management, Erasmus University Rotterdam, Rotterdam, The Netherlands; [2]Department of Sociology/ICS, University of Groningen, The Netherlands

Introduction

I think the discussion about the 'American model' is not very clear. It is assumed that the USA has the largest non-profit sector in the world, but research has shown that the sector relatively speaking is stronger in The Netherlands, Ireland, Belgium and Israel. And even if the percentage of volunteering in the population is higher in the US, the difference is not so big compared with some European countries.

The real difference, I believe, is not in the scope of volunteering or the sector, but in the way the work is organised. It is not primarily volunteering that is different – that's a result – it is the volunteer organisation that is different. In Europe we have a membership tradition, in the US a service delivery tradition. In the former everything starts with the members. They form an organisation, they decide what it should do, and they do the job. In the latter an organisation starts with the task and then recruits volunteers to do the work. The first model is strong on democracy, the second on service delivery. If helping people is your major aim, the service delivery model is obviously much more efficient. From my European perspective, to combine the strength of the two into one organisation seems to be the best solution. But is that possible?

(Christer Leopold, Senior Officer, Volunteering, International Federation of Red Cross and Red Crescent Societies (Leopold, 2000))

This quote from Christer Leopold shows that there is no generic model that can be applied to all volunteering/volunteer management contexts. Volunteering, volunteers and the way they are organized and managed differ from context to context. This chapter delves further into the growing understanding of the diversity of volunteering and volunteer management. The chapter focuses on the different settings in which volunteering takes place. These different settings are linked to different management approaches: membership and programme management. The first part of the chapter draws the differences between a membership and a programme approach to managing volunteers (based upon Meijs and Hoogstad, 2001). In the second part these two approaches are linked to different organizational and emotional settings in which people volunteer. The final part draws conclusions on the relation between organizational context and the way that volunteers should be managed.

Two Different Management Approaches

Meijs and Hoogstad (2001) observe that European (Dutch, in particular) volunteer organizations take a fundamentally different approach to the management of volunteers than do American volunteer organizations. In their typology, management systems most often focus either on the volunteers themselves (membership management) or on specific operational tasks (programme management). In the former system, common to European organizations, tasks are created such that they fit the expectations of the volunteers existing within the group. Conversely, organizations adopting the more 'American' style of programme management begin by identifying the tasks to be done and then find volunteers to do them. The international literature on volunteer management is dominated by this programmatic approach, which can also be typed as the workplace model (see e.g. Brudney, 1990; Wilson, 1990; Ellis, 1996). The membership model is less known, although some writers explain that this is also important (Smith, 2000).

Membership management is capable of generating broad, multi-faceted involvement of volunteers, leading perhaps to greater overall satisfaction with the volunteer experience. By focusing first on the volunteers (who are treated as members and have a strong sense of belonging to the organization) and their goals, the membership-managed organization shapes itself to the needs and desires of its membership annex volunteers. Through careful attention to who is to be admitted to membership, it guards against the introduction of members whose goals may be contrary to those of the existing membership. This leads to a very 'our breed of volunteers' way of selecting volunteers and a difficulty in working with diversity. Because it is tailor-made to the specifications of the membership, it would be difficult for a member to find such a good fit with any other organization. Because the costs of both entry and exit are high, the membership-managed organization may cultivate considerable loyalty among its individual members. Entry costs are high because people need to develop trust with the organization (typically this is done by all kinds of social activities such as playing cards with existing volunteers). Exit costs are high because people lose long-time friendships when leaving. By these means a strong organizational culture is developed.

However, membership management does not always pro
basis for the continuity of an organization. While individual vc
indeed remain loyal to the organization for long periods of tin
ization itself risks stagnation, lack of growth and eventually e̱ ̱̱
practical challenge of membership management is that it assumes the necessity of a close connection between the board and the volunteers. While the
extensive and prolonged involvement of board members in this system provides continuity to the organization, it makes it very difficult to adapt to environmental changes or even demographic shifts in the membership base. In
many cases the board is more 'old fashioned' than the volunteers, while the
volunteer is outdated compared to the diversity in the population and the
needs that must be addressed. Because of this, the membership-managed
organization may eventually face a slow and painful death! Consider the
example of traditional women's emancipatory organizations, which are
unable to change their organization to attract younger women, who do not
need the traditional development activities within the safe organizational
setting anymore. It also means that in membership management the border
between leisure and volunteering is unclear because there is so much social
activity involved.

Programme management, on the other hand, is designed with an eye
toward continuity for the output and impact. The general focus on carefully
specified tasks guards against any one volunteer becoming indispensable. The
limited scope of involvement expected of any volunteer facilitates both the
entry and the exit of volunteers, who may affiliate with the organization only
for the purpose of performing one specific, time-limited task. Because the
tasks to be accomplished take priority over the aims of the volunteers
performing them, the programme-managed organization is capable of
maintaining smooth, consistent operations over extended periods of time.
Because each task is, for the most part, a self-contained unit, change in
response to environmental shifts involves only the reworking of single components rather than an overall shift in ideology or target population. The
programme-managed organization is resilient and flexible.

Programme management, however, may not cultivate – and may even
discourage – loyalty on the part of volunteers. Members who join an organization in order to participate in programmes of limited duration or those
focused on specific activities are less likely to identify themselves as members
of the organization than are those whose involvement is broader (see Karr,
2001). While capable of continuity over time, the programme-managed
organization is dependent on the availability of fresh supplies of volunteers,
thus risking high turnover, impersonality and cooptation.

In national organizations, membership management results in local
branches that carry out the same activities as the national body, while programme management leads to national organizations with local branches (if
there are any) that are much less diverse. So in the Dutch case the national
animal protection organization runs three 'tasks': animal shelters, animal

ambulances and campaigning for animal rights. In the Dutch situation the expectation is that local groups perform all three tasks although the local situation may ask for a larger regional area for the ambulances than for the shelters. On the other hand, in many cases volunteers do not want to do all three tasks, so some tasks are 'stepchilded'.

To show the differences between the two approaches two exhibits are presented. The first one describes how, within a typical Dutch sport association, programme and membership management would lead to different solutions. The second exhibit describes the differences between Girl Scouts USA and Scouting Netherlands on the different steps in the organizational process (based upon Karr and Meijs, 2002). It shows that the US model is based upon a programme approach, exemplified by the 'on my honor' opening sentence of their vow. The Dutch model is membership-based, which is shown by the 'you can count on me' last sentence of the Dutch vow.

Exhibit 1: Going from membership to programme management in a sport association

Hoogendam (2000) looks at four ways to reduce the workload within local sport associations (in the Dutch context typical mutual support organizations using a membership approach) for the current volunteers:

1. *Discarding tasks or activities.* Organizations should make a critical appraisal of the present parcel of tasks. Certain of these tasks were probably introduced some time ago and are now carried out largely as a matter of course. The organization might conclude that some of these tasks should be dropped.

2. *Obligation.* Members should be obliged to take on some of the less pleasant routine jobs such as serving at the bar or cleaning. Although this method has been criticized as conflicting with the true spirit of volunteering, studies have shown that it is increasingly being applied in mutual support organizations, particularly sports clubs. Janssens (2000) reports that the proportion of sports clubs in which the volunteer is obliged to carry out one or more organizational tasks was still only 43% in 1998, but had already risen to 62% by 2000. What is remarkable is that so many members took a positive attitude towards this obligation: 42% were in favour, 15% neutral, 40% against and 3% undecided.

3. *Flexibilization.* The third method suggested for relieving the workload of active volunteers is what Hoogendam calls 'flexibilization'. The principle behind this is that the organization should use the talents and potential of the members as efficiently as possible. For example, the situation often arises where certain members are available for short periods only, when they can help with large one-off jobs. This means that the 'permanent' volunteers do not have to concern themselves with these jobs.

4. *Professionalization* is the final option. This means assigning tasks to paid staff, who can be either hired for the occasion or employed on a project basis.

Meijs and Hoogstad (2001) translate these into programme management:

- The first solution, *discarding*, is a common occurrence in programme management. That is to say, when an organization starts a new programme with a fresh combination of tasks, it may at the same time discard the existing tasks and programmes.
- The option of making tasks mandatory (*obligation*) is not open to organizations practising programme management, because they start with the tasks that need to be done and only then do they look for suitable volunteers to carry them out. However, making tasks mandatory does occur in another form, representing an important source of volunteers for many organizations. Organizations practising programme management are often able to recruit from amongst groups that are more or less forced to make a contribution: for example, offenders doing community service, students volunteering as a part of the school curriculum or employees taking part in corporate volunteering.
- The third solution, *flexibilization*, is inherent in programme management. The basic idea is, after all, to match the demand (volunteers) to the existing supply (the tasks within the organization). In this way, organizations attempt to achieve a perfect fit between the nature of the tasks and the potential and availability of the volunteers.
- *Professionalization* can also play a part in programme management: for example, a paid manager may direct the volunteers in the performance of the required tasks and coordinate the entire programme.

Exhibit 2: An illustration from the world of Scouting (based upon Karr and Meijs, 2002)

	Girl Scouts of the USA (GSUSA)	Scouting Netherlands (SN)
Vow	On my honor, I will try: To serve God and my country, To help people at all times, And to live by the Girl Scout Law. (Girl Scouts of the USA, 2003)	I promise to do my best to be a good leader for you, and help you to be good Scouts. I also promise consciously both to seek and to carry out that which is good. I will accomplish this together with the other leaders of our group. You can count on me. (Scouting Nederland, 1992)

Continued

	Girl Scouts of the USA (GSUSA)	Scouting Netherlands (SN)
Development	Founded 1912 National organization within 3 years Top-down roll out.	1910: formation of several geographically dispersed groups of boys. After some years groups joined to form five national Scouting organizations. 1973: merging of all into SN.
Integration	National level grants charters and oversees the work.	A national level, 48 regions and more than 1000 local groups. The national level attending mainly to its own agenda and the local units attending largely to theirs – often to the extent of ignoring each other altogether. This disconnection does not lead to chaos.
Local troops	Primary vehicle for delivering the Girl Scout programme, structurally the weakest entity. A troop committee, consisting largely of parents of the girls in the troop, provides the leaders with assistance and support. Troops maintain financial responsibility, but fund-raising is controlled at the council level (Girl Scouts of the USA, 1993).	Primary vehicle for delivering the SN programme and structurally strong link. A group board, consisting of parents and previous leaders, officially governs the group. Troop leaders (being 17–25 years and not parents) are highly self-governed. National level does not control and is not aware of financial situation of local groups.
Recruitment	Recruitment activities for adult volunteers are carried out throughout the entire annual work cycle of a Girl Scout council. **1.** Major recruitment drives for girl members at the beginning of each school year. Membership in a troop is highly dependent upon the availability of sufficient adult volunteers. **2.** In spring, as existing leaders decide whether to continue their activities. **3.** Campaigns may be carried out through community clubs, churches and other associations to recruit leaders for new troops to be formed in the autumn. There is an application, a review	Scout leaders in SN tend to be 'home-grown'. The most prominent goal of the SN programme is to teach young people to take more responsibility for themselves. Beyond the age of 17 or 18, they are generally considered too old to remain as members of the playgroups, and are faced with the choice of either leaving Scouting or becoming a troop leader. It is also possible for them to form or join an existing group for older members ('stam'), which serves the dual functions of providing recreation for its members and a support system for other Scout leaders. The primary recruitment tool in SN appears to be peer pressure.

	Girl Scouts of the USA (GSUSA)	Scouting Netherlands (SN)
(Recruitment continued)	process, a written job description and a letter of agreement signed by the new leader and the designated council representative.	
Training/ socialization	A new Girl Scout leader is usually required to participate in at least one formal training course. During special meetings, new leaders come into contact with experienced leaders, participate in Girl Scout games, ceremonies and songs, and gradually come to understand the meanings behind particular Girl Scout expressions and traditions.	Training and socialization are two entirely separate and 'conflicting' processes in SN. About one-third to one-half of all Scout leaders have completed this obligatory basic training, depending on the availability of trainers in their areas and their own willingness to be trained.
Retention	The retention of volunteers in Girl Scouting is strongly related to the retention of girl members, and both are vital to the continuing healthy operation of Girl Scouting at all levels. A highly developed system of formal volunteer recognitions at the national, council and local levels exists. Volunteers are able to nominate their fellow volunteers for appropriate recognition, in the form of patches, pins or other tokens for activities such as completing training courses, participating in activities, or turning in required forms and reports on time.	Retention poses a double challenge for SN. The first retention challenge is that of keeping members of around the age of 12–14 involved in the organization. The age that younger members become volunteers corresponds closely to the age at which they are finishing secondary school and preparing for entry into higher education or the workforce. In many cases they keep involved in Scouting because volunteering and membership in the 'stam' fulfils the need of young adults to maintain ties with their hometowns and social circles. The greatest retention problem therefore occurs several years after a member has finished school. There is no official policy for recognition in SN. Meijs and Olde Hanter (2002) report that there is an ongoing debate in some local groups regarding the position of the 'speltak' leaders. In some groups, the board members define 'speltak' leadership as Scouting for grown-ups, and simply refuse to give recognition.

Table 9.1 summarizes the differences between the two approaches (for a more detailed explanation, see Meijs and Hoogstad, 2001).

Organizational Settings and Volunteer Management

In this section a number of existing organizational settings are reviewed. The first is based on the sector in which the volunteering takes place. The second classification is concerned with the relationship between paid staff and volunteers. The third is based on the goals of the organization, and the final classification makes use of the recently developed 'contingency approach' for small local volunteer organizations.

By sector

Non-profit organizations are: organized, institutionalized, privately managed, separate from the government and not aimed at making profit – any profit made is not distributed among shareholders or members but is applied towards the goal (the 'non-distribution constraint'). In addition, the organization is responsible for its own administration, is able to manage its own activities and has considerable input from volunteers, in the form of either voluntary financial support or volunteering. This is the basic approach used by the Johns Hopkins Third Sector Comparative Research project. In The Netherlands, most volunteers are connected with non-profit organizations, which is a bit different from the USA, where volunteers are also involved in government (Brudney, 1990). But as Hupe and Meijs (2000) make clear, the distinction between government and non-profit in The Netherlands in many cases is unclear to the people involved, as with parent participation in primary education.

The sector, whether business, government or non-profit, is relevant to volunteering if the volunteers have a strong personal motivation. In a government agency, there is little or no room for the transfer of one's own standards and values; this is one of the most important points about volunteer management in the government sector (Brudney, 1990). On the other hand, a non-profit organization can be entirely based on its own standards and values; the volunteers might share an interest in, say, old sailing boats, table tennis or butterflies (Meijs, 2000) but also, of course, religious norms and values (West and Meijs, 2001). However, in organizations that are legally seen as non-profit organizations, personal norms and values are in many cases not supposed to be used (see Box 9.1).

Table 9.1. Comparison between programme management and membership management (from Meijs and Hoogstad, 2001).

Criteria	Programme management	Membership management
Structure		
Flexibility of approach	From task to volunteer	From volunteer to task/assignment
Integration	Free-standing programmes	Integrated approach
Direction of integration in national organization	Vertical	Horizontal (i.e. per branch)
Management	One single manager	Group of 'managers'
Executive committee	Arm's length	Close by
Culture		
Organizational culture	Weak	Strong
Volunteer involvement	Low	High
Volunteer involvement in more than one organization	Often	Sometimes
Level of homogeneity among volunteers	Low	High
Relationships between volunteers	People do not know each other	People know each other well or very well
Volunteers' motivation 1	Goal-orientated	Socially orientated
Volunteers' motivation 2	Increase in external status	Strengthening internal status
Process		
Cost of admission	Low social costs	High social costs
Cost of transfer	Low	High
Expectations	Explicit	Implicit
Recognition	On basis of performance	On basis of number of years as member
Hours spent/invested	Low	High
Environment		
Necessity of conforming to environment	Major	Minor
Possibility of conforming	Good	Poor

Box 9.1. The importance of personal standards and values in volunteering.

When it comes to running summer camps, there are successful and less successful organizations. Traditionally, the programmes of such camps set out to combine the provision of leisure opportunities, the teaching of skills and the passing on of standards and values. The camp volunteers find that their motivation is based on the same kind of combination: their involvement affords them pleasure and allows them to pass on to the children skills and values that they believe will benefit them. As already stated, non-profit organizations can be firmly based on a set of distinctive standards and values – as in the case of evangelical summer camps. On the other hand, it is possible for a non-profit organization to be a public body and be regarded as part of the government, which is essentially 'neutral'; by contrast, such an organization does not, and cannot, have its own set of standards and values.

Many of the summer camps are offered by semi-governmental organizations such as community centres and umbrella welfare bodies. As a result, the camps fail to profit from a very important set of motivations, especially among those who work with children. Many summer camp programmes have a strong missionary element, which community centres and umbrella welfare bodies cannot satisfactorily include. (Note that the personal standards and values we are discussing are not necessarily religious standards and values.)

Source: Meijs and Hoogstad (2001)

By relationship between paid staff and volunteers

Another classification of volunteer organizations takes into account the relationship between paid staff and volunteers. Meijs and Westerlaken (1994) make the following distinctions:

- The *volunteer-governed organization* is one in which volunteers set the goals and form the management/board, but where the preparation and execution of policy is in the hands of paid staff.
- In the *volunteer-supported organization*, paid staff are mainly responsible for formulating goals and policy and for carrying out the primary process. Volunteers are only involved to a limited extent, in carrying out specific tasks. Some organizations are both volunteer-governed and volunteer-supported, which means that there is no real connection between the two groups of volunteers and that paid staff are performing most of the primary processes.
- In *volunteer-run organizations*, the goals of the organization are set and realized by volunteers. Paid staff might support them in this.

There is a big difference in the way that volunteer-supported and volunteer-run organizations work with volunteers. The former will continue to operate even when there are no volunteers present. If the volunteers disappear, the quality of service may deteriorate, but the organizations themselves will not be in any danger. This makes possible a more demanding approach to managing volunteers. In these organizations the metaphor of the workplace is and can in many cases be used. In volunteer-run organizations the situation is different. Caroll and Harris (1999, p. 16) explain that in the campaigning and volunteering organization context of Greenpeace in the UK, the workplace model simply does not work. As Meijs and Westerlaken (1994) make clear, volunteer organizations by contrast face discontinuity when volunteers drop out. Volunteers will drop out, either by leaving (voting with their feet) or by just doing what they see as appropriate instead of what the 'manager' sees as appropriate (voting with their hands).

By goal

Another means of classification, as proposed by Handy (1988), recognizes three distinct types of non-profit organization. According to the goals of the organization, a distinction can be made between 'service delivery', 'campaigning' and 'mutual support/mutual benefit' organizations. Meijs (1997) has described this threefold division for volunteer organizations operating nationally.

1. *Service delivery organizations* aim to provide a service to an actual customer or client outside the organization. The volunteers and employees of these organizations usually try to deliver a good service to the customers. This means that they are prepared to submit to management, selection, recruitment and coordination. Volunteers can only work for a service delivery organization if they possess the required qualifications. This sometimes means that the volunteer has to undergo training – as in the case of AIDS buddies or telephone help lines – but there are also many fields (such as visiting) where the volunteer does not have to undergo training or possess specific skills. Service delivery organizations are characterized by a high level of professionalism and by customer orientation. This professionalism, defined as doing one's job well, can be seen among both paid staff and volunteers.

2. The *campaigning organization* does not have individual customers or clients, but sets out to convince the entire world. For this type of organization, the rule is that every 'believer' counts – anyone who supports the cause can be accepted as a volunteer. Any contribution is welcome and cannot really be rejected. This results in a situation where there is scant acceptance of management – organization is not an issue in a campaigning group. Most of the volunteers, and even the paid staff, feel that the organizing will just have to be done by someone else. Within campaigning organizations, the fiercest discussions usually concern the effectiveness of methods and the correctness of ideology, and such discussions are firmly based on a specific set of values.

3. The *mutual support organization* exists because a certain group of people have come together around an issue that links them: for example, a particular illness, a sport or a shared interest in collecting teacups. Such organizations set out to encourage mutual support and assistance among their members, or to gain a mutual advantage for them. Solidarity and camaraderie are the most important qualities. Mutual support organizations have a culture of 'doing things together': the people involved work together to set up the organization. The major frustrations in such organizations arise when the others just want to play sport, collect postage stamps or be ill and avoid volunteer work that supports these interests. The real strength of mutual support organizations can be seen when the 'hobby energy' of individuals is freed for the benefit of an activity or the organization itself – then, just about anything becomes possible.

To some extent, nearly every organization displays a combination of the three organizational types: for example, it is very difficult to raise funds without campaigning. Handy states that non-profit organizations can find themselves in trouble if they combine these three types of organization without being aware of the internal tensions between them.

By 'contingency'

Van Walsem (2001) has specifically researched the all-volunteer organization at the local level (see also Smith, 2000). He has developed a 'contingency approach' that recognizes four distinct types of local branches of national organizations. The four types are not completely separate entities, but can be seen as the successive forms through which a local volunteer organization develops.

According to Van Walsem, such an organization will, in principle, start up as a local initiative: a small group of volunteers come together to pursue a single goal or to carry out one particular programme. The organization is characterized at this stage by a *simple structure*: everyone is busy trying to achieve the mutual goal, and the means available to do this are very limited. In addition, the contact between the volunteers is informal and the organization is internally orientated. As the number of volunteers and members grows, the organization will develop into a *simple structure plus*. The form of the organization is much the same as before; however, an important group of volunteers have now formed themselves into an executive committee. The next step is the development towards a more externally orientated organization, known as the *policy structure*. This step makes greater demands on the (new?) members of the executive committee; after all, in addition to the basic, often internally orientated activities, they now also have to deal with policy and planning activities (externally orientated towards the current environment or to the future). The manner in which the organization is set up will also exhibit more formal characteristics; however, the informal character and the overall goal of the organization still remain important. In contrast, the following *complex structure* will pursue several programmes at the same time and with equal emphasis. This usually requires a formal organizational structure in which there is a division of labour and task specialization: for example, in the form of committees and/or branches.

By emotion

Cultural factors such as language and social perception may also affect the way that people perceive volunteering and how they expect to be treated by the organization. For example, Dekker (2002) argues that cross-national differences in the culture of volunteer work may be traced, in part, to language and the words that are used to discuss volunteer work. For example, volunteering in the USA and the UK is most often perceived as unpaid labour. In Sweden, however, volunteer work is commonly perceived as *ideellt arbete* (idealistic work), implying extra effort on behalf of associations of which a person is already a member. The German *Ehreamt* (honorary post) refers for the most part to involvement in a board or other governance function.

In the setting of unpaid labour, public appeals are often the most effective means of recruiting volunteers, followed by the offer of such instrumental rewards as status and marketable skills. Immediate rewards are of least importance. In the context of *ideellt arbete*, appeals from the membership and peer pressure are of greatest influence in this setting, followed by such immediate first-order rewards as fun and excitement. Status rewards come only from within the group itself, and are therefore of less influence. In this context, public appeals and status rewards are the strongest motivators, with less emphasis placed on immediate enjoyment. Such perceptual differences will probably lead to markedly different styles of volunteering. It will also lead to different managerial approaches to managing volunteers. The concept of unpaid labour leads to more rigid styles than the *ideellte arbete*. The concept of *Ehreamt* is less clear because it simply leads less to the idea of volunteers being managed too!

Recent research into cross-national perceptions of volunteering suggests important differences in the types of work individuals in different countries consider to be volunteer work (see e.g. Handy *et al.*, 2000; Meijs *et al.*, 2003), and supports the distinctions made by Dekker (2002). For example, in the USA, working overtime without pay is much more likely to be considered volunteer work than it is in The Netherlands, some element of gain-seeking in the American perception. On the other hand, assuming additional responsibility within a membership association – such as leading a group of joggers at your country club – is less likely to be perceived as volunteer work in the USA than it is in The Netherlands. These two differences suggest that the Dutch perception of volunteer work assumes a stronger normative component.

Discussion

Now the question can be posed: in which context should membership or programme management be used?

The effects on managing volunteers in the different organizational settings can be analysed from the point of the possible and needed use of less or more rigid management approaches, simplified as the difference between membership- versus programme-management approaches. So looking at the difference between volunteer management in public and private organizations, due to the fact that there is more need to control the (mis)use of private norms and values, and that the organizational setting generally is more bureaucratic, volunteer management in public organizations must be more in control than in private organizations. Controlling the volunteer is much easier in a programme approach, in which volunteers can more easily be dismissed individually.

The same type of reasoning can be applied to volunteer-supported versus volunteer-run organizations. In a volunteer-supported organization, volunteers perform tasks that are less crucial to the continuity of the organization. Also volunteers perform tasks that are less integrated into the organization.

For service delivery organizations, the idea that there is a customer outside and that there is the all-felt urge to do a good job opens the door to more rigid managerial approaches such as in programmes. This is in contrast to the mutual support organization in which the social relations between the volunteers are more important. Mutual support organizations are in essence membership-based, so the management system should also be membership-based. Campaigning organizations can probably be less clearly put in the dichotomy, although Caroll and Harris (1999) say that the workplace model does not work in campaigning organizations. Campaigning organizations face a dual primary process of decision making and activism to put this opinion forward. This dual primary process in many cases leads to a dual managerial system. Decision making in many cases is based upon membership models because trust in the others norms and values is needed. Activism leads to more programmatic approaches because in many cases the more people that support the good cause, the better it is.

In the contingency approach for small local non-profit organizations, the 'we are all in this together' way of working in the first two models leads to membership-based ways of managing volunteers. In the other two models management must be much more clearly defined, which leads to a more programmatic approach, although in the complex model there is room for membership management within the separate parts of the organization.

Table 9.2. Linking organizational contexts to programme and membership management.

	Programme management	Membership management
By sector	Public	Private
By relationship between paid staff and volunteers	Volunteer-supported	Volunteer-run
By goal	Service delivery	Mutual support
		Campaigning?
By contingency		
		Simple structure
		Simple structure +
	Policy structure	
		Complex structure?
By emotion	Unpaid labour	*Ideellte arbete*
		Active citizenship

Looking at the emotions the picture is clear for *ideellte arbete* (which is active membership) and unpaid labour. The first is membership management, the second fits into a programme approach. The issue of active citizenship is more complicated (see Table 9.2).

The next question, of course, becomes what happens with management if contexts mix. As can be observed in The Netherlands, the emotion of active membership (*ideellte arbete*) and the tradition of membership management also lead to the dominance of this model in service delivery organizations such as the Red Cross. According to reactions at workshops on the Meijs and Hoogstad (2001) paper, sport associations in the USA are blocked by a dominant perspective of programme management in all the normative, recipe-like books they can get. As always, more research is needed!

References

Brudney, J.L. (1990) *Fostering Volunteer Programs in the Public Sector. Planning, Initiating, and Managing Voluntary Activities.* Jossey-Bass, San Francisco.

Caroll, M. and Harris, M. (1999) Voluntary action in a campaigning context: an exploratory study of Greenpeace. *Voluntary Action* 2(1), 9–18.

Dekker, P. (2002) On the prospects of volunteering in civil society. *Voluntary Action* 4(3), 31–48.

Ellis, S.J. (1996) *From the Top Down: the Executive Role in Volunteer Program Success*, rev. edn. Energize Associates, Philadelphia, Pennsylvania.

Girl Scouts of the USA (1993) *Safety-wise*. Girl Scouts of the United States of America, New York.

Girl Scouts of the USA (2003) Official website for Girl Scouts of the United States of America, http://www.girlscouts.org.

Handy, C. (1988) *Understanding Voluntary Organizations, How to Make them Function Effectively from the Author of Understanding Organizations.* Penguin Books, London.

Handy, F., Ram, A., Cnaan, J.L., Ascoli, U., Meijs, L.C.P.M. and Ranade, S. (2000) Public perception of 'Who is a volunteer?': an examination of the net-cost approach from a cross-cultural perspective. *Voluntas, International Journal of Voluntary and Nonprofit Organizations* 1, 45–65.

Hoogendam, A. (2000) Wat te doen als je te veel werk hebt voor te weinig mensen? *Sport Vrijwilligerskrant* 512, 2–3.

Hupe, P.L. and Meijs, L.C.P.M., with cooperation of M.H. Vorthoren (2000) *Hybrid Governance. The Impact of the Nonprofit Sector in the Netherlands.* Work document No. 65. Social and Cultural Planning Office, The Hague.

Janssens, J. (2000) Steeds meer verenigingen stellen taken verplicht. *Sport Vrijwilligerskrant* 512, 3.

Karr, L.B. (2001) Organization and association: an examination of issues relating to cooperation in the context of a national volunteer-run membership organization. MSc. thesis, The University of South Carolina, Columbia, USA.

Karr, L.B. and Meijs, L.C.P.M. (2002) ON MY HONOR, YOU CAN COUNT ON ME: management strategies and organizational commitment among volunteers. Paper presented at the 31st Arnova Conference, Montreal, November.

Leopold, C. (2000) International Federation of Red Cross and Red Crescent Societies, http://www.e-volunteerism.com/fall2000/intlexchintro.html.

Meijs, L.C.P.M. (1997) *Management van Vrijwilligersorganisaties.* NOV Publikaties, Utrecht.

Meijs, L.C.P.M. (2000) Thema: 'Management van vrijwilligersorganisaties: een specialiteit', 'Management van vrijwilligers', 'Een typologie van vrijwilligersorganisaties'. *Goed bestuur: Stichting en vereniging: financieel, fiscaal en juridisch nieuws en advies* 3(5), 6–10.

Meijs, L.C.P.M. and Hoogstad, E. (2001) New ways of managing volunteers: combining membership management and programme management. *Voluntary Action* 3(3), 41–61.

Meijs, L.C.P.M. and Olde Hanter, A.L.G. (2002) *Evaluatie en toekomstgericht onderzoek van het Steunpunt Scouting Gelderland: Naar een betere ondersteuning van georganiseerd jeugd-en jongerenwerk.* The Erasmus University Rotterdam, Business Society Management, Rotterdam.

Meijs, L.C.P.M. and Westerlaken, C. (1994) Vrijwilligersorganisaties en HRM, Talenten: beleid of misleid? *Personeelbeleid* 6, 37–43.

Meijs, L.C.P.M., Handy, F., Cnaan, R.A., Brudney, J.L., Ascoli, U., Ranade, S., Hustinx, L., Weber, S. and Weiss, I. (2003) All in the eyes of the beholder? Perceptions of volunteering across eight countries. In: Dekker, P. and Halman, L. (eds) *The Values of Volunteering: Cross-cultural Perspectives (Nonprofit and Civil Society Studies).* Kluwer Academic/Plenum, New York, pp. 19–34.

Scouting Nederland (2003) Official website for Scouting Nederland, http://www.scouting.nl.

Smith, D.H. (2000) *Grassroots Associations.* Sage Publications, Thousand Oaks, California.

Van Walsem, R. (2001) *Parameters van lokale vrijwilligersorganisaties.* The Erasmus University Rotterdam, Business Society Management, Rotterdam.

West, A. van and Meijs, L.C.P.M. (2001) Vrijwilligerswerk in een levensbeschouwelijke omgeving. *Tijdschrift voor Humanistiek* 8, 76–85.

Wilson, M. (1990) *The Effective Management of Volunteer Programs.* Johnson, Boulder, Colorado.

Encouraging the Next Generation: Sustainability and Youth Volunteering

This section bears on the situation of young volunteers and how, in the face of the demands of work and the lure of casual leisure, to sustain the interest of all volunteers in altruistic activities. Two of the chapters centre on policy in this area, while the third reports data from research on meaning and motivation among a set of high school volunteers. The chapters are set in Brazil, Australia and the UK.

In Chapter 10 Geoff Nichols draws on earlier research on volunteers in sport and in the Guide Association in the UK (now called GirlGuides UK) to demonstrate the importance of such people in these areas. Then, using the same research, as well as findings from a national survey of volunteers, he examines some of the general pressures on the volunteer sector. The pressures include growing demands on time, growing demands for professionalism, increased complexity of volunteer skills, and increased choice of, and competition among, leisure activities for youth. Nichols concludes with a set of research questions for volunteering. More study is needed, he says, to substantiate the extent and felt intensity of these pressures.

Stephen Wearing outlines in Chapter 11 how to better understand best practice in volunteer tourism. This he does by examining the focus of and motivation for such tourism and the dynamic social interrelationship between it and the host community. In the course of treating volunteer tourism as a form of serious leisure, Wearing describes the idea of 'best practice' there. Best practice includes striving for excellence, keeping in touch with innovations, avoiding waste and concentrating on outcomes central to community interest. The goals of volunteer tourism are, in general, to provide sustainable alternative travel that can assist community development, scientific research or ecological restoration. Moreover, pursuit of these goals should lead to ideologically sound travel experiences that contribute to the natural, economic, social and cultural environments. A range of non-governmental organizations have programmes that offer, through tourism, possible personal development, programmes that, in the past, have not been characteristic of tourism organizations.

In the final chapter, Antonio Carlos Bramante examines a set of concepts that helps explain the development of voluntary human resources for work and, in addition, helps explain involvement in leisure pursuits among young Brazilians. For him, knowledge and altruistic activity can be combined in human life with having significant leisure experiences. This presupposition led him to a study of serious leisure volunteering by youth living in the Brazilian city of Sorocaba. Some youth there had been involved in volunteer activity for many years. Their commitment inspired Bramante to initiate a project that he dubbed 'Volunteering, Taking Leisure Seriously'. Its aim was to cultivate, even at a young age, a spirit of solidarity as generated through interest in serious leisure, in particular career volunteering. At the end of the chapter Bramante presents some of the findings from his study of young participants in this project.

Pressures on Volunteers in the UK

Geoff Nichols

Introduction

This chapter draws on research into volunteers in sport and in the Guide Association in the UK (now called GirlGuides UK) to show the importance of volunteers in these areas. It then uses the same research, as well as findings from a national survey of volunteers, to examine general pressures on the voluntary sector. It concludes with a set of research questions for volunteering.

The Importance of Volunteers in Sport and Guiding in the UK

Modern sport first developed in the UK in the second half of the 19th century through the establishment of the governing bodies of the major sports and a proliferation of sports clubs (McIntosh, 1987; Holt, 1990). These small amateur sports clubs still provide the foundation for the structure of organized sport; however, their fragmented nature makes it difficult to measure the voluntary activity they represent. Research in 1995, conducted by the Leisure Industries Research Centre (Gratton et al., 1997, p. ii) for the Sports Council (now Sport England), concluded that there are nearly 1.5 million volunteers in UK sport, each contributing an average of 2.5 hours a week for 48 weeks of the year. Eighty per cent of these volunteers are involved in the running of voluntary sports clubs. The 1995 survey was conducted by interviews and questionnaires with officials in the national governing bodies and clubs in the most important sports. These results were aggregated to give a

UK-wide estimate over all sports. The research was thus an estimate based on the best data available, although care was taken to always err on the conservative side. Volunteering in sport was defined as 'individual volunteers helping others in sport, in a formal organisation such as clubs or governing bodies, and receiving either no remuneration or only expenses' (Gratton et al., 1997, p. i). This survey of volunteers in sport was repeated in 2002, by the same research team, but just for sport in England.

An alternative estimate of volunteers in sport can be derived from the 1997 National Survey of Volunteering (Davis Smith, 1998). In this survey volunteering was defined as 'any activity which involves spending time, unpaid, doing something which aims to benefit someone (individuals or groups) other than, or in addition to, close relatives, or to benefit the environment' (Davis Smith, 1998, p. 13). The survey distinguished between formal and informal voluntary activity. Formal activity was carried out for, or through, an organization or group of some kind. This could be either a formal entity, such as a national voluntary organization or statutory agency, or a more loose-knit grouping such as a residents' committee or a sports club. The important defining characteristic of formal volunteering was its context of an organizational boundary. Informal volunteering accorded with the general definition of volunteering, but took place outside an organizational context and on an individual basis, such as helping a neighbour. The two types of volunteering were asked about separately in the questionnaire. The survey used an interview-administered, random sample of adults aged 18 or over in the UK. It found that 48% (1486) of respondents had been involved in volunteering for a formal organization in the last year. This is estimated to equate to 21.8 million volunteers. It found that 26% of formal volunteers were in the area of sport and exercise (Davis Smith, 1998, p. 43). This was the highest single category of area of involvement, and would equate to 5.7 million volunteers (approximately 12% of the population). Thus, both surveys show the importance of volunteers in sport but the differences in their results illustrate some of the difficulties in measuring volunteering. The 1997 National Survey estimate is much bigger than the 1995 sports volunteers' survey partly because it includes all those who volunteered just for one occasion in the last year. The National Survey, although using a relatively small sample, will pick up all volunteering in sport, whereas the methods used in the 1995 sports volunteers survey was based on estimates made by respondents in the national governing body structures of the 27 sports which were most important for volunteering.

In 1997 the Guide Association was the largest voluntary youth organization in the UK with a total membership of almost 661,000 women and girls. In 1995 it had 65,455 uniformed members over the age of 25, all taking voluntary leadership roles. Research conducted in 1997 (Nichols and King, 1998, 1999) involved a postal survey yielding 1494 responses from uniformed unit leaders. This showed that each leader contributed on average 3.57 voluntary hours per week.

Thus, sport and Guiding are major areas for volunteering in the UK but what difficulties do volunteers face? Research into both sets of volunteers provides a comparison.

Difficulties Faced by Volunteers

The results in Table 10.1 are from self-completion questionnaires completed by sports club committee members in 47 sports clubs and by 1494 Guiders. In both cases responses were prompted by a question asking which of the statements, as reproduced in the table, applied to their work as volunteers.

In both surveys volunteers felt that the most important difficulty was the lack of others to volunteer, followed by the feeling that work was increasingly left to fewer people. The Guider questionnaire asked a wider range of questions than the sports one; however, in both, the need for volunteers to have specialist skills, the conflict with family commitments and the feeling that things could be better organized were also significant.

The National Survey of Volunteering asked a similar question of those who volunteered regularly, defined as once a month, for a formal organization. This only gave a sample of 419 regular volunteers, but from this the

Table 10.1. The difficulties faced by leaders in the Guide Association and by volunteers in sports clubs.

Reported difficulties	A (%)	B (%)
There are not enough other people to volunteer	74	71
Increasingly the work is left to fewer people	55	59
Dissatisfaction with parents' contributions		41
There is little time left after your paid work	19	39
Rules and regulations of the Association		28
Conflict with family commitments	16	25
Increasingly my work as a volunteer needs specialist skills	23	20
Things could be better organized in the Association so you feel that your efforts are sometimes wasted	16	16
Poor support from other leaders		12
Attitude of the members of the unit you lead		10
There is little time left after your partner's work commitments		9
Poor support in training offered by the Association		8
Your children are no longer involved in the Association so you feel less motivated		5

Column A shows results from the survey of sports club committee members (Gratton *et al.*, 1997; sample size 353). Column B shows results from the Guide Association survey (Nichols and King, 1999; sample size 1494). Sports volunteers were asked a more limited range of questions.

major drawbacks of volunteering were: things could be much better organized (71%), you sometimes get bored with it (34%) and it takes up too much
of your time (31%). The same survey found that of 173 non-volunteers who
would 'like to get involved', 58% did not think they had enough time to spare,
53% did not know many people who are interested in that sort of thing and
52% felt they had not got the right skills or experience to help (Davis Smith,
1998, p. 96). These survey results, combined with qualitative data from the
studies of sports volunteers and Guide leaders, suggest several pressures on
the voluntary sector (Nichols et al., 1998).

Time pressures on potential and existing volunteers

The results in Table 10.1 and those from the National Survey of Volunteering
show that time pressures are a major difficulty. Nineteen per cent of sports
club committee members and 39% of Guiders reported that a major problem
was little time left after paid work. It is debatable whether there has been a
recent increase in working hours in the UK (Holliday, 1996; Martin and
Mason, 1998) or if a perceived time squeeze is merely the consequence of
an increased and competing range of leisure opportunities (Robinson and
Godbey, 1999). It seems likely that time pressures are felt most by males in
'professional'/managerial jobs, and who are parents with dependent children (Gershuny, 2000); exactly the groups who comprised the majority of
sports club committee members in the survey reported above. The results
above show that for 16% of sports volunteers and 25% of Guiders, 'conflict
with family commitments' was a significant problem, which implies pressures
from time spent with children or partners. The UK General Household
Survey (Goddard, 1994) also asked questions about volunteering and found
that A/B socioeconomic groups have the greatest propensity to volunteer;
and the propensity to volunteer is also positively related to the number of
dependent children. This again confirms that time pressures will fall dispro-
portionately on those who volunteer the most. Thus, time pressures may
come from the demands of paid work, but may also come from family commitments and the greater range of opportunities to use leisure time. Time
pressures from paid work will not apply to those who are retired or not in
paid employment, although time pressures from an increasing intensity of
life, as noted by Robinson and Godbey (1999), will. In general there is greater
competition for leisure time, expenditure and commitment. Thus sports clubs
and organizations such as Guiding will need to compete more voraciously for
volunteers, and, as discussed below, also for participants.

A contributory factor to time pressures is the change in the labour force.
It was estimated that by 2001 females would account for 47.6% of all
employment in the UK; a significant amount of this in part-time work
(Department for Education and Employment, 1996). The increase in female
employment is reflected in the increase in the proportion of dual-income

households between 1981 and 1993 (Hills, 1995, p. 49). This change means that the households with two earners will be experiencing a greater time squeeze. This is likely to impact particularly on organizations such as the Guide Association, who depend almost entirely on female volunteers. However, the gradual convergence in time use between males and females, such as unpaid work distributed more evenly within households (Gershuny, 2000), will also reduce the propensity of males to volunteer.

The National Survey of Volunteering was able to compare volunteering in 1981, 1991 and 1997. It found that the only age groups to increase volunteering between 1991 and 1997 were the 65–74-year-olds and the over 75s. It was only this increase that had held the total numbers of volunteers over this period roughly constant. One would also expect these older volunteers to give more time each and this is confirmed by the national survey, which found that the 65–74 and the 75+ age groups contributed 4.1 and 4.9 hours per week, respectively; above the average of 4.0 (Davis Smith, 1998, p. 27).

A demand for 'professionalism'

In both sports clubs and the Guide Association volunteers felt they had to increasingly deliver services in ways that are common to, and comparable with, those of the private or public sectors. For example, a sports club secretary explained that

> Organisation five years ago was more of a back of a cigarette packet job, now it is all computers, with things going out on the internet, which is much more professional. And if you put something forward it has to look good, it can't just be hand written and passed around the boys, it has to go to one committee and on to the next.
>
> (Nichols *et al.*, 1998, p. 42)

Pressures for professionalism can arise from within organizations, as illustrated by the expectations of members in the quote above. But they can also come from external organizations, including: national governing bodies of sport; central government via conditions attached to support from Sport England; local authority conditions attached to support; and legal requirements. Houlihan and White (2002) have shown how the finances of national governing bodies (NGBs) of sport have become increasingly reliant on grants from Sport England and UK Sport. These have become increasingly tied to development plans that incorporate government objectives; for example, to promote world-class competition. Since the 1996 research into sports volunteers child protection legislation has been introduced nationally. From April 2001, grant aid for an NGB became contingent on it demonstrating to Sport England that an active child protection policy was in place (Brackenridge, 2002). This, in turn, was a new funding criterion from the Department for

Media, Culture and Sport. This had been preceded in 2000 by a Sport England criterion for gender and race equity. Thus Sport England funding initiatives are a double-edged sword for volunteer administrators because while they provide substantial extra finance, for example through the World Class Programme, which distributed £50 million in 1998, they also require additional administration.

Similarly, all youth organizations, including the Guide Association, have had to use police checks for volunteers. This has meant that even a helper taking Guides to a supermarket must have been police checked and means that any organization finds it more difficult to use casual volunteers who just help occasionally.

Since the sports volunteers and Guide research was conducted, another significant factor has been increased fear of litigation. Several high-profile cases, combined with the introduction into the UK of the ability of solicitors to take on cases on a no win–no fee basis, have resulted in an increased concern by volunteers to make sure they are covered both by insurance and by rigidly sticking to procedures. As one example, the British Mountaineering Council in the UK is forced to raise its subscriptions considerably because they include third party cover for members against claims of negligence. Another consequence is the tightening up of regulations and a reduced willingness of volunteers to put themselves in situations where they may be sued.

Several examples were given by Guiders when discussing new walking regulations and the requirement to take a walking safety test:

> Unless you do it you cannot leave your meeting place. [Guide HQ] are putting a total stop on any outside activities.

> I've been to Switzerland, I've been to the Lake District and to Derbyshire at weekends and I'm not now allowed to do it and all those years I've been doing it.

> If you are going on pack holiday and they will be walking down the road you must put that on the form so that the parents know they will be walking. They're not just going to be in an enclosed space. This is because people have now got what I call sue happy.

> In one quick swoop they took away our confidence of taking children out because then we suddenly thought oh what if something happens to them. This year we're going for our pack holiday to Edale and I think we'll just look through windows.

Paradoxically, these restrictions will reduce the ability of organizations such as the Guide Association to contribute to their objective of the development of young people (Nichols, 1998).

When the 1996 sports volunteers research was conducted a major external pressure on sports clubs was bidding for and meeting the requirements of the National Lottery. This required business plans and development plans to show both financial viability and, again, the meeting of Sport England policy objectives. Local government sometimes offered specialist support to clubs making these bids (Nichols and Sparrowhawk, 1999). Since then the funds available have been reduced and making bids has become a lower priority for clubs.

Increased complexity of voluntary skills

The pressures towards professionalization all contribute to a demand for more specialist skills for volunteers, be they making National Lottery applications, dealing with legislation, learning specialist coaching or leadership skills, or word-processing skills. Skills might also include handling relations with 'partner' organizations. Twenty-three per cent of sports volunteers and 20% of Guiders felt that their work as volunteers required more specialist skills. The National Survey of Volunteering found that of those who had thought of volunteering but had not actually volunteered, 52% felt they had not got the right skills or experience to help.

Increased choice and competition

The demands of 'professionalism' and increasing skill requirements are related to the increasing competition the voluntary sector faces from the private and public sectors. Potential sports club members are more able to choose alternative provision from the private or public sectors, for example, for sports such as badminton, squash and tennis. Similarly, Guide leaders claimed that young people had an increasingly wide range of activities to choose from and Guiding had to compete more strongly for their interest, even if it was against a television soap opera. This illustrates that competition is not just direct, but rather competition for time from the increasing array of other leisure opportunities (Robinson and Godbey, 1999). Not only are there more choices but those alternatives are more fiercely promoted as competition for consumers' time becomes more intense.

A changed attitude to volunteering

The overall impression from the sports volunteers and the Guide Association research was that there had been a reduction in the number of volunteers. In both surveys volunteers reported that there were not enough other people willing to volunteer in the club and that the work was left to fewer people. For example, a respondent involved in football administration for the sport's governing body reported that

> I have a council of 30 people. At 60 I am the third youngest. What used to happen is that you played to a certain age and then took up refereeing or

administrative work. What happens now is that people play up to the age of 30 and then go and do other things.

(Nichols *et al.*, 1998, p. 39)

These surveys were snap shots, and could not show trends. Perhaps the respondents were all pessimists! But there is evidence to support changed attitudes towards volunteering from the National Survey of Volunteering. Between 1991 and 1997 the drop in the proportion of those volunteering from 51% to 48% equates to a reduction of 1.4 million volunteers, although as the report notes, the sample sizes mean that a fall of 4% would be required for it to be significant at the 95% confidence level. At the same time the mean hours spent volunteering in the past week rose from 2.7 to 4.0. Overall, this suggests an increase in volunteering time commitment, but given by fewer volunteers. As noted earlier, the proportion of total time given by volunteers aged 65+ had risen. Conversely, time given by volunteers aged 18–24 fell from 2.7 hours per week to 0.7. Does this represent an attitudinal change between generations?

Eley and Kirk (Eley, 2001; Eley and Kirk, 2002) reported that the young volunteers they studied were initially highly motivated by the desire to develop leadership skills and to help them with their future career in paid work. After 9 months, the motivation of 'working in the community' gained in importance, still behind 'increasing leadership skills', but now more important than enhancing their CVs. Sample sizes were small in this study, but it indicated the important motivations for young volunteers. In some areas of work, for example heritage or conservation, voluntary experience is a virtual prerequisite for full-time employment. Perhaps young people view volunteering in a very different way to older volunteers?

A hegemonic redefinition of the voluntary sector

The pressures above could be understood as part of a hegemonic redefinition of the voluntary sector such that it is increasingly equated to the understanding of leisure as consumption, a commodity to be bought and sold (Clarke and Critcher, 1985, pp. 225–229). For both Henry (1993) and Hedley and Davis Smith (1992), the rights and responsibilities of citizens are being replaced by the rights and responsibilities of consumers. This erodes the sense of obligation to volunteer, to contribute to society, and supports the hegemonic view that relations must be mediated by the cash nexus. Relationships are increasingly defined in terms of economic costs and benefits. This explains the comments by sports volunteers that parents use their junior sessions as cheap child-minding facilities for their children. It helps to explain why 41% of Guiders were dissatisfied with parents' contributions.

A volunteer in orienteering put it this way:

I think the increase in the responsibilities of volunteers is to do with the socioeconomic changes in the country. I think people who are in work, are having to work much longer hours, which means less time for voluntary activity. If there is time they want to be paid for it. At the same time there are others who are in work, but under a lot of stress because they are thinking they may lose their job, or they are in and out of work a lot. They are obviously under pressure which takes their minds off voluntary activities like sport. Then you have the unemployed who are desperately looking for jobs. We find it is much more difficult now to get people who are willing to go and work with juniors, travel overseas etc., than it was 5 or 6 years ago. Orienteering is extremely heavy on volunteer help because we make all our own maps, and organise all our own competitions. I think it is a great tragedy the way the market philosophy has hit sport, it has certainly hit the opportunity of thousands of youngsters.

(Nichols *et al.*, 1998, p. 41)

Increased geographical mobility

Formal volunteering is made possible by the network of organizations which use volunteers, which is itself a component of a neighbourhood's social capital. The relationship between social capital and volunteering has to be clarified (Davis Smith, 2001) but clearly volunteering can contribute to this and is more likely to occur if there is a rich and diverse range of opportunities. However, it takes time to become aware of these opportunities if one moves to a new area. The research into Guiding showed that young volunteers were lost as they moved away from their home area, normally to take places in higher education. In the UK the percentage of under 21-year-olds in higher education rose from 12% in 1981 to 30% in 1995 and the government has a target of 50%. Not all of these will leave their home area, but for those that do there is a discontinuity with the volunteering opportunities with which they are familiar. The Guide Association research showed that even if contact was made with opportunities for volunteering in a new area, it was difficult to break into the social networks of the new volunteering situation. These young guiders would often continue to volunteer in their old neighbourhood when they returned in college holidays.

The increase in participation in higher education is only one factor leading to higher geographical mobility. Another will just be the willingness to travel to find work or promotion. The extent of this, and its impact on volunteering, is a research question, but it is likely to be a significant factor.

Conclusions

How significant are these pressures and are they replicated elsewhere? The sports volunteers research and that into the Guide Association were both snapshots rather than longitudinal studies. They might just show that volunteers are pessimistic, and they might reflect the bias of a pessimistic researcher! (Nichols and Garret, 2001). A survey in 2000 of 3038 sports clubs in Scotland found that 46% had been established before 1970 and 15% before 1900 (Allison, 2000). The Guides Association was founded in 1910. This is a picture of continuity rather than change. However, social change appears to happen at an exponential rate. In the UK the best picture we have of changes in volunteering is from the National Survey of Volunteering, conducted in 1981, 1991 and 1997, used extensively in the discussion above. Even so, the sample was relatively small.

Interestingly, Cuskelly (2002, personal communication) has compared longitudinal data on volunteering in Canada and Australia. In Canada he notes the same apparent trends as in the UK: the volunteer workload in sport is being shared amongst fewer volunteers. In contrast, in Australia it appears that the number of volunteers in sport is on the increase and each volunteer, on average, has less work to do. However, he notes methodological concerns with the Australian data, which reflect the general difficulties of measuring volunteering. He notes the same pressures on the voluntary sector in sport: a 'professionalization', the impact of regulations and government conditions of funding that exacerbate this; a drop in volunteer engagement; an increasing diversity of leisure choice; and increasing direct competition from private providers.

Major research questions are: How exactly is the voluntary sector changing and why are these changes occurring? How important are the pressures identified above? Are these changes and pressures international? To what extent do they erode the potential of the voluntary sector to contribute to social capital and to what extent do they themselves reflect a dilution of that capital? We have indications of the answers, but more research is required in this enigmatic area of study.

References

Allison, M. (2000) *Sports Clubs in the New Scotland – Report on a Study for SportScotland*. Centre for Leisure Research, University of Edinburgh, Edinburgh.

Brackenridge, C. (2002) '. . . so what?' Attitudes of the voluntary sector towards child protection in sports clubs. *Managing Leisure* 7, 103–123.

Clarke, A. and Critcher, C. (1985) *The Devil Makes Work; Leisure in Capitalist Britain*. Macmillan, Basingstoke.

Davis Smith, J. (1998) *The 1997 National Survey of Volunteering*. National Centre for Volunteering, London.

Davis Smith, J. (2001) The inflatable log: volunteering, the state and democracy. *Voluntary Action* 3(3), 13–27.

Department for Education and Employment (1996) *Meeting the National Skills Challenge*. Department for Education and Employment, Nottingham.

Eley, D. (2001) The impact of volunteering on citizenship qualities in young people. *Voluntary Action* 4(1), 65–83.

Eley, D. and Kirk, D. (2002) Developing citizenship through sport: the impact of a sport based volunteer programme on young sport leaders. *Sport, Education and Society* 7, 151–166.

Gershuny, J. (2000) *Changing Times: Work and Leisure in Postindustrial Society.* Oxford University Press, Oxford.

Goddard, E. (1994) *Voluntary Work.* HMSO, London.

Gratton, C., Nichols, G., Shibli, S. and Taylor, P. (1997) *Valuing Volunteers in UK Sport.* Sports Council, London.

Hedley, R. and Davis Smith, J. (1992) *Volunteering and Society.* Bedford Square Press, London.

Henry, I. (1993) *The Politics of Leisure Policy.* Macmillan, Basingstoke.

Hills, J. (1995) *Inquiry into Income and Wealth.* Joseph Rowntree Foundation, York.

Holliday, S. (1996) Trends in British working time: has the British worker's increasing workload become a barrier to leisure participation? In: Gratton, C. (ed.) *Work, Leisure and the Quality of Life: a Global Perspective.* Leisure Industries Research Centre, Sheffield, pp. 68–83.

Holt, R. (1990) *Sport and the British.* Oxford University Press, Oxford.

Houlihan, B. and White, A. (2002) *The Politics of Sports Development.* Routledge, London.

Martin, W.H. and Mason, S. (1998) *Transforming the Future Quality of Life; Rethinking Free Time and Work.* Leisure Consultants, Sudbury.

McIntosh, P. (1987) *Sport in Society.* West London Press, London.

Nichols, G. (1998) Things we did yesterday. *Horizons* 2, 25.

Nichols, G. and Garret, R. (2001) Research questions for volunteering in leisure. In: Graham, M. and Foley, M. (eds) *Leisure Volunteering: Marginal or Inclusive?* Leisure Studies Association, Eastbourne, pp. 11–20.

Nichols, G. and King, L. (1998) Volunteers in the Guide Association; problems and solutions. *Voluntary Action* 1(1), 21–32.

Nichols, G. and King, L. (1999) The changing motivations and frustrations facing volunteers in youth programs: a study of the Guide Association of the United Kingdom. *Journal of Applied Recreation Research* 23, 243–262.

Nichols, G. and Sparrowhawk, J. (1999) Local authorities' role in distributing the lottery to sport. *Local Government Studies* 25(3), 1–15.

Nichols, G., Shibli, S. and Taylor, P. (1998) Pressures that contribute to a change in the nature of the voluntary sector in British sport. *Vrijetijdstudies* 16(2), 34–46.

Robinson, J. and Godbey, G. (1999) *Time for Life: the Surprising Ways Americans Use Their Time.* Pennsylvania State University Press, Pennsylvania.

Examining Best Practice in Volunteer Tourism

Stephen Wearing

Youth Challenge Australia/School of Leisure, Sport and Tourism Studies, University of Technology, Sydney, Australia

Introduction

This chapter will present an outline of how to better understand best prac-tice in volunteer tourism by examining the focus and motivations for volun-teer tourists and the dynamic social interrelationship between them and the host community. Many non-governmental organizations (NGOs) and non-profit organizations are committed to undertaking projects and programmes in developing nations. These programmes have evolved from a tradition of overseas volunteer organizations that work on projects of community service, medical assistance and scientific discovery.

A range of NGOs undertake programmes that focus on the personal development potentiality in tourism, which, in the past, has not been char-acteristic of tourism organizations. These organizations and their projects seek to be locally identified and sustainable, while providing the tourist with an opportunity to learn and become involved in development issues. These projects incorporate many of the key elements that are considered to be essential to the underlying concept of alternative tourism.

The adoption of a broader conceptual framework for the understand-ing of alternative tourism practices in relation to an operator such as an NGO allows for the complexity of interactions that make up the tourist relationship, specifically those between developed and 'other' cultures found in international tourism. The complexity of cross-cultural issues inhering in the tourist experience is often omitted in the analysis of tourism. The adoption of a broader conceptual framework may allow the exploration of these relational issues and their consideration in the tourist experience.

In mass tourism marginalized communities have rarely (if at all) had their voices heard; that is, the host communities who are the recipients of mass tourism have little or no ability to influence its construction. Some NGOs offer volunteer tourism as an alternative and, as an example of best practice, provide the basis for a particular critique of this position from what could be characterized as Foucauldian in suggesting the changing nature of the tour operator and their removal from the centrality of power whereby the exchange between discourse and power, applied to community and operator, which is fundamental to the way in which developing countries are used as destinations, is rewritten.

Volunteering for Serious Tourism

The development of organizational volunteering and specifically here international volunteering has occurred without it having been considered as a form of tourism. The modern phenomenon of travelling overseas as a volunteer appears to have begun in about 1915 (Gillette, 1968; Clark, 1978; Australian Volunteers Abroad 1989, Beigbeder, 1991; Darby, 1994) and has involved a variety of organizations and groups throughout the world, with Australian Volunteers Abroad operating in Australia and similar types of organizations, such as the Peace Corps USA and Voluntary Service Abroad NZ, operating in other countries. The Organization for Economic Co-operation and Development (OECD) estimates that in 1990 over 33,000 overseas volunteers were involved with projects, primarily in developing countries. The investment in over 18,000 volunteers for 1986 was US$389 million, a growth of 400% since 1976, according to OECD figures (Beigbeder, 1991, p. 103).

International volunteerism generally involves some form of travel and, as this brief outline will demonstrate, the underlying concepts comprising specific forms of alternative tourism and organizational volunteering overlap to a substantial degree, thus providing for a more specific form of tourism (cf. Wearing, 2001) which falls outside the context of mass tourism and within a conceptualization that involves altruistically motivated travel. Significantly, there are a number of studies (cf. Dickson, 1976; Clark, 1978; Darby, 1994; Wearing, 1998) that focus on the range of volunteer programmes for the 17–25-year-old age group, which provides a perspective that allows for elaboration on the specificity of the conjunction between volunteer and tourist experiences[1] (Fig. 11.1).

It is generally agreed that the volunteer is one who offers service, time and skills to benefit others (Beigbeder, 1991, p. 109), provides voluntary personal aid while living in developing communities (Clark, 1978), and gains mutual learning, friendship and adventurousness (Gillette, 1968). Definitions of volunteers necessarily include the recognition that they are those who provide assistance, or unpaid service, usually for the benefit of the commu-

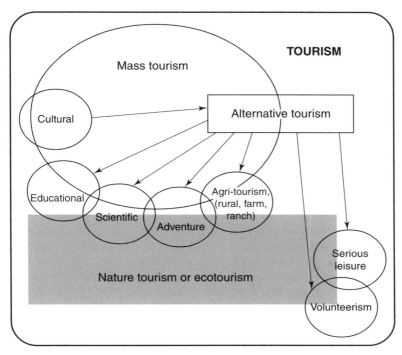

Fig. 11.1. A conceptual schema of alternative tourism and its relationship to ecotourism, serious leisure and volunteering.

nity (Australian Bureau of Statistics, 1986). This may be through formal involvement as a volunteer in an organization, and/or independently as an individual. For the purposes of this chapter, the concept of volunteering is defined as an action perceived as freely chosen, without financial gain and generally aimed at helping others (van Til, 1979; Stebbins, 1982, 1992), and volunteer tourism as applies to those tourists who, for various reasons, volunteer in an organized way to undertake holidays that might involve the aiding or alleviating the material poverty of some groups in society, the restoration of certain environments or research into aspects of society or environment (Wearing, 2001, p. 1). There have been suggestions that there are enough developed nations already working in developing countries (Chavalier, 1993) and increasing this level through alternative tourist activity is not going to help resolve local problems (Wearing and Neil, 1999). One fundamental danger is that volunteers can reiterate the ethos of the 'expert', thus promoting deference in the local community to outside knowledge, therefore contributing to the curtailment of self-sufficiency.

A tourist experience that allows for the opportunity to live and work with people of other cultures may provide a type of alternative tourism (Holden, 1984; Cohen, 1987, 1995; Vir Singh, 1989; Pleumarom, 1990; Smith and

Eadington, 1992; Weiler and Hall, 1992; Wearing, 1998, 2001) that is able to meet effectively some of the concerns raised by destination communities about the impacts of tourism. Younger tourists are possibly more likely to use the knowledge gained from their volunteer tourism experiences to influence other areas of their lives, such as the choice and development of career paths, particularly if these experiences allow for inclusiveness of issues and impacts that relate to natural environments and destination communities.

The research in the area of volunteerism has shown that people working and living together on jobs of social significance often results in facilitating understanding and friendships that are more important to the participants than the physical construction itself (Clark, 1978, p. 13). Whatever the genesis of the programme, it is the personal encounter between the volunteer and the community that is essential (Clark, 1978, p. 4). Additionally, research on international volunteer organizations has demonstrated an orientation towards reviewing the issues around personal development. The links between volunteering and tourism can possibly be made more apparent when viewed as leisure experience and the research on personal development and international development volunteer programmes initially provides some background for positing such a conjunction in alternative tourism experiences.

In reviewing the international volunteering literature,[2] there is a focus on personal development and the role of learning in changing or influencing the self, which introduces to the alternative tourism experience issues relating to self-identity and change. It is proposed that the concept of international volunteering, as an element within the context of alternative tourism experience, highlights learning as a central element of the interaction with the destination culture and environment. The research of Weinmann (1983) and Carlson (1991), in considering exposure to a new culture, found personal development related to: (i) greater tolerance; (ii) a more compassionate understanding of other people and their individual differences; and (iii) the gaining of a more global perspective and insight into new values, beliefs and ways of life.

Learning components within this exchange included academic learning, the development of personal knowledge, self-confidence, independence, cultural awareness and social abilities. Similarly, Stitsworth (1987) indicated that participants, as part of a group for 6 weeks, contributed to their own personal growth and development while gaining a better understanding of the role of developed countries, particularly the issues surrounding development in experiencing another culture. The AFS Impact Study (American Field Service, 1986) of over 1000 high school students found that participants' greatest amount of positive change was in awareness and appreciation of the host country and its culture. In this way, the studies of volunteering provide an added dimension to the examination of alternative tourism experiences and as a result lead me to speculate that this type of tourism provides us with a 'best practice' example of tourism.

Best Practice

Edwards and Prineas (1995) detail 'best practice' as including: striving for excellence, keeping in touch with innovations, avoiding waste and focusing on outcomes which are in the community interest. Others such as Hennessy (1995) and Rodski and Falls (1995) note that best practice is about managing change, continual improvement and that it is a holistic approach encompassing all of an organization. Possible examples of 'best practice' are aiming to increase customer service, improvements in productivity or in the management of people. From these differing views it can be seen that 'best practice' is not limited to particular types of organizations or bodies, nor to particular aspects or issues within those organizations or bodies. Rather, it is an extremely diverse practice which can be implemented in an array of different situations to serve different purposes. Although these differences were noted in what 'best practice' encompasses, a central theme was present, being that it was related to, or associated with, some form of change within an organization or body. Here we can see how volunteer tourism is leading the way for the tourism industry by providing a change in focus from the tourist and their experience to the community and their participation in the creation of an experience. Additionally, the focus on paying for the experience and the expectation that the more you pay the better the experience is questioned. The programmes run by NGOs are more inclined to examine the benefits to local, social, economic and natural environments, the tourism experience being linked to this and thus enabling the parameters of the experience to move beyond the economic benefit and the tourist consumption of the marketer's images. Volunteer tourism offers a model of 'best practice' that shifts the evaluative criteria to what the tourist can put into the host community and how the host community has integrated this into their lifestyle. These ideas are built around a very different conceptualization of tourism from the parameters currently dominating the tourism industry. The next section explains how these experiences are differently constructed and why they shift tourism to 'better practice'.

Volunteering as Alternative Tourism

The time contributed to participation in international volunteering can be considered serious leisure (Stebbins, 1982, 1992; Henderson, 1984) and many organizations rely on this 'free' time in order to operate (Bishop and Hogett, 1986). It is evident that the travel component of volunteerism in these alternative tourism experiences is an essential component of the appeal of organizations operating in developing countries. Rather than travelling simply as a 'tourist' the volunteer may regard travel as an activity for the stimulation and development of character. The appeal of travelling with a purpose, working with communities in developing countries and spending time to assist in saving natural environments, provides a strong platform for expanding the conceptualization of tourist experience.

Stebbins (1992), in defining 'serious leisure', uses the fields of amateurism, hobbyist and volunteering to encompass the range of specific characteristics. Similarly, Parker (1992) links 'serious leisure' to a range of activities such as volunteering, suggesting that these activities fundamentally affect individual values. Two distinguishing features of volunteering identified by Stebbins that may contribute to our understanding of alternative tourism experiences – particularly in relation to volunteer tourism – are that volunteers are usually motivated by a sense of altruism, and that they are often delegated tasks to perform, making them a 'special class of helper in someone else's occupational world' (Floro in Stebbins, 1982). Furthermore, in identifying a number of components that contribute to volunteerism – including: demonstrated perseverance; significant personal effort based on special knowledge, training or skill; durable benefits relating to self-actualization, self-enrichment, recreation or renewal of self; feelings of accomplishment; enhancement of self-image, self-expression, social interaction and belonging; lasting physical products of the activity; and a unique ethos demonstrating a subculture with intrinsic beliefs, values and norms – Stebbins (1982, p. 257; 1992, p. 18) provides significant overlapping qualities between some alternative tourists and volunteerism.

Significantly, research by Parker (1992) and Stebbins (1982, 1992) indicates that some volunteers do not perceive themselves as being 'at leisure', but rather involved in working through a sense of 'good citizenship concern for the community'. The addition of volunteering to the analysis of alternative tourism experiences enables us to differentiate it from forms of mass tourism that are inclined towards a specific focus on relaxation and excitement. This is not to deny that relaxation and excitement are components of alternative tourism experiences, but allows for volunteering as a significant differentiating component.

The examination of motivation is significant in linking volunteer experience, serious leisure and volunteer tourism forms. Neulinger (1982) and Henderson (1984) both note that volunteerism and leisure fulfil higher-level needs such as self-esteem, belonging and self-actualization. In addition, Stebbins (1982, 1992), in further examining 'serious leisure', sees 'career volunteering' as a specific example. In his consideration of 'serious leisure', Stebbins points out that it is an important part of people's lives in its relation to personal fulfilment, identity enhancement and self-expression (1982, p. 253).

The research[3] on volunteerism which focuses on individual motivation acknowledges that volunteers seek to gain considerable personal benefits from their endeavours, including self-satisfaction and social and personal well-being (Henderson, 1981, 1984; Stebbins, 1982, 1992; Frank, 1992). Motivations, such as being useful (Independent Sector, 1990), altruism and being needed (Beigbeder, 1991), personal satisfaction and being cared for by the organization (Tihanyi, 1991) are all considered to be important by the volunteers. Alternative tourist experiences could be studied within this rubric, as a fundamental motivating element for the participant is the desire to assist communities in developing countries.

Volunteer Tourism and Serious Leisure

The consideration of serious leisure with its component of volunteering thus becomes an element that provides a significant broadening of the analysis of alternative tourism experiences.[4] The early literature that attempted to clarify the concept of leisure (cf. Wearing and Wearing, 1988) did so without adequately considering the relationship between leisure and cultural relationships, focusing instead on the ideas of non-work time and individual activity. It is this limitation that serves to obscure elements of leisure, such as volunteerism in the context of volunteer tourism. A more inclusive approach beyond the simple paradigm of work/non-work serves to question the theoretical construction of leisure as individually conceived, arguing instead that it should be built around the micro-social dynamic exchanges that are a part of the participant's experiences. The use of such an approach allows the incorporation of the interaction of cultural or social influences such as those between the host community, the participant and the site. Budowski (in Valentine, 1991) draws attention to the two-way interaction between ecotourists and the environment upon which their experience depends, in that the environment consists, in part, of the dynamic social exchange which establishes much of the experience of the natural environment. What is at issue here is, fundamentally, the dynamic social exchange between and within social groups (the host community and the tour group), which forms the basis of the participant's experience and the way they construct their ideas of the experience.

Motivation for Volunteer Tourism

The ideas developed here may be applied to a range of areas of tourism research, for example the characteristics that differentiate volunteer tourists through an analysis of tourist motivation. Further, demographic and psychographic characteristics, the needs of volunteer tourists, the images and attitudes volunteer tourists ascribe to a destination, and the influence of social, cultural and physical environments could be examined whereby – with a wider frame of reference informed by the areas of serious leisure and volunteering – we may be able to address the managerial implications for organizations operating in the realm of volunteer tourism.

By understanding the nature of the target market, tourism operators can alter marketing mix components according to the needs of an altruistically motivated consumer. One way in which we can identify particular forms and styles of tourism is through an examination of what factors motivate tourists.

Motivation is aroused when individuals think of certain activities that are potentially satisfying. Since people act to satisfy their needs, motivation is thought to be the ultimate driving force that governs travel behaviour. Therefore, tourists' motivation could be informed by the literature on serious leisure and volunteering. Motivational research in tourism is based on the early works of Dann (1981), who identified that 'push' and 'pull' factors are central in motivating tourists. Push motives are internal to the individual while pull motives are aroused by the destination. Push factors establish the desire for travel and pull factors explain actual destination choice (Bello and Etzel, 1985). Crompton (1979) modified the push/pull model in identifying a tourist's desire for pleasure and the desire for a break from routine. He identified nine motives in determining causal factors resulting in a tourist's departure. 'Push' factors are motives concerned with the social and psychological status of the individual while 'pull' factors, on the other hand, are 'motives aroused by the destination rather than emerging exclusively from the traveller himself' (Crompton, 1979, p. 410).

Crompton (1979) conceptualized motives as being located along a disequilibrium continuum. When disequilibrium arises due to a feeling of dissatisfaction in relation to one or more push factors, it can be rectified by a break in routine, thus restoring homeostasis (equilibrium) – that is, through travel (Uysal and Hagan, 1993). For Crompton (1979) the destination site is merely a medium through which motives are satisfied. Significantly, Iso-Ahola (1983) found that the individual possessed an inclination to travel primarily for intrinsic rewards. Intrinsically motivated activities are engaged in for their own sake, rather than any external remuneration. The connection between intrinsic motivations and push and pull factors was made by McGehee (1996), who recognized that most of the push factors are intrinsic motivators. It is important here to note that satisfaction for the volunteer tourist may come not only from the experience itself but from the external reward of having promoted community development and environmentally sound travel and having made a contribution to the destination region. In this way, serious leisure which provides sound information on intrinsic motivation is able to better inform us about motivation.

The tourist motivation framework developed by Pearce (1993) based on Maslow's hierarchy of needs provides an expansive framework to identify the needs that a tourist is fulfilling when travelling. A 'casual leisure' tourist is more concerned with fulfilling lower-level needs of relationship, stimulation and relaxation whereas the volunteer tourist is more concerned with development and fulfilment, which includes self-education. If the focus of volunteer tourism is community development, often intrinsically aroused, with a degree of education about destination cultures and interpretation of the natural environment, it stands to reason that volunteer tourists are more focused on the self-actualization and higher-level needs than needs identified at the base of Maslow's hierarchy. As Mayo and Jarvis (1981, p. 155) note, intellectual needs can in some instances take precedence over some of the lower-order needs. For example 'curiosity, exploration, the desire to learn, the desire to understand – these are sometimes pursued even at great cost to the individual's safety'.

A study conducted by Kretchman and Eagles (1990) also found that the motivations of, for example, an ecotourist and those of the general tourist differed in relation to intrinsic versus extrinsic motivations for travel. The study found that the general tourist in most cases liked to feel at home when away from home. The results from this study align strongly with the 'push' and 'pull' factors that influence tourist motivation. This is not to say that 'pull' factors alone provide enough stimulation for a trip departure, because despite the fact that 'pull' factors are paramount for volunteer tourists, push factors still do (to varying degrees) influence the departure decision. The application of Crompton's (1979) theory illustrates that 'pull' factors are necessarily ranked higher for volunteer tourists than mainstream tourists, based on their psychographic characteristics.

However, accurately gauging the motivations of volunteer tourists is difficult. To begin with, defining tourists' motivations using the push and pull model is more complex when applied to a specific market niche such as volunteer tourists, rather than mainstream travellers. The internal push motives of discovery, enlightenment and personal growth are important to volunteer tourists but features of a destination are more than simply pull motives to this group, for volunteer tourists see physical locations in developing countries as motivation in themselves while they are also attracted by many of the elements that make up a mainstream tourism experience. For example, to describe this as a 'pull' phenomenon is to overlook the importance, in ecotourism, of the destination communities' surrounding natural environment as a motivator (Eagles, 1991). The following quote gives some further insight into volunteer tourist motivations:

> There is a lot that needs to be done to make the world a better place. No one person can do everything, but each of us can do something. We need to find something that moves us and then act on it. The projects that you'll find on our site were started by people who saw a need and acted on it . . . Every community needs people willing to volunteer their time, energy and money to projects that will improve the living conditions for its inhabitants. No one needs to travel around the world to find a good and worthy cause to dedicate their efforts to. Volunteering should be something we do as a regular part of our lives, not just when we can take a month or two off, or when we have extra money to spend on travel. Your actions are your voice in the world, saying loudly and clearly what you think is important, what you believe to be right, what you support.
>
> (Explorations in Travel, 2002)

Goals of Volunteer Tourism

The goals of volunteer tourism are generally to provide sustainable alternative travel that can assist in community development, scientific research or ecological restoration (cf. Wearing, 2001). It could be further stated that they should be ideologically sound travel experiences that contribute to the natural, economic, social and cultural environments. The provision of tourism services is becoming central to many developing countries' local communities, particularly in a shift away from the dependence on agricultural commodities such as coffee and extractive industries. A combination of volunteer tourist needs and the image they have of the destination pre-departure creates expectations that a volunteer tourist assumes will be satisfied. By understanding the volunteer tourist motivations the local community will be in a better position to meet these needs and expectations, and by understanding various community members' expectations of the volunteer tourist the tourist can also understand the communities' expectations.

The tailoring of products using motivational research is important in any sector of tourism and also recognizing that the motives of volunteer tourists differ. Owing to reduced numbers of tourists but longer stays, the likelihood of reduced impacts and interest in an educative component, roles and rules for volunteer tourists may be redefined. This can result in higher rates of satisfaction for the tourist and the community.

Research on visitor expectations was used in the ecologically sustainable management of whale shark tourism in Queensland. Respondents felt that regulations allowed divers to swim too near to whale sharks. Management used this research to modify guidelines, increasing the distance, which enhanced protection of the species, while still offering a satisfying experience for ecotourists (Birtles, 1995). This demonstrates a differing managerial response to the market, based on their unique needs and characteristics.

Motivation alone exemplifies differences between volunteer tourists and mainstream tourists and the way the ideas of serious leisure and volunteering can help expand this area; other areas of tourism research could also be explored to expand our understanding of tourism behaviour.

Serious Fun or Community Development

Alternative tourism experiences, when contextualized in relation to the differential elements of volunteerism, serious leisure and volunteer tourism, illustrate the centrality of the interactions that take place within the destination area in conjunction with the exploration of personal identity and development through enabling the tourist to contribute to the community development of local areas. This has significant implications in relation to tourism research and future policy as it enables researchers to be able to examine local communities and volunteer tourism as socially constructed institutions and draw on wider social constructs within theory such as 'serious leisure' rather than simplify the experience and over-generalize. This provides policy with a more specific understanding of the differing types of tourist experiences, which may redirect resources in terms of funds being provided for tourist development in a more diverse way than just looking at direct economic return within the very limited framework currently dominating the tourism industry.

If we are able to better understand alternative tourism experiences, such as volunteer tourism, and are able to come to more specific understandings of these experiences by, for example, better analysis of what motivates the tourists, then both tourism policy providers, local communities and industry will be better able to understand the tourist and the experiences that they seek. Kenny (1994) notes that the dominant characteristics of community development are participation in decision making, acceptance of individual differences and involving the transference of skills that are held but not controlled by professionals. It involves multi-sector and multi-issue approaches to the whole and sees the interrelations between the parts. In this way it is a systemic (looking at the operations of the overall social system as a whole) rather than systematic (looking at parts sequentially and separately) approach, involving the breaking down of the barriers to cooperation, understanding the wider implications of issues, linking people together on issue-based actions, adopting a task orientation, exchanging knowledge and skill, and constant renewal and consolidation of the relationship, whereby support is maintained, trust continued, realistic tasks set and achieved and those involved rewarded. The perspective encapsulated and understood through serious leisure and volunteering is quite different from that of the tourism industry as a whole, which is predominantly focused on a profit ethos. Instead, these concepts place far more importance on accessing the information networks of people and, in particular, groups forming around particular issues. Alternative tourism experiences – such as volunteer tourism – when differentially analysed in terms of its volunteering and serious leisure components, actively facilitate the type of interaction and exchange identified here, thus significantly shifting the analysis of tourism research, and the provision of tourist experiences, into a realm that enables the elaboration of the specificity of component elements that sustain particular tourist experiences.

Determining Best Practice

If this shift occurs then the industry needs to look not just at the theoretical context where the focus has shifted but also at the means by which it can learn and adopt better practices. For example, this shift in focus, while maintaining the sociological context of a tourist experience, allows for the active construction of the role of the community in the 'tourist experience'. The idea of experience can be informed by a number of different elements in respect to the individual, the individual's social groups, their travel experience and the interrelating elements that sustain the experience. Wearing (1998) has differentiated alternative forms of tourism – specifically here, volunteer tourism (cf.

Wearing, 2001) – through the placing of experience as a nodal point. This then allows for the elaboration of the conceptual, theoretical and practical differences and overlaps between specific tourism forms. This provides the basis for the introduction of other ideas that can inform us of these experiences and thus contributes to the movement towards an understanding and elaboration of the potential benefits of particular tourism experiences as a holistic interchange rather than chiefly evaluated through economic analyses. This thereby opens up parameters of best practice that incorporate a range of indicators not hereto considered.

For example, an essential feature of volunteer tourism is sustainability. The Bruntland Report introduced the concept of sustainable development, defining it as: 'development that meets the needs of the present without compromising the ability of future generations to meet their own needs' (Mieczkowski, 1995, p. 457). Similarly, The World Tourism Organization guidelines concluded that:

> Sustainable tourism can only take place if carrying capacities for key tourism sites are conducted and then rigorously implemented through a system of effective planning and operating controls. These studies and regulations will constitute the cornerstones of long term, local tourism management strategies and plans . . . it also requires acceptance of the concepts of validity and cooperation in its implementation from the tourism private sector, as well as the participation of local communities and tourists themselves.
> (World Tourism Organization, 1990, p. 47).

Volunteer tourism, then, appears to fit into the general construction of sustainability and ecotourism, having minimal impacts, being small scale and requiring little specialized infrastructure, and therefore not contributing to damaging the environment on which ecotourism (and all other forms of tourism) depends.

Notes

[1] For a detailed account of volunteerism see Darby (1994).
[2] The initial studies considered the more widely researched area of personal development and the university student or college experience (Terenzini and Wright, 1987; Kuh, 1988; Karen, 1990), as well as personal development through culture shock (Weinmann, 1983). These studies were followed by research on university student study abroad (Kauffmann and Kuh, 1984; Carlson, 1991); youth programmes and national service (Thomas, 1971; United Nations Department of Economic and Social Affairs, 1975); and international youth exchange (Stitsworth, 1987). Studies of international development experience include, specifically, youth-based Canadian Crossroads International and Operation Raleigh USA as well as government-based volunteer programmes – United States Peace Corps (1980, 1989; Winslow, 1977) and Volunteer Service Abroad (Clark, 1978).
[3] Phillips (1982); Allen and Rushton (1983); Rohs (1986); Independent Sector (1990); Luks and Payne (1991); Darby (1994).

⁴ See, for example, Bishop and Hogett (1986) on the leisure profession and the
   consideration of available time for travel; serving communities through leisure
   (Neulinger, 1982; Henderson, 1984); the provision of purpose for leisure (cf.
   Roberts, 1981, p. 61; Stebbins 1992, p. 19); the high correlation between individual description of their volunteer efforts and their perception of leisure
   (Henderson, 1981); the degree of involvement and its correlation to commitment and more satisfying and rewarding experiences (McIntyre, 1994).

References

Allen, N.J. and Rushton, J. (1983) Personality characteristics of community health
   volunteers: a review. *Journal of Voluntary Action Research* 12(1), 36–49.
American Field Service (1986) *The AFS Impact Study: Final Report*. American
   Field Service, Washington, DC.
Australian Bureau of Statistics (1986) *Volunteering in NSW*. Australian Government
   Publishing Service, Canberra.
Australian Volunteers Abroad (1989) *Australian Volunteers Abroad: 25 Years
   Working for the World*. Australian Government Publishing Service, Canberra.
Beigbeder, Y. (1991) *The Role and Status of International Humanitarian
   Volunteers and Organizations*. Martinus Nijhoff, London.
Bello, D.C. and Etzel, M.J. (1985) The role of novelty in the pleasure travel experi-
   ence. *Journal of Travel Research* 24(1), 20–26.
Birtles, A. (1995) Incorporating research on visitor experiences into ecologically sus-
   tainable management of whale shark tourism. In: Richins, H., Richardson, J. and
   Crabtree, A. (eds) *Ecotourism and Nature-based Tourism: Taking the Next
   Steps. Proceedings of the Ecotourism Association of Australia National
   Conference*. Alice Springs.
Bishop, J. and Hogett, P. (1986) *Organizing Around Enthusiasms – Mutual Aid in
   Leisure*. Comedia, London.
Butler, J.R. (1992) Ecotourism: its changing face and evolving philosophy. Paper pre-
   sented at International Union for Conservation of Nature and Natural Resources
   (IUCN) IVth World Congress on National Parks and Protected Areas, Caracas,
   Venezuela, 10–12 February.
Carlson, J.S. (1991) *Study Abroad: the Experience of American Undergrauates
   in Western Europe and the United States*. Council of International Educational
   Exchange, New York.
Chavalier, C. (1993) Letter to the Editor, *The Times*, London, 3.
Clark, K. (1978) *The Two-way Street – a Survey of Volunteer Service Abroad*. New
   Zealand Council for Educational Research, Wellington.
Cohen, E. (1987) Alternative tourism critique. *Tourism Recreation Research* 12(2),
   13–18.
Cohen, E. (1995) Contemporary tourism – trends and challenges: sustainable authen-
   ticity or contrived post-modernity? In: Butler, R.W. and Pearce. D. (eds) *Change
   in Tourism: People, Places and Processes*. Routledge, London, pp. 12–29.
Crompton, J.L. (1979) Motivations for pleasure vacations. *Annals of Tourism
   Research* 3, 408–424.
Dann, G. (1981) Tourist motivation: an appraisal. *Annals of Tourism Research* 8,
   187–219.

Darby, M. (1994) International development and youth challenge: personal development through a volunteer experience. MA thesis, School of Leisure and Tourism Studies, University of Technology, Sydney, Australia.

Dickson, A. (1976) *A Chance to Serve*. Dennis Dobson, London.

Eagles, P.F. (1991) The motivation of Canadian ecotourists. In: Weller, B. (ed.) *Ecotourism Incorporating the Global Classroom*. Bureau of Tourism Research, Canberra, pp. 12–17.

Edwards, G. and Prineas, T. (1995) Plans, networks and lines: workshop on planning for networks of regional open space. Presented at the First International Urban Parks and Waterways Best Practice Conference, Workshop 3, Melbourne, 26 February to 1 March.

Explorations in Travel Inc. (2002) Explorations in travel: volunteering. http://www. volunteertravel.com/philosophy.html (last accessed 20 January 2002).

Frank, D. (1992) Volunteers . . . a force to be reckoned with! *Australian Journal of Leisure and Recreation* 2(3), 33–39.

Gillette, A. (1968) *One Million Volunteers*. Pelican (Penguin), Ringwood, Victoria.

Henderson, K.A. (1981) Motivations and perceptions of volunteerism as a leisure activity. *Journal of Leisure Research* 13, 260–274.

Henderson, K.A. (1984) Volunteerism as leisure. *Journal of Voluntary Action Research* 13(1), 55–63.

Hennessy, J. (1995) Achieving organizational change. Presented at the First International Urban Parks and Waterways Best Practice Conference, Business Seminar 2, Melbourne, 26 February to 1 March.

Holden, P. (ed.) (1984) *Alternative Tourism: Report on the Workshop on Alternative Tourism with a Focus on Asia*. Ecumenical Coalition on Third World Tourism, Bangkok.

Independent Sector (1990) *Giving and Volunteering in the United States*. Independent Sector, Washington, DC.

Iso-Ahola, S.E. (1983) *Towards a Social Psychology of Leisure and Recreation*. Wm. C. Brown Company, Dubuque, Iowa.

Karen, C.S. (1990) Personal development and the pursuit of higher education. Paper presented at the annual meeting of the American Educational Research Association, Boston, 16–20 April.

Kauffmann, N.L. and Kuh, G.D. (1984) The impact of study abroad on personal development of college students. Paper presented at the American Educational Research Association, New Orleans, 4–7 April.

Kenny, S. (1994) *Developing Communities for the Future: Community Development in Australia*. Thomas Nelson, South Melbourne, Australia.

Kretchman, J. and Eagles, P. (1990) An analysis of the motives of ecotourists in comparison to the general Canadian population. *Society and Leisure* 13, 499–508

Kuh, G.D. (1988) *Personal Development and the College Student Experience: a Review of the Literature*. New Jersey Department of Higher Education, New Jersey.

Luks, A. and Payne, P. (1991) *The Healing Power of Doing Good*. Fawcett Columbine, New York.

Mayo, E. and Jarvis, L. (1981) *The Psychology of Leisure Travel*. CBI, Boston, Massachusetts.

McGehee, N.G. (1996) The Australian international travel market: motivations from a gendered perspective. *Journal of Tourism Studies* 7(1), 45–57.

McIntyre, N. (1994) The concept of 'involvement' in recreation research. In: Mercer, D. (ed.) *New Viewpoints in Australian Outdoor Recreation Research and Planning.* Hepper Marriot, Melbourne.

Mieczkowski, Z. (1995) *Environmental Issues of Tourism and Recreation.* University Press of America, New York.

Neulinger, J. (1982) *To Leisure: an Introduction.* Allyn and Bacon, Boston.

Parker, S. (1992) Volunteering as serious leisure. *Journal of Applied Recreation Research* 17(1), 1–11.

Pearce, P. (1993) Fundamentals of tourist motivation. In: Pearce, D. and Butler, R. (eds) *Tourism Research: Critiques and Challenges.* Routledge, London, pp. 113–134.

Phillips, M. (1982) Motivation and expectation in successful voluntarism. *Journal of Voluntary Action Research* 11(2/3), 118–125.

Pleumarom, A. (1990) Alternative tourism: a viable solution? *Contours* 4(8), 12–15.

Roberts, H. (ed.) (1981) *Doing Feminist Research.* Routledge and Kegan Paul, London.

Rodski, S. and Falls, S. (1995) The changing nature of work. Presented at the First International Urban Parks and Waterways Best Practice Conference, Business Seminar, Melbourne, 26 February to 1 March.

Rohs, F.R. (1986) Social background, personality, and attitudinal factors influencing the decision to volunteer and level of involvement among adult 4-H leaders. *Journal of Voluntary Action Research* 15(1), 85–99.

Smith, V.L. and Eadington, W.R. (1992) *Tourism Alternatives.* University of Pennsylvannia Press, Philadelphia.

Stebbins, R.A. (1982) Serious leisure: a conceptual statement. *Pacific Sociological Review* 25, 251–272.

Stebbins, R.A. (1992) *Amateurs, Professionals, and Serious Leisure.* McGill–Queen's University Press, Montreal.

Stitsworth, M. (1987) Third world development through youth exchange. Paper presented at the Annual Third World Conference, Chicago, 9–11 April.

Terenzini, P.T. and Wright, T.M. (1987) Student's personal growth during the first two years of college. Paper presented at the annual meeting of the Association for the Study of Higher Education, 14–17 February.

Thomas, M. (1971) *Work Camps and Volunteers.* PEP, London.

Tihanyi, P. (1991) *Volunteers, Why They Come and Why They Stay.* Centre for Voluntary Organizations, London School of Economics, London.

United Nations Department of Economic and Social Affairs (1975) *Service by Youth.* United Nations, New York.

United States Peace Corps (1989) *Final Report from the Returned Peace Corps Volunteer Pretest (RPCV) Survey.* United States Peace Corps, Washington, DC.

United States Peace Corps Evaluation Division (1980) *A Survey of Former Peace Corps and VISTA Volunteers.* United States Peace Corps, Washington, DC.

Uysal, M. and Hagan, L.A.R. (1993) Motivation of pleasure travel and tourism. In: Kham, M.A., Olsen, M.D. and Turgut, V. (eds) *VNR's Encyclopaedia of Hospitality and Tourism.* Van Nostrand Reinhold, New York, pp. 798–821.

Valentine, P.S. (1991) Ecotourism and nature conservation: a definition with some recent developments in Micronesia. In: Weiler, B. (ed.) *Ecotourism Incorporating the Global Classroom.* Bureau of Tourism Research, Canberra, pp. 4–10.

van Til, J. (1979) In search of volunteerism. *Volunteer Administration* 12, 8–20.

Vir Singh, T. (1989) *Towards Appropriate Tourism: the Case of Developing Countries*. Peter Lang, Frankfurt.

Wearing, S.L. (1998) The nature of ecotourism: the place of self, identity and communities as interacting elements of alternative tourism experiences. PhD thesis, Charles Sturt University, Albury, NSW, Australia.

Wearing S.L. (2001) *Volunteer Tourism: Seeking Experiences that Make a Difference*. CAB International, Wallingford, UK.

Wearing, S.L. and Neil, J. (1999) *Ecotourism: Impacts, Potential and Possibilities*. Butterworth-Heinemann, Oxford, UK.

Wearing, B.M. and Wearing, S.L. (1988) All in a days leisure: gender and the concept of leisure. *Leisure Studies* 7, 111–123.

Weiler, B. and Hall, C. (eds) (1992) *Special Interest Tourism*. Belhaven Press, London.

Weinmann, S. (1983) *Cultural Encounters of the Stimulating Kind: Personal Development Through Culture Shock*. Department of Humanities, Michigan Technological University, Michigan.

Winslow, E.A. (1977) *A Survey of Returned Peace Corps Volunteers*. Office of Special Services, United States Peace Corps, Washington, DC.

World Tourism Organization (1990) *Tourism to the year 2000*. World Tourism Organization, Madrid.

12

Fostering Human Resources in the Leisure Field: 'Serious Leisure' and the Potential Role of Volunteers. A Proposal for Developing Countries

Antonio Carlos Bramante

Department of Leisure Studies, College of Physical Education, State University of Campinas, São Paulo, Brazil

Introduction

The purpose of this chapter is to examine the concepts involved in the development of voluntary human resources for work in fostering and encouraging more involvement in leisure activities among young Brazilian people. Knowledge/intervention is combined with living significant meaningful leisure experiences in this human life dimension (Stebbins, 1992). It concerns the engagement of the youth segment of the population considering an experience related to leisure volunteering that has been going on for more than 25 years in the city of Sorocaba, State of São Paulo, Brazil.

In spite of the perceivable changes that have occurred over the past years all over the world, leisure continues to be constrained by work and suffers from serious discrimination concerning its priority in the field of public social policy, especially in developing countries.

Within the actual world situation of complex relations paradoxes are becoming routine, rationality operates side by side with emotionality, expression with numbness, creativity with boredom, objectivity with subjectivity. These polarities have a dialectic relationship.

The rise of a world culture within the globalized market – another example of polarization/dialectic relationship – brings to leisure new challenges at the beginning of this millennium. The relatively harmonious coexistence (nobody knows for how long) between endemic and structural unemployment and a genuine spirit of celebrating popular culture with strong playful components has become common in countries like Brazil. If the *global* affronts, the *local* is re-signified, expressed in new life styles in the ambit of 'obligations' – notably professional occupations – as well as in the 'non-obligatory' ones, especially leisure.

In this context there also coexists the *programmed* with the *spontaneous* in the leisure field. This challenges those who still believe that we ought to develop the broader sense of human *'being'* rather than the narrower materialist consumer, so that people can find new ways of coexisting and being tolerant, where solidarity prevails over rampant individualism.

Therefore, preparing personnel who are able to re-balance the offer of meaningful leisure experiences against the pressure of those of immediate pleasure is a considerable task to be achieved. This is a challenge to be faced and answered by those who conceive, organize, apply and evaluate programmes for preparing people to work in the leisure field.

Pina (1995), when presenting 'strata' in the area of programmed intervention in the leisure field, gave a special place to the high vertex of the pyramid, a small group of *general professionals* ('managers and consulters') who should have 'very inclusive (ample and diverse) preparation, knowledge and experience' (p. 126). They would supervise two other strata. *Specialized professionals* in the case of leisure, adopting the taxonomy proposed by Dumazedier (1979) and Camargo (1986), would be professionals who bring about viable leisure experiences within physical sports, artistic, social, intellectual, manual and cultural tourism-related contexts. At the base of this pyramid – but in greater numbers – are the *volunteers* who, after acquiring specific knowledge and skills, share their experiences with other people who want to learn about new leisure opportunities.

With the advent of the 'Leisure Programme' proposed by the City of Sorocaba in 1977, a list of 'impact events' was included in the programme. One of them was 'Férias Quentes' (Hot Vacation), an activity for children aged between 5 and 12 years old, which continues to be offered to the community today. This 'vacation camp' is for poor children who cannot travel during the school vacation. The combination of excessive demand with limited available resources on offer became problematic. The City responded by recruiting groups of volunteers from the 'School Teachers Course', a programme which trains teachers to teach children who are beginning their school education. This stimulated the creation of a new module named the 'supervised stage', which became an obligatory addition to the training programme being delivered to these future professionals.

Over the course of 25 years, with two annual sessions involving more than 60,000 children, the project evolved quantitatively as well as qualitatively. However, for the purposes of this chapter it is important to point out that the voluntary activity of these young people continued throughout this period. In 2001, it inspired the project 'Volunteering, Taking Leisure Seriously', which had the purpose of 'cultivating', even when young, a spirit of solidarity by means of playfulness. Thus, leisure would fuse with volunteering and volunteering with leisure, the main theme of this book.

A Short History of Volunteering in Brazil

Forty-three years after Brazil was discovered by the Portuguese settlers (or colonizers) in 1500, there occurred the first incident of volunteer service with the foundation of the first Santa Casa de Misericordia (Holy House of Mercy – a community hospital) in the then-called Vila de Santos, today the city of Santos, on the coast of the State of São Paulo.

Leaping forward in the history of volunteering in Brazil and arriving at the events of the 20th century, in 1908 the Red Cross began to operate in Brazil, followed by the Boy Scouts in 1910; both of these institutions had the purpose of helping others on any occasion of need. Only in 1935 was the Law of Public Utility promulgated; it established norms for State collaboration with philanthropic institutions that were (and continue to be) administrated by volunteer groups. In 1942, the then-President of the Republic Getulio Vargas created the Legião Brasileira de Assistência (LBA, Brazilian Legion of Assistance) with the essential purpose of attending those families considered to be suffering extreme need.

The struggle for a more inclusive society in relation to special people gave impulse to the pioneer institution Associação de Pais e Amigos do Exceptional (APAE, Association of Parents and Friends of Exceptional Persons). From 1961 to the present, APAE, with its great number of volunteers, has been working in all the Brazilian states. Another project involving volunteers and making great national and international repercussion is the Child Care Pastoral Project, created in 1983 by the Brazilian National Conference of Bishops. With the slogan 'so that all children may have life', the task of this group of the Catholic Church is to act in the areas of health, nutrition and education from the maternal womb to the age of 5. This action takes place today in more than 30,000 Brazilian communities and involves 133,000 volunteers. Regarding youth, most probably it was the Rondon Project, created in 1967, that was the pioneer. This government project had the purpose of taking university students on vacations to the most distant regions of the country to do interdisciplinary work to attend to the basic needs of the population of numerous Brazilian municipalities whose people suffered social problems related to great deprivation.

The worldwide economic crisis of the 1970s resulted in pruning the federal government's resources for social projects. This situation went on deteriorating and, in the 1990s, volunteer initiatives began to look more intensively for partnerships with businesses. In 1993, the sociologist Herbert de Souza created the 'Citizens Action against Hunger and Misery and for Life'; this sought to establish a process for organizing society to combat hunger. After a year, the number of local committees jumped from 300 to more than 5000, all staffed by volunteers. Ten years later, the new Brazilian government, led by President Luis Inacio Lula da Silva, not only launched its major governmental project 'Zero Hunger' but also transmitted the necessity of attending to this emergency by a response, based on human solidarity united to a great extent by the voluntary action of society, in the World Social Forum in Porto Alegre, Brazil, as well as in the World Economic Forum in Davos, Switzerland, both held simultaneously at the end of January 2003. This national/world mobilization, mostly by means of voluntary action, faithfully pictures the growing need for more solidarity in the world.

The UN nominated 2001 as the 'International Volunteer Year'. Brazil had already marked the recent history of volunteerism with three occasions: (i) in 1995, the Federal Government created the 'Community of Solidarity' programme as an incentive for civil society to participate in solving national social problems; (ii) in 1997, the first Volunteer Centres were created in Brazil – a type of 'pool of volunteers' that could help mediate the equation of 'supply/demand' in this field; and finally (iii) in 1998, the Law of Voluntarism (Law No. 9,608) was enacted to deal with conditions for exercising voluntary service, including establishing terms of enrolment for both parties. This legislation, in a way, has revolutionized voluntary service in Brazil, with employment law preventing disputes and bad faith on the part of the ones who offered their service as well as of those who used it.

In this short history of volunteer action in Brazil, it is worth noting that a greater number of these people were retired. Furthermore, many of them were adults, predominantly women, doing volunteer services invariably related to mitigating in some way the suffering of the poorest segments of the population.

In a country like Brazil, although it is gradually passing through a process of 'getting old', as reported in recent censuses of the Brazilian Institute of Geography and Statistics (IBGE), the majority of the population is considered to be young.

How to link pleasure to a type of voluntary action involving young people that is modelled on human solidarity is a tremendous challenge for a country replete with social injustice. And, who are these Brazilian young people?

Profile of Brazilian Youth

Brazil is conceived of and recognized as a 'young country' even though it has existed for 503 years. This demographic profile, nevertheless, has been changing during the last decades. A certain type of 'flattening out' of the pyramid corresponding to the ages that compose the Brazilian population has been observed in the last three censuses of the IBGE in 1980, 1991 and 1999. There has been a growing diminishment of children ranging from 0 to 9 years old and an increase corresponding to the age range from 10 to 19 years old. This has had repercussions on the rest of the age groups, especially those above 60 years old. This represents a demographic dynamic that has combined the gradual reduction of births per family with the implementation of public social policies that are co-responsible for the greater longevity of Brazilians, along with the progressive advances in technology.

A recent report about the situation of adolescence in Brazil, produced by UNICEF Brasil (2002a), revealed advances, but it also pointed out serious problems suffered by a significant part of Brazilian youth. The report analyses youth (12–17 years old) in all Brazilian municipalities (5507) based on seven basic criteria: (i) literacy; (ii) schooling; (iii) participation in community life; (iv) violence; (v) adolescent pregnancy; (vi) health; and (vii) culture, sports and leisure.

It is important to point out that the publication of this report coincided symbolically with a 'passage' from the state of 'childhood' (until 12) to 'adolescence' (12–18) according to the introduction of the Statute of the Child and Adolescent in 1990. This is the most modern document concerning protecting infancy and youth. It is considered a truly 'civilizing law' (Rivera, 1991) by treating this segment of the population as 'citizens with rights and responsibilities'; implementing article 227 of the 1988 Constitution of Brazil.

Today, Brazil has approximately 21 million adolescents, representing 12.5% of the country's population.

Illiteracy affects 2 million young people between 15 and 24 years old, with only 41% being able to complete elementary/junior high school (first 8 years of compulsory education). One-third of them go on to high school (another 3 or 4 years after the previous period) and an impressive number of 2.2 million adolescents are out of school.

A survey of 5280 adolescents in Brazil (UNICEF Brasil, 2002b) showed that for 85% of those interviewed the family is the institution with the greatest responsibility for guaranteeing the rights of adolescents and their welfare. For 95% of respondents, it is the most important institution in society, reinforcing the ties of affinity and solidarity that are customarily typical to the family environment. In a way, these data contradict, at least in Brazil, the opinion of common sense that attributes a certain aversion to family values among youth.

Passing directly to the object of this study related to sports, culture and leisure, this survey showed that 'to go over to a friend's house' is cited by 53% of those interviewed as the principal entertainment of adolescents. Television follows as the second source of having fun and leisure activity. Among 20 possible options (not exclusive) presented in the questionnaire, 51% of them cited television. This percentile surpasses those attributed to more dynamic activities like 'walk around the street' and 'play sports' (both with 47%). The average time dedicated daily to television is 3 hours and 55 minutes, an index that, more than merely revealing a preference for television, can be explained by the lack of other options.

Only 24% of the adolescents interviewed said they had opportunities of participating in some artistic cultural activity outside of school; 83% do not have access to leisure clubs of any kind; 74.5% cannot go to see movies;

60% do not play sports, and more than 80% do not have public or community equipment which assures them the right to sports, culture and leisure free of charge.

This information is part of the explanation behind the violence that adolescents are involved in, especially in urban areas (which represents more than 80% of the country's population). Principally in the poverty belts, lack of wholesome socializing activities leads to another type of socialization among peers resulting in anti-social acts involving 'gangs' or 'supporters'. Various studies have demonstrated that creating space for the development of artistic, cultural and sports activities has a strong impact on the reduction of violence in communities previously deprived of them. It can be noted that the greatest way to promote participation in these activities in their distinct forms and nature is to develop the values that make people turn to the aesthetic and also a more humane moral stance. This dimension of alterability is the fundamental ingredient for the construction of affectionate social ties.

Regarding volunteers, this study also indicated that the participation of youth in these initiatives that involve solidarity constitutes a strong indication of the potential they represent in consolidating democracy in the country. Therefore, strengthening a healthy social environment by supporting these initiatives and stimulating the creation of new forms of participation is a task for all sectors involved with the adolescent segment of the population.

The Perspective of Solidarity in Leisure: the Role of Volunteers

Although the relationship of leisure to solidarity is not new in literature, it was only during the 1990s that it became more vigorously developed, principally beginning with the works of Stebbins (1992) and with the 6th World Congress on Leisure, held in Bilbao, Spain, in July 2000, with the principal theme of 'Leisure and Human Development'.

Cabeza (2000a), presenting the contemporary dimensions and manifestations of leisure that he categorized as 'humanistic', described leisure in five distinct categories: (i) the playful dimension of leisure; (ii) the creative; (iii) environmental—ecological; (iv) the festive; and (v) solidarity. In this last dimension, Cabeza considers leisure

> as committed and altruistic social coexistence giving satisfaction rooted in disinterestedly helping others, independent of the activity in itself. Exemplified in groups of volunteers and associations of leisure, the development of the solidarity dimension corresponds to actions in open communities where there exists responsibility and commitment and whose fundamental principals are voluntarism and free choice.
>
> (Cabeza, 2000a, p. 13)

In another work, Cabeza completes his humanistic concept of leisure in its solidarity dimension, emphasizing 'its altruistic and social coexistence, being at the same time a need to participate and "make part of" within a perspective that he refers to as "mature leisure"' (2000b, p. 135).

Therefore, the solidarity dimension of leisure is based on satisfaction proportionate to the free help and detachment dispensed, appearing principally in communication (knowledge), cooperation (sharing the benefits) and help (disinterested selflessness in benefit of others), better expressed in the practical life of the vast world of the volunteer (Cabeza, 2000b, p. 136).

Leisure in Brazil

In order to establish a connection between this landmark concept of 'humanistic leisure' and the reality of this important dimension of human life in Brazil, it seems to be worthwhile, even in an abbreviated way, to recall some historical data about knowledge and intervention in Brazil, followed by turning our attention to the people who 'animate' (give *anima*, soul, life) to these cultural manifestations.

Requixa (1977) points to the work of Acacio Ferreira (1959) as the beginning of more elaborate studies about leisure in Brazil ('the first Brazilian to deal with leisure', p. 22). However, more recent historical studies covering the decades of the 1920s and 1930s in Porto Alegre, 1930s and 1940s in São Paulo, and 1940s and 1950s in Rio de Janeiro show that leisure was already the object of studies and action in innumerable community experiences (Werneck, 2003).

With regard to the training of professional personnel for service in the leisure field, although the previously mentioned studies included sporadic initiatives, only in the 1970s did this area truly become the object of research and more accurate analysis.

In 1970, the first college course for a Bachelor's degree in Tourism opened in São Paulo. Today, there are more than 500 tourism college-level programmes spread around the country. Repeating the phenomenon occurring in other nations, postgraduate courses arose before graduate ones in the specific area of leisure in Brazil. Also in the beginning of the 1970s, there began the first specialization courses for graduates in distinct areas of knowledge and professional branches; it became evident that leisure was (and continues to be) an interdisciplinary field and multi-professional by nature. For 10 years these courses were offered, principally, in the south of Brazil.

At the beginning of the 1990s, the first certification for recreation and leisure as a Bachelor's programme in Physical Education was introduced at the Physical Education College of the State University of Campinas (FEF/Unicamp). In 1998, the first specific graduate courses in 'Leisure Management' in the country were implemented. It is worthwhile pointing out that the first master's and doctoral degree programmes in leisure were also implemented by the FEF/Unicamp.

The author who had the greatest influence on leisure studies in Brazil was the French sociologist Joffre Dumazedier. During the decade from the mid-1970s to the mid-1980s, Dumazedier, as 'father of leisure sociology', came to Brazil many times as consultant to the Social Service of Commerce (SESC) in São Paulo, one of the most prestigious institutions in this field in the country.

This European influence disseminated in Brazil the concept of 'social–cultural animator', the title in France of that professional who provides leisure services and the adoption of the concept of 'community action' was assumed as the basis of the interventions of voluntary service in the leisure field.

The methodology of community action in the leisure field became very well known and was practised at the end of the 1960s and beginning of the 1970s, especially by SESC. Even today, it remains one of the principal means of the public sector to address the community in the leisure field.

Two decades ago, the article 'Training volunteers for community leisure activities' (Carneiro, 1983) was published, wherein the author offered concepts and elements for intervention that were especially significant to the era.

Requixa (1973) understands community action as

> a social—educational activity that consists of a deliberated intervention in a
> determined community through activities programmed together with the
> people and local institutions. Its aim is to arouse and deepen consciousness
> about the community's problems, encourage mobilization and coordination of
> leadership. This is intended to predispose it for action leading to the solution
> of those problems, or the attempt to fulfill aspirations related to the
> community as a whole.
>
> (Requixa, 1973, p. 9).

The first preparation of volunteers given by SESC occurred in Rio de Janeiro in 1973 and, 6 years later, the Leisure Sector of the National Department of this institution, responsible for the community action programme, included this training programme in its strategic planning.

The volunteer concept expressed in the documents of the 1970s indicated a person predisposed to live and work in a group, understanding that, once organized, the community would be capable of discovering its values, resources and needs; and it would find adequate solutions for bettering the quality of life. The volunteer, therefore, would serve as a link between the personal world and collective needs.

The basic programme of this training lasted 40 hours, divided into 20 hours of predominantly conceptual content and the other 20 hours of practical interventions within the community. The participants discovered that they were able to help others at the same time that they helped themselves.

What was observed during the course of this literature research was evidence that Brazil had a clear potential for voluntary action that would extend 'beyond emergencies'. Leisure was found to be a special time/space dimension of the human being where meaningful play experience could be undertaken both as an 'end' – volunteer service – and as a 'means', whereby volunteers could act as facilitators of the play experience.

Leisure in Sorocaba

The city of Sorocaba, with its 348 years of existence, is located 90 km from São Paulo. It is connected to various other large population centres at this same distance, including the city of Campinas (more than 1 million inhabitants), resulting in a human conglomerate of more than 15 million people.

The city of Sorocaba itself, with its 600,000 inhabitants, has a rich history of the vocational pursuit of leisure, which is widely recognized (Rodrigues, 2003).

In 1977, the city of Sorocaba officially approved its first policy for the leisure sector. It became one of the pioneer cities regarding this item in the country by undertaking a set of actions articulated by local public authority to increase the offer of leisure experience to the population. This action foreseen by this policy considered four basic programmes:

1. *Community recreation*: attending the requests of neighbourhoods, sending mobile leisure equipment or, in the case of those communities that did not solicit this, using a conscience-raising process for intervention in this area of services.

2. *Recreation in the municipal parks*: interpretative education was performed within the leisure framework, exploring the different spatial characteristics of each municipal park, from small neighbourhood parks to the city's zoo.

3. *Recreation in micro-environments*: actions in specific spaces such as hospitals, companies, centres for the elderly, among others, taking playful activities to these people.

4. *Impact events*: consisting of a set of different community projects that target distinct types of people with the principal purpose of increasing awareness and consciousness of the important role of leisure in improving lifestyles.

As was previously mentioned in this chapter, the 'Hot Vacation' project was selected among 'impact events' to illustrate the role of volunteering in leisure experiences within the *Leisure Programme* in Sorocaba city.

The principal purpose of this project is very simple: to offer leisure opportunities to children between 5 and 12 years old who do not have the financial means to travel during school recess. The first time this was offered, four Municipal Sports Centres were used, attending to 400 children in the afternoon for 2 weeks. The overall supervision of the project as well as the specific coordination at each location was handled by professional personnel.

The animation of the activities was taken care of by a group of 40 young people who were in the last year of teacher training (today, unified as Middle School Education). These youths passed through a 1-week training course; and all they received for their voluntary work was a bus pass for the trip back and forth to the event, daily lunch, the T-shirt of the project and, at the end, a certificate that would add some points to their résumé if they applied for a job as a public servant.

The political and social worth of this project are demonstrated by the fact that in Brazil, during these 25 years, the seven mayors from different political parties who passed through the City Hall not only maintained but even expanded the project. In the last three sessions (2001/2002), small alterations were made to improve its quality. One was the creation of an 'adult group' of mothers who brought the children and remained until the end of the day; they constituted a group and were invited to participate in different leisure experiences during all the period they were waiting for their children. A 'Family Hot Vacation Day' at the close of the event encouraged parents and their families to participate and become involved in the programme. Finally, there was the adoption of themes with the object of directing the programming to relevant issues in the community such as 'the role of communication', 'attention to special people' and 'World Peace'. During these last sessions, more than 4000 children, distributed over 17 locations, attended each event. Three hundred volunteers participated in the training programme, working together with the children and the community as a whole.

Volunteers in leisure: a new moment

In January 2001, the author of this study assumed the direction of the Sports and Leisure Department of the city of Sorocaba; this department became the principal public body responsible for the organization and execution of the 'Hot Vacation' project when this project was included in the new Policy for the Sports and Leisure Sector of the City (Bramante, 2001a). This policy, adopted within its 'conceptual framework', was influenced by the writings of the authors Stebbins and Dumazedier, especially with regard to the development of professionals and volunteers to work in the community.

After a detailed diagnosis of the needs of the city in the leisure field, we turned to the fortunate existence of the traditional project of 'Hot Vacation' in the city, specifically involved with personnel working in the leisure area. It had celebrated a quarter of a century of existence at the time of the UN's determination of the 'International Volunteer Year'.

In Brazil, the impact of this commemoration surpassed all the best expectations because it aroused in an extraordinary way a spirit of solidarity in a large part of the population; this was expressed in the innumerable actions of all social-economic classes and cultures in the most diverse fields.

Within the calendar of commemorations in Brazil that culminated on

4 December 2001 with the International Day of Voluntarism, each month had a theme. In March, when 'Sports and Leisure' were the areas selected, the project 'Volunteering, Taking Leisure Seriously' was strongly associated with the concept of 'serious leisure/casual leisure' as expressed by Stebbins (Bramante, 2001b).

The objectives of this project were to:

- Prepare the team of volunteer monitors, qualifying them personally and professionally, showing the recognition due to the relevant role they played in society and strengthening the ties between 'Public Authority and the Volunteer' regarding sports and leisure action.
- Stimulate volunteerism as one of the strongest characteristics of citizenship and solidarity.
- Encourage volunteers to develop and improve their knowledge and skills in the sports and leisure field.
- Prepare volunteers in the sports and leisure fields not only to benefit the community but also for their own benefit.

The methodology adopted in this project was based on ten meetings, one per month, from March to December 2001. Two procedures prevailed in these meetings: presentation, reflection and discussion of themes relevant to volunteer work in the sports and leisure field; and presentation of possible alternatives of action for the volunteers in these fields.

After a diagnostic evaluation of themes which could be treated in meetings with a sample of volunteers, ten topics were determined:

1. The importance of volunteers for the development of community.
2. Recreational activities for children and adolescents.
3. The volunteer and social inclusion.
4. Art and its manifestations.
5. The volunteer and community action in sports and leisure.
6. Physical sports activities as cultural content of leisure.
7. Introduction to psychology development.
8. Application of group dynamics to diverse age groups.
9. The volunteer and the media: the power of mobilization.
10. Volunteerism: future perspectives.

As can be seen, attempts were made to select themes in such a way that those of a more theoretical nature alternated with those more related to applied actions.

To our pleasant surprise, within 48 hours all the 200 positions offered for this volunteer preparation course were filled. This immediately created administrative difficulties in organizing the group; but these were at least partially taken care of over the months that followed.

The formative evaluation that was performed at the halfway point of the project in July 2001 presented some important data for the maintenance/reorientation of action. By means of the application of a questionnaire

($N = 154$), it was observed that, although for 30% of people this was the first time that they had participated in 'Hot Vacation', the remaining 70% had already participated more than five times in the project. Two people said they had been participating as volunteers for the past 10 years!

Other important data, which justify the association between 'solidarity' and 'leisure', showed that 35% of the respondents had already been 'children of Hot Vacation'; this participation as a child varied between 'one time' (41%) and 'more than five times' (33%). It can be inferred that a 'Hot Vacation 'culture' had been created in the city; that is, many people who had benefited as child participants are today repaying the community by accepting this opportunity to put into practice a real sense of solidarity by providing leisure experiences to others.

Two-thirds of those who were attending the project 'Volunteering, Taking Leisure Seriously' considered that it was contributing significantly to their performance in the 'Hot Vacation' project. In this survey it was important to verify that among these young people actions moulded by the spirit of solidarity of pleasurable volunteerism (in the case of 'Hot Vacations') did not necessarily transfer to other volunteer services; only one in ten said they had developed other volunteer work besides that in the sports and leisure fields. It seems reasonable, therefore, to infer that, for groups of young people to develop a process of solidarity action through voluntary service, the inclusion of attractive elements like leisure experiences performs an important role.

The profile of this group consisted principally of students (89%) who were in high school (86%), single (96%) and predominantly female (79%). When questioned about their housing situation, 85% answered that they lived in a house owned by the family, earning a per capita income measured by the 'minimum salary' ('MS'), equivalent to US$67.00 with the prevailing category being 'between three to five "MS"' (44%), followed by 'more than five/less than 10 "MS"' (20%).

These data were essential for ratifying the importance of the 'Hot Vacation' project as a moment of expressive contagious feelings about the maintenance of volunteer groups for community leisure. Even with the periodic evaluations and realignments of the project 'Volunteering, Taking Leisure Seriously', it was noted that the *response* ('easy engagement') of volunteers was significant (practically every call for volunteers for a given action received an immediate positive response); but the same cannot be attributed to the *sense of commitment* of those who started in the project but dropped out of the group during its course. At the end of the first year of the project, of the 200 initial participants only 120 had completed the whole sequence of ten meetings.

In order to prepare the programme for 2002, an evaluation took place in the last meeting of 2001 ($N = 96$) principally to identify the reasons for the dropouts. It became evident that communication with the volunteers was very effective since 96% indicated they had received all the correspondence at least 4 days before the dates of the meetings. It is important to point out that these letters only reiterated the date, theme, location, time and leader responsible for each meeting, all of which had been previously disseminated at the beginning of the project.

Six out of ten alleged that the causes of the dropout during the course of the year were 'incompatibility of time' (21%), 'disinterest' (10%) and 'misinformation' (6%). The rest of the reasons (work, the occasion of other commitments, among others) were considered to be beyond the control of the Sports and Leisure Department.

Furthermore, it ought to be pointed out that this project was conceived of and accomplished in collaboration with the University of Sorocaba. It had as its objective to pass on to the young volunteers the idea of 'acquiring new knowledge' and to make them aware of the commitment that the University had with the community. In this regard, all ten meetings were held in the buildings of the three campuses of the University of Sorocaba according to the needs of the themes and available space at the university (the study revealed that, unfortunately, alterations in these arrangements influenced the dropout rate of the group). What can be inferred from this experience is that being connected with a university in working with groups of young volunteers is very important. The whole process of the socialization of these young people while still in high school is facilitated by the support that the university can offer to community intervention moulded by volunteers.

When they were asked about the principal reason for their participation in a project for the preparation of volunteers for working in sports and leisure, they gave various answers: (i) 'looking for new knowledge' (41%); (ii) 'belonging to a group of volunteers working side by side every month' (22%); and (iii) 'doing volunteer work itself' (14%). Various other reasons completed this picture.

One hundred per cent of the answers positively classified the themes selected and 97% felt that they had a 'very good/good' level of participation in the meetings. 'Supporting work done by non-governmental organizations and social entities' was a predominant strategy (54%) for improving the practical insertion of volunteers in actions programmed by the Sports and Leisure Department. This strategy serves to alert public authorities to the need to make the opportunities for volunteer service in diverse projects more apparent, since what is observed is a compartmentalized view of each area within the public sector: 'Each and everyone in its own niche'.

The continuation of the project in 2002 received the approval of 98.5% of the respondents and only one-third presented some suggestion of change. It is worth saying that these suggestions were extensively applied in 2002 by creating principally two training groups of volunteers: one now with only 100 positions ('updating' for the group that had concluded the project in 2001) and another 100 positions for a new group of interested young people. The long-term aim of this project is very ambitious: to prepare 500 young volunteers for sports and leisure in Sorocaba city before the end of 2004.

At the end of the second year of this experience (even without the evaluated data at hand) it seems fitting to propose that one of the alternatives for attending to the growing demand for leisure services in the public sector is the preparation of young volunteers. Here are some of the positive factors of working with young volunteers: (i) they begin to think about their neighbour in an age of extreme individualism; (ii) the full exercise of their citizenship through participation in community life, a right which is often denied to this population segment; (iii) to associate 'work' with 'pleasure and fulfilment' volunteer action presupposes spontaneous engagement, the fact that, in this age group, to live together with experiences that bring pleasure is essential; and (iv) the positive occupation of their 'free time' so that they are able to channel their energy to the well-being of society. All these possible benefits, however, do not exclude the grave danger of the public sector turning these young people into so-called 'cheap labour', where, far from promoting new knowledge and significant interventions that promote the human being, they get lost in essentially functional, utilitarian and repetitive tasks that do not lead to the inventive and creative spirit so essential for their age group.

In conclusion, it is evident that one of the great challenges in this field is to overcome another 'polarity' that is beginning to emerge in the leisure field, that which exists between the 'serious' and the 'casual', as Stebbins teaches us. We could associate this polarity with that of '*a sense of commitment*' and '*easy participation*', respectively. The dialogical relation between both should always exist. For the '*easy engagement*' of this age group, the appeal of the leisure experience itself had been enough for the time being. But '*a sense of commitment*' could only come about by the virtuous and systematic combination of the two major elements during the course of time: the promotion of new knowledge associated with significant interventions that favour the community as well as serving the volunteers' needs and desires.

After all, leisure education seems to go hand in hand with the education necessary for being a volunteer.

References

Bramante, A.C. (2001a) *Política setorial de esporte e lazer de Sorocaba* [Leisure Policy of Sorocaba 2001–2004]. Secretaria de Esportes e Lazer/Prefeitura de Sorocaba, Sorocaba.

Bramante, A.C. (2001b) Voluntariado, lazer levado a sério [Volunteers, leisure taken seriously]. In: Villela, M. (ed.) *Sonhando Juntos*. Pearson Education do Brasil, São Paulo.

Cabeza, M.C. (2000a) Introducción. In: Cabeza, M.C. (ed.) *Ócio y desarrollo humano* [Leisure and Human Development]. Universidad de Deusto, Bilbao, Spain.

Cabeza, M.C. (2000b) *Ocio humanista* [Humantistic Leisure]. Universidad de Deusto, Bilbao, Spain.

Camargo, L.L. (1986) *O que é lazer* [What Leisure Is]. Editora Brasiliense, São

Paulo.

Carneiro, M.P. (1983) Treinamento de voluntários para atividades comunitárias de lazer [Training volunteers for community leisure activities]. *Boletim de Intercâmbio* 4(16), 31–42.

Dumazedier, J. (1979) *Sociologia empírica do lazer* [Empirical Sociology of Leisure]. Editora Perspectiva, São Paulo.

Ferreira, A. (1959) *Lazer operário* [Workers Leisure]. Livraria Progresso Editora, Salvador.

Pina, L.W. (1995) Multiplicidade de profissionais e funções [Multiplicity of professions and functions]. In: Marcellino, N.C. (ed.) *Lazer: formação e atuação profissional* [Leisure: Professional Formation and Performance]. Papirus Editora, Campinas, SP.

Requixa, R. (1973) *Lazer e ação comunitária* [Leisure and Community Action]. Serviço Social do Comércio, São Paulo.

Requixa, R. (1977) *O lazer no Brasil* [Leisure in Brasil]. Editoria Brasiliense, São Paulo.

Rivera, D. (1991) *Pelo amor destas bandeiras* [For the Love of these Flags]. Ministério da Ação Social, Brasília, DF.

Rodrigues, E.C. (2003) Construindo uma política pública de lazer: espaço ou programa. O que garante a animação? [Constructing public policy for leisure. What guarantees the animation?]. Master's dissertation, Faculdade de Educação Física da Universidade Estadual de Campinas, São Paulo, Brazil.

Stebbins, R.A. (1992). *Amateurs, Professionals, and Serious Leisure*. McGill-Queen's University Press, Montreal.

UNICEF Brasil (2002a) *Relatório da situação da adolescência brasileira* [Report on the Situation of Brazilian Adolescence]. UNICEF, Brasília, DF.

UNICEF Brasil (2002b) *A voz dos adolescentes* [The Voice of the Adolescents]. UNICEF, Brasília, DF.

Werneck, C.L.G. (2003) Significados de recreação e lazer no Brasil: reflexões a partir da análise de experiências institucionais (1926–1964). [Meanings of recreation and leisure in Brazil: reflections from the analysis of institutional experiences (1926–1964)]. Doctoral thesis, Faculdade de Educação da Universidade Federal de Minas Gerais, Brazil.

Epilogue 13

Leisure Volunteering: Future Research and Policy

There is an abundance of research opportunity within this under-researched field and this publication touches on some of the key issues that need to be raised in future research projects. The best way to forecast the paths that volunteering research will follow in the future is to consider external forces alongside the topics and issues raised directly and indirectly throughout this book

Volunteering as Leisure

Leisure volunteering as social capital constitutes an enormous reservoir of skills, energy, and local and special interest knowledge. Volunteering as leisure gives participants a sense of purpose, provokes serious contemplation, encourages concern for others, provides the opportunity to further an interest, and to have fun and enjoyment. Moreover, the substantial forms of volunteering can generate a sense of deep personal fulfilment. Finally, volunteering can be said to build societies, encourage community participation and contribute to life-long learning through the provision of volunteering experiences.

Yet the informality of volunteering as time spent outside work makes it difficult to measure its economic importance in terms of quality-of-life impacts. Host organizations are inclined to have a lack of comprehensive data because many of the activities that volunteers are involved in are unplanned and unrecorded. This makes it difficult to explore theoretically volunteering's

© 2004 CAB International. *Volunteering as Leisure/Leisure as Volunteering: an International Assessment* (eds R.A. Stebbins and M. Graham)

unique complex relationship with paid work. Further research in this field is crucial for the future preservation of volunteering in all its serious–casual forms as a type of leisure participation. Making this clear distinction will guard against volunteers compromising their leisure experience by being viewed, assessed and valued in the same way as paid staff.

At this stage it is worth pondering that if future research projects are to maximize their effectiveness, inter-disciplinary collaboration and broadening dissemination of outputs beyond peer groups is going to be critical.

Volunteering in all its substantial variations needs to be understood in the context of community resources and benefits rather than as commercial assets. Against this background the future of volunteering can be propagated and meaningfully progressed to respond to the very diverse needs of different individuals and groups. A greater understanding of volunteering as leisure among stakeholders will serve as a catalyst in the formation and review of objectives and policies. This will contribute towards communicating the scope and variety of images of volunteering to a wider audience, raising opportunities to coach and develop more volunteers for the benefit of future generations.

/Politics of Volunteering

The politics of volunteering must be a primary focus when setting a framework for future volunteering research. At an international governmental level the benefits of volunteering's role in the development of societies is recognized and being included in future policy planning agendas. This was further advanced at the European Parliament in Brussels on 24 June 2003 with the launch of the European Volunteer Centre (EVC) Manifesto for Volunteering in Europe. The manifesto is part of EVC's strategy to enhance social and economic cohesion within the EU community (EVC, 2003). The objectives of the manifesto are to increase volunteering opportunity through the creation of an EU infrastructure that allows for greater recognition of volunteering and the provision of support for its effective future development.

Therefore, stakeholder interest in volunteering is likely to expand considerably on a global scale in the future. This undoubtedly will have a knock-on effect in widening research interest and opportunity in the topic, encouraging more international collaboration. Hence research as a tool to inform future policy in the field of leisure volunteering will have a significant impact on future debate, drawing together more urgently practitioners, academics, politicians and other stakeholder agencies. This stakeholder exchange approach offers the potential to make future research projects more informed, relevant and open to wider scrutiny than they presently are. More importantly it will provide the armoury to justify, advance and apply policy decision making more confidently.

Value of Volunteering

Volunteering as a developmental concept can be interpreted as an exchange of improvement benefits secured in equal measure by volunteers and the cause(s) they support. Political interests undoubtedly centre around more robustly promoting the benefits of volunteering to a wider section of society as a mechanism to achieve various goals of achievement related to economic development and social improvement. However, politicizing the growth of volunteering can be viewed either as a sign of social progress by a responsible society or more cynically as increased state control over society to the determination of how citizens spend their leisure time.

In this light, what immediately springs to mind is the threat that the opportunity would be ripe for future volunteering to improve the quality of volunteers to assign them to redesigned welfare-related roles that replace paid work. Taking this perspective, three rather controversial research questions emerge:

1. To what extent would future policy for volunteers systematically swing the balance away from volunteering as leisure towards volunteering as a form of coerced, obligated civil labour?
2. To what extent would future policy for volunteers aim to more rigorously control and channel volunteering as a means of social control, making the boundaries between work and leisure merge?
3. In view of the political advancement of volunteering as serious leisure can it be realistically separated from achieving the same goals as paid work? And to what extent can personal gains be viewed as replacing payment incentives (Stebbins, 2004)?

Widening Civic Engagement

Perhaps the most difficult challenge for researchers would be undertaking research projects focused on objectives geared towards encouraging the next generation to participate in a variety of volunteering experiences. This is particularly the case when volunteering is in competition with other leisure pursuits that are marketed more prominently in popular media. Therefore the long-term future of volunteering depends on how its image is portrayed and presented within this highly competitive market place. This need not challenge the traditional ethos of volunteering, which promotes philanthropic ideals that actively demonstrate care and concern for communities alongside opportunities for self-improvement.

Research into the value of volunteering, its contribution and its impact on individuals and communities, with more focus on how it enhances work, leisure, domestic and community life, would make a valuable contribution to the field.

Research objectives should consider projects that will explore a vast range of volunteering experiences and benefits that are likely to promote volunteering as an alternative leisure pursuit. This would include identifying different types of volunteer teams, what type of people they welcome to volunteer, their distinctiveness from other volunteers and the reasons why others do not choose to volunteer. Issues can be addressed such as identifying among non-volunteers (latent), what gives volunteering its negative image, key strengths of other competing leisure interests and any conflict between volunteering and paid work, domestic and education-related commitments.

Pressures and Unfulfilled Expectations

Further research into the negative impacts of volunteering such as those identified in this book by Perkins, Benoit and Nichols will serve to highlight the need to address pressures on volunteers as well as their unfulfilled expectations. Alongside this there is a need to understand more clearly the competing pressures on volunteer host organizations to ensure that volunteers help to fulfil their organizational obligations.

In this way the focus will shift from volunteering experiences to the preparation and support provided by the organizations who host them. Further research using Edwards' institutional approach and Meijs' cost–benefit models of volunteer management would be beneficial in this field.

Management

The volunteer participation debate tends to obscure the fact that some revolutionary policy and accounting impacts on host organizations have changed their views of volunteers. More and more of these organizations are increasingly being forced to make economic rather than ideological choices. Volunteer leadership reared on inherited traditions of community duty is faced with a shift in values and priorities. Although they are more accountable to develop the capacity to adapt and establish a new relationship with volunteers, little is known about the extent of discontinuities experienced by volunteers and how they are organized.

The impact of legislation and changing priorities that push management to change the concept of their responsibilities is a field ripe for research. Researching organizations who host volunteers tends to be problematic because of a lack of comprehensive data. However, as these organizations are being pressed to behave more like commercial providers, there is more pressure to scrutinize and manage volunteers more formally. And so the thorny issue of designing appropriate management models for organizing and scheduling volunteers continues to be a particularly hot research topic.

Goals of achievement would need to prioritize flexibility and customization to inspire, protect, develop and retain a vast range of volunteers in order to sustain volunteering for the future.

Conclusion

This publication provides an insight into the diversity and variety of leisure volunteering experiences, the causes they support and key topical research problems being tackled worldwide within this field. The main strengths of this book are undoubtedly the international and multi-disciplinary profile of the authors and the scope of their theoretical approach to tackle and explain their research questions. It also presents a solid grounding of knowledge on which future research can build and develop to help academics and practitioners understand volunteering more fully.

References

European Volunteer Centre (EVC) (2003) Launch of the European Volunteer Centre Manifesto for Volunteering in Europe. Press Statement, 25 June, European Parliament, Brussels.

Stebbins, R.A. (2004) *Between Work and Leisure: a Study of the Common Ground in Two Separate Worlds*. Transaction Books, New Brunswick, New Jersey.

Index

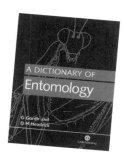
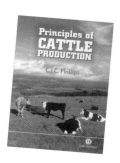